THE SKY TRAMPS

PETER JACKSON

The Sky Tramps

The story of
Air Charter

SOUVENIR PRESS
London

*Printed in Great Britain by
The Central Press, Aberdeen*

For

SARAH LOUISE

Contents

Contents

Illustrations

1*

Cliff Luxton hears Hughie Green reconstruct their escape from Russian fighters in the Berlin air corridor.

Helicopter pilot Alan Green switches to a horse between flights in the mountains of Iran.

One of the Bristow Helicopters fleet engaged in off-shore oil operations in the Arabian Gulf.

Freddy Laker, once a scrap dealer and now managing director of British United Airways. The movements of his world-wide fleet of aircraft are plotted at Gatwick Airport by Captain Cecil Bebb.

Acknowledgments and thanks are due to the British Overseas Airways Corpn., Flight, Bassano, Fox Photos, and The Sun for permission to use their photographs.

Prologue

THE ninety passengers on board Britannia GAR Whisky Zulu of British United Airways include farmers, factory workers, hoteliers, housewives, civil servants, typists, two wardens of a Girls' Friendly Society hostel at Bournemouth, a bank manager, and a 17-month-old baby who sleeps all the two hours and fifteen minutes of Flight BR 315 from the early morning mists of Surrey to the Mediterranean glare of Majorca. They travel at 390 m.p.h. and 19,000 feet high in the char-a-banc of the second half of the 20th Century . . . the charter plane.

Like the char-a-banc in its day, the charter plane is a form of transport of the widest popularity moving in a cloud of public suspicion. When its efficiency is not in question, its morality most certainly is. The char-a-banc was attacked as a menace to health, a ravager of the countryside, the purveyor of roadside orgies. The charter plane has become associated with death and disaster, scandal and bankruptcy, and economy with the smell of cheapness. It is a label which remains although British charter companies operate only by increasingly strict Government licences, demanding the highest safety standards and advance proof of ample financial resources. But the cheapness to the customer is still there.

The passengers on board Whisky Zulu, sipping their duty-free brandy after a chicken lunch high above France, are paying between £50 and £60 for a fortnight's inclusive holiday at a first class hotel in Majorca. Only £18 of that price is taken for the round trip in a £250,000 airliner capable of flying the Atlantic non-stop. This is less than half the return fare by scheduled service. It is the reason why three million passengers will fly on 50,000 charter flights from Britain this

11

year, why charter flying is the fastest growing section of civil aviation.

Only forty-six years have passed since Lieutenant Bill Lawford flew one passenger and a cargo of newspapers, leather, grouse and Devonshire cream from London to Paris on August 25, 1919. That was the beginning of the world's first daily passenger service to be operated internationally over a sustained period—generally regarded as the effective birth of commercial aviation. But charter flying was already leading the way six months before when Sir Woodman Burbidge, managing director of Harrods, hired an ex-World War I bomber to fly him from Hendon to Brussels for a business meeting. The flight was illegal, made in defiance of a war-time ban on civil flying still in force after four months of peace, and immediately establishing the charter operator's sturdy distaste for bureaucracy.

Early airliners were invariably converted bombers and two passengers on a flight from Brussels to London on November 11, 1919, were sitting in front of the pilot in an open cockpit where the forward gun turret used to be. At 11 a.m. on this, the first Remembrance Day, the pilot switched off his engine at 2,000 feet above the English Channel to observe the two minutes' silence. One of the front passengers was caught in the air-stream and almost blown over the side when he insisted on rising to his feet in the cockpit and saluting the gallant war dead. The pilot started the engines again and passed forward a hastily scribbled note, asking the passenger to return to his seat and reminding him of the disastrous results for all on board should an object as small as a flying helmet fall from the cockpit and be blown into the arc of the wooden propellers.

Gordon Percy Olley, one of the great charter pioneers, was a pilot on the London-Paris service in the early 1920's when fully laden planes taking off from the Handley Page base at Cricklewood needed to fly the length of the Edgware Road to get to 500 feet over Marble Arch—and were said to be fast enough to overtake the red open-top buses on the No. 16

route only when the buses stopped to pick up passengers. Navigation was by landmarks and if a pilot got lost he could only land in a field and ask the way. With no blind flying instruments he had to fly round or underneath bad weather. If the weather closed down he would have to land where he could and wait for it to clear. Olley established the uncomfortable record of no less than seventeen forced landings on one flight from London to Paris, including a crossing of the Channel at such low level that his passengers were helping to keep a look-out for ships ahead.

Airliners of the day were thoughtfully equipped with a clock on one wall of the passenger cabin and a calendar on the other. During a flight to Brussels, Olley ran into heavy snow and had to land in the grounds of a monastery near the French-Belgian border. He and his passengers spent the night in monks' cells. The flight was resumed next morning but Olley had to make another emergency landing, this time in the middle of a World War I battlefield. The passengers went on to Brussels by horse and cart, motor car and train. He moved into an old German dug-out and lived there for the next few days while supervising local farmworkers in the construction of a make-shift airstrip across a shell-blasted stretch of no-man's land. The aircraft's calendar recorded a full week before he took off to the cheers of the farmworkers and the journey continued once more.

This was flying with a covered wagon mentality, the resolve to reach an objective whatever stood in the way. A passenger, who recovered consciousness in a North London garden after being thrown clear of the aircraft in one of the first crashes of the London-Paris service, was determined to keep a business appointment in the French capital. He climbed out of the garden, walked to Golders Green, took an underground train to Victoria, and caught the Golden Arrow ferry train to Paris where he read newspaper reports of his death in the crash. Another accident, two years later in 1922, led to civil aviation devising the beginnings of air traffic lanes. There was a head-on collision between British and French airliners, killing a 16-year-old cabin boy who served coffee from a flask in flight—one of the first air stewards.

British and French interests were already in a state of collision over a problem which still divides aviation. Should airlines be subsidised? The French companies were, the British were not. In 1921 the British airlines were forced out of business and re-started operations only when Winston Churchill, then Secretary of State for Air, helped to bring about a limited subsidy. This was only a temporary solution and within three years the State-aided Imperial Airways was formed from the four surviving private companies. Like all subsequent mergers it was a melting pot not big enough to contain all the individual energy and ambition inspired by flying. When Edward Henry Hillman, an Essex motor coach operator, felt he had a grievance against the authorities for restricting his road services he formed his own airline and went into competition with Imperial Airways. Starting with a Puss Moth biplane and day-trip flights to Margate and Clacton, he built up a fleet of modern airliners within the space of three years. At his death in 1934, Hillman's Airways was operating international services to Paris, Brussels and Antwerp, domestic services to Liverpool, Glasgow and Belfast, and carrying mail between London and Northern Ireland. Within another year, Hillman's was merged with other aggressively competitive independents to form British Airways which eventually found the need to receive a Government subsidy and was merged with Imperial Airways in 1939 to create the British Overseas Airways Corporation.

An ex-B.O.A.C. pilot, Captain John Treharne, now captains British United Airways' Flight BR 315 to Majorca. In many ways, a full circle has been completed. B.U.A. came about to serve the original purpose of British Airways in the 1930's, an umbrella organisation for a miscellany of small independent airlines facing too many rainy days. It is an umbrella under which Treharne is well content to find a place. He gained his first charter experience along the hastily improvised air corridors of the Berlin Airlift. Today he flies the sleek, sophisticated airways of Europe—Amber 26 to Paris, Red 25 to Toulouse, and Blue 31 to Palma. Radar screens cover his departure, watch his progress, and prepare for his landing. He is in constant touch with a chain of VHF radio stations along the route, which in turn report by teleprinter to British United's operations centre at Gatwick Airport.

Whisky Zulu's flight details are entered on a blackboard stretching the length of two walls of the room—along with VC-10 jets bound for Africa and South America, BAC-111's flying to and from Italy and Spain, other Britannias taking Servicemen and their families to the Far East, DC-6's ferrying horses to a military tattoo at Copenhagen and tourists from Corfu, Viscounts coming and going between France, Holland and Belgium and all points of the British Isles.

The blackboard is supervised by the Regional Operations Manager, Captain Cecil Bebb, a small middle-aged man with thinning, gingerish hair, who displays a pair of blue braces as he works at his desk in shirt-sleeves.

Fog at Le Touquet, head winds over the Mediterranean, a replacement engine needed at Johannesburg, and a catering delay at Gatwick all make demands on his judgement, and his decisions make their mark on the blackboard with fresh deployments of the fleet. He watches the chalking of the safe arrival of BR 315 at Palma with the satisfaction of a bank clerk completing a neat page in his ledger. But Bebb knows that no set of figures can tell the real story of a flight any more than a mass of statistics can be presented as the whole story of charter flying.

The duty officer's assistant begins chalking up one more flight sequence, recording the progress of another Britannia carrying 110 holidaymakers to the Canary Islands. Bebb looks over his shoulder and, in a pause between telephone bells and teleprinter chatter, he sees in these latest figures on the blackboard a vivid picture of himself setting out for the same destination as a young man when flying was young as well . . .

CHAPTER ONE

Revolution in the Air

CAPTAIN Cecil Bebb was the pilot for a holiday charter
flight which left Croydon Airport for Las Palmas on the
morning of July 11, 1936. The aircraft was a twin-engined,
six-seater de Havilland Rapide, GAC-YR. Passengers were
Major Hugh B. C. Pollard, his 19-year-old daughter, Diana
Pollard, and her friend, Dorothy Watson. They would be
spending a few days in the Canary Islands doing all the
things that English tourists would be expected to do. Bebb
knew they also planned to so something very different.

Gordon Olley, managing director of Olley Air Services,
had not tried to pretend this was an ordinary holiday charter.
He talked to Bebb about the flight in the presence of Louis
Bolin, a Spanish journalist. " Mr. Bolin wants you to take
some English friends of his to the Canaries," said Olley.
" They will behave like tourists but I think it is only fair
to tell you that they are part of a plot to bring about a rising
of the Riff tribes in Morocco. The real job as far as you are
concerned is to fly a Riff leader from Las Palmas into Spanish
Morocco and there he will start a revolution. What a passenger cares to do when he leaves the plane is no concern of
yours, and not at all your responsibility. I'm only telling
you this because there is always the risk that the plot is
betrayed and there might well be attempts to intercept you.
So I can't blame you if you would rather not take the trip."

The idea of helping to start a Riff rising was not something Bebb could take very seriously at this time. His current girl friend was an actress with a touring company of *The Desert Song* and all that came to mind in Olley's office was a picture of the male chorus rushing to the attack singing a selection of Sigmund Romberg melodies, with lyrics by Oscar Hammerstein. There seemed merely an extra touch of melodrama about Bolin's undertaking to insure Bebb's life for £2,000 and to insure the Rapide against total loss. As for the secret emissaries, Major Pollard was a quiet caricature of the country sportsman and the two girls revelled in an air of mystery borrowed from some repertory company thriller. Pollard left Croydon regretting that he was missing the first day of the Eton-Harrow cricket match at Lords and, during a refuelling stop at Bordeaux, was obviously moved to note no less than eight Old Etonian ties among a group of fellow conspirators waiting at the airport to wish him well. Bebb was to find later that Pollard's soft drawl and huntin'-shootin'-fishin' mannerisms were most misleading. He was a fine athlete and a champion shot with a revolver, a firearms expert often consulted by Scotland Yard.

From Bordeaux, Bebb set off to fly to Lisbon but met bad weather over the western Pyrenees and was forced to turn back and land at Biarritz. He borrowed a large scale map of the area and, over lunch in the flying club, worked out a way of flying underneath the cloud by following a valley through the mountains.

The flight was then resumed, with the Rapide picking its way along a narrow, twisting tunnel having grey rock on three sides and the dark mass of the storm on top. At times the valley was so narrow that Bebb hunched his shoulders as if to withdraw the wingtips a few precious inches. He could fly at little more than stalling speed, and tried to calculate the difference in fuel consumption between an aeroplane winding along a mountain path and following a crow between two points. When the Rapide eventually found its way out of the Pyrenees and landed at Oporto the fuel tanks had only the slightest swill of petrol, not enough for five more minutes in the air.

The act of flying in 1936 was still very much an adventure in itself, regardless of the revolution waiting to be started at Bebb's destination. Crews chosen for a night mail service to Germany being planned by British Airways would take off only after being issued with parachutes. And Croydon magistrates fined an Imperial Airways passenger £10 for endangering an aircraft by smoking on a flight from London to Paris less than four months before Bebb's charter plane followed a mountain path through the Pyrenees.

After an overnight stop at Oporto, Bebb flew by way of Lisbon to Casablanca in North Africa. Pollard had more friends waiting for him there and Bebb began to wonder at the motives of such people in wanting to bring about an Arab revolt in Morocco. The major and the two girls seemed in no hurry to leave Casablanca until late the next evening when they heard news that Calvo Sotelo, one of the outstanding Right Wing leaders in Spain, had been murdered. Pollard became suddenly agitated.

" We must get to Las Palmas," he told Bebb. " Prepare the plane to leave as soon as possible to-morrow morning."

Bebb made the necessary preparations overnight but the Rapide did not leave until mid-morning. The delay was due to Diana Pollard and Dorothy Watson turning up with large quantities of French dresses they had bought in Casablanca. There was difficulty in packing them into the aircraft and Bebb complained that all this excessive baggage was seriously overloading the plane for a crossing of a long stretch of desert and 300 miles of ocean. Pollard insisted the dresses should stay on board, suggesting they helped the party's pose as innocent tourists. In fact, the Rapide reached Las Palmas without difficulty.

Pollard and the two girls took a boat to the island of Tenerife, explaining that the Riff leader was living there and they would be attempting to make contact with him. Bebb was left with various passwords and signals by which he could recognise other members of the plot who might need to tell him of any change of plans. No passwords were offered by the soldiers who forced their way into Bebb's hotel room the following afternoon and led him at gunpoint to a car waiting at the rear of the building. He was driven to a large villa in the hills outside the town and there he was interrogated by a group of high ranking officers. The most insistent questions about why he was in the Canary Islands came from a general whose mood was openly hostile. Bebb insisted in reply that he was a charter pilot employed to bring three English tourists on holiday and he was merely waiting to take them home again.

To all questions about his views on the political situation in Spain he could plead a genuine ignorance. He was genuinely puzzled, too. What had party politics in Madrid got to do with his own little production of *The Desert Song* in Morocco?

"You are placing yourself in great danger if you interfere in another country's affairs," said the general. "There is sentence of death for any conspiracy against the State."

Bebb was returned to his hotel in a highly confused state of mind. The excursion to the villa in the hills had the same streak of melodrama which made it difficult to regard the whole enterprise with any seriousness. But the soldiers were real enough and the talk of the situation in Spain obviously had some link with Pollard's reaction to the murder of Sotelo. Bebb was not inclined to worry about the general's threats. So far he had flown three highly respectable British citizens into a friendly country and there could be no crime in that.

Mention of the death sentence had little meaning for a young man fresh from two years as an aerobatic pilot with Sir Alan Cobham's world famous air circus. Death, as Bebb well knew, always happened to other people. It was a kind of technical error to be analysed over the wreckage and then filed away as something not to do.

Like a bull fighter or racing driver, he had enjoyed the nearness of death as proof of his own immortality. Did that general know he was talking to someone who earned £1,000 a year picking handkerchiefs from the ground with a wing-tip, who had his propeller disintegrate in a 170 m.p.h. dive only 300 feet above an audience of 10,000 people and still landed safely?

Flying was the one thing that Bebb, the son of a London dentist, always wanted to do. He entered the R.A.F. in 1921 as a 16-year-old apprentice. By 1926 Bebb was a fighter pilot and already beginning to fret over the lack of variety in his R.A.F. duties. In 1930 he resigned his commission and took a job with F. G. Miles who was operating an air-taxi service from Shoreham. When Bebb moved on to Cobham's air circus in 1932 Cobham was already an international figure, hero of survey flights to Australia and South Africa. Bebb found him a dynamic little man, bristling with ideas and enthusiasm which Lady Cobham steered to good purpose. As director of forward publicity for the air circus, Lady Cobham made sure that her husband's vision of bringing aeroplanes to the masses made the most of its commercial possibilities.

The circus flew from farmers' fields and factory sports grounds, drawing crowds of 3,000 up to 30,000. For Bebb, living in a tent between ceaseless travelling from one town to another, there was the aristocratic status of a stunt pilot, with queues of fans paying 6d each for his photograph—6d extra for his autograph. He was a wealthy young man, averaging £20-a-week in all from a basic wage of £5 and 5/- for every hour he was in the air and thrilling the crowds.

His Tiger Moth had two separate fuel systems, one inverted so that he could circle the field upside down at 15 feet. His speciality was the " death dive " which culminated in an upward roll from ground level. That was the manoeuvre which lost him his propeller during a performance at Glasgow. He did his display in the midst of thirteen or fourteen other circus planes, some giving formation exhibitions, others sky-writing, and most of them offering joy-rides to the public. The cheapest flight was 5/-, the most expensive was

£2 and included a flick roll and loop performed by P. P. Phillips, a tall studious pilot from Truro. His passengers sat without seat belts in an open cockpit and were still there afterwards for the same reason that water remains in a bucket swung over one's head. Phillips' wry humour liked to assess which passengers came out of the loop with a stomach feeling like the water in just such a bucket.

The circus had a variety of characters. There was Ivor Price, the parachutist who earned £5 every time he jumped from the wing of Bebb's Tiger Moth. Planning a world record of ten drops within an hour at one Scottish performance, he packed the nine extra parachutes himself and took a pre-packed parachute from the stores for his first jump. Bebb watched him leave the wing at an altitude of 1,200 feet, saw the parachute unfurl but not open, and followed Price's fall to the ground. Women in the crowd were still screaming when Bebb landed beside the body. He saw blood spilling from Price's mouth. Then ambulance men were cutting away the tangled parachute and the world record attempt ended with an ambulance driving slowly from the field and the crowd standing in respectful silence. Three hours later there was frantic applause as Price limped back on the field. He had landed on ground left soft by heavy rain and had expertly taken the impact on his left thigh and shoulder. Except for flesh grazes and bruises he was unharmed. The blood Bebb saw was caused by biting his lip in the jolt of landing. Price was jumping as usual the following day. He was eventually killed trying a double delay jump with a girl parachutist.

Even an air circus needed a clown and Cobham engaged Martin Hearne to play this role. In true tradition, Hearne was a sad clown. He was a small, neat Lancashire man, an engineer by trade and a cynic by way of apology for choosing to earn a living in an air circus.

" I'm only doing this for quick money," he used to assure Bebb. " My real ambition is to have my own engineering company and have Cobham dirty his hands working for me."

Hearne would blacken his face and wear baggy clothes for a comedy routine with a Model T Ford which Bebb bombed from his Tiger Moth with bags of flour. Another part of Hearne's act was to walk the wing of an Avro Tutor single-engined training plane, also flown by Bebb. Wearing a tight-fitting white suit and rubber shoes, Hearne would climb out of the cockpit on to the wing and walk about with no form of harness, then sit on the edge of the wing and climb down on to the landing wheels while the plane did a loop. Bebb needed to put the Tutor into a steep dive and build up to a speed of 130 m.p.h. to overcome the extra drag of a man dangling from the wheels. Hearne's features were distorted by the wind tearing at his face. To Bebb it was an expression which always suggested a mask beaten to the shape of a cynical smile.

Hearne lost his smile when another pilot took over from Bebb for three weeks during the circus's tour of South Africa. Bebb was taken ill with typhoid fever and was still weak when Hearne began to plead with him to return to the show.

"I know something is going to happen with this other chap," said the clown, utterly serious and sincere. "I've got a premonition he's going to have an accident or get killed. I don't want to do the act with him any more. In fact, I don't even want to travel in his plane when we move on to Capetown tomorrow."

The tour was nearing its end and Cobham wanted Bebb to have a look at a small airfield not far from Capetown and see if it was good enough for an extra show before the circus returned to England. Bebb agreed that Hearne could fly to Capetown with him by way of this airfield. The circus commentator went with the other pilot on a direct flight to Capetown. Bebb and Hearne arrived a few hours later, after their detour, having established the small airfield was not suitable for a public performance. They reached Capetown to find the rest of the company mourning the loss of a star pilot and the commentator. Hearne's premonition had been tragically fulfilled. The plane in which he should have travelled reached its destination without incident, went into a loop over the airfield to celebrate a safe arrival, and plunged into the ground, killing pilot and passenger.

The death of the circus commentator was a personal blow to Bebb. They were good friends and worked closely together during one of the highlights of his display—diving at a row of six coloured balloons and shooting them down from his cockpit with a Colt revolver. Bebb always missed with his first shot and the commentator explained to the crowd that the pilot was having to calculate such technicalities as wind and drift and light. Bebb would swoop towards the balloons and miss a second time, giving the commentator ample scope to build up the suspense. " Is Captain Bebb going to fail at long last? Six balloons to hit and only four bullets left. Can he possibly save his reputation as the ace marksman of the skies?" The third time Bebb fired, one of the balloons exploded and so, to mounting applause, it was with his fourth and fifth bullets. Finally, with the commentator unable to control the tremble in his voice and the crowd gasping with uncertainty, Bebb would approach the balloons at a sharp angle, fire his last bullet and burst all three of the remaining balloons.

The commentator took to his death the secret that he " shot " the balloons while Bebb fired only blank cartridges. The balloons were filled with hydrogen and connected to an electrical circuit running from the target stand to the commentary box. By pressing a button the commentator could explode whichever sequence of balloons gave most drama to his commentary.

At midday on his third day in Las Palmas, Bebb had reached the opinion that Pollard's whole mission was as big a pretence as that aerial attack on the balloons. The major was putting on a great act as a conspirator but there was no real action to justify all the furtiveness. The business with the soldiers, Bebb decided, was nothing more than a routine interview carried out in what were probably very normal circumstances by local standards. He would believe the story about a Riff leader when such a character was produced for him.

Bebb received the note from Pollard shortly after 2 p.m. as he was sitting in the hotel lounge. The note was delivered by two Spaniards and the message read: "Take these two fellows to Mutt and Jeff." The schoolboy flavour of such a password brought a snigger from Bebb when Pollard had warned him to expect this message from Tenerife.

Now the message was here and there was nothing very funny about it any more. The meaning was that he should go with whoever presented the note and accept them and their friends as members of the conspiracy. The car waiting at the rear of the hotel seemed familiar to Bebb. So did the beginning of the drive out of the town. When the car climbed into the hills and stopped in the grounds of the same villa, Bebb was reconciled to the shock of Pollard's plot having been betrayed. He prepared to maintain his story of an innocent holiday flight no matter how fierce the interrogation should be. But this time the general received him as a friend. He introduced himself as General Orgaz and said: "I do apologise, Captain Bebb, for the manner of our first meeting but you do understand that we had to test your loyalty to our cause. We were most impressed by your behaviour. Now there is no need for pretence on either side. Events have begun which will give you your passenger to Morocco before very long. Your safety is now most important and I think it will be better if you stay in this house until it is time to go to the airport."

Bebb discovered from Pollard afterwards that the events mentioned by General Orgaz started with the murder that day of the military governor of Las Palmas.

His funeral was to be held the following day. This provided an excuse for the mysterious figure who was to be Bebb's passenger to leave the house on Tenerife where he was virtually under arrest and visit Las Palmas as one of the mourners. He travelled on the early morning ferry boat, reaching Las Palmas at 7 a.m. Pollard, his daughter and Dorothy Watson crossed from Tenerife on the same boat. Diana Pollard later described the scene: "Every deck was packed with picturesque but sinister gentlemen in raincoats bulging with revolvers."

The day of the funeral, July 17, passed quietly for Bebb at the villa in the hills. Pollard arrived at 5 p.m. with news that the Riff leader had gone into hiding on a fishing boat after the funeral. He would be close at hand to join the Rapide whenever there was an opportunity to make the flight to Morocco. Bebb was got out of bed at three o'clock the next morning. "Now is the time to prepare your aeroplane," he was told. "You must leave Las Palmas at dawn." Pollard was waiting in a car outside the villa. They were driven, with an armed escort, to the airport. Bebb glimpsed groups of soldiers standing guard over road junctions and at bridges. There was a sound of gunfire on all sides. The airport seemed prepared to withstand a siege. Machine guns were mounted on all sides and when Bebb went to his aircraft he found it surrounded by a detachment of soldiers.

Their officer assured Bebb the Rapide had been closely guarded night and day since he arrived. Once more Bebb wondered at the Spanish Army being so closely involved in an attempt to start an Arab rising in Morocco. General Orgaz was in personal command of the forces at the airfield and an intense air of expectancy was directed towards the side of the airfield which adjoined the sea. That was where Bebb's passenger was due to arrive. The Rapide was ready to leave for 6 a.m. but at noon there was still no sign of the passenger. Pollard came back from one of several conferences with General Orgaz and explained that the man they were all waiting for had spent the night on a fishery gunboat which had since disappeared from the main harbour. At 4.30 p.m. the gunboat was seen approaching from out at sea. It anchored off the airfield and five men were rowed ashore in a dinghy. The leader of them was wearing the uniform of a Spanish general. He was a short, square man, received by

General Orgaz with the eager respect which acknowledged a superior.

" This is your man," said Pollard, now displaying openly the excitement he had been trying to hide since leaving Croydon a week before. " There won't be room for me and the girls to come with you and if you should run into any trouble your story is that we gave up our seats to some Spanish businessmen with an urgent appointment in Morocco. Sorry about the Riff leader business. It was a cover for something much, much bigger. You'll get the full story on the way to Morocco." Bebb had his first clue before he could follow the general and his four companions on board the Rapide. A colonel watching the departure was moved to seize Bebb's hand and say: " Take great care, captain. You are about to fly the future leader of Spain."

During the brief flight to Agadir on the African mainland, Bebb was formally introduced to General Franco, now on his way to take command of the Spanish Foreign Legion for the start of a Right Wing rising against the Spanish Government. " This is the moment of history for our country," one of his party said fiercely. General Franco changed into civilian clothes soon after take-off and suggested Pollard's fictional business friend on his way to see a client rather than a great war leader keeping an appointment with destiny. He sat quietly amongst his lieutenants throughout the flight and remained on board the aircraft when Bebb landed at Agadir to send a cable to an address in Casablanca. The text had been dictated by Pollard back at Las Palmas: " Father left for you at 1900—Hugh." Bebb did not want the cable to be linked with their appearance at Agadir. He persuaded the local Shell manager to send the signal for him, then flew on to Casablanca. Two cars were waiting for them when they arrived there in the late evening and they were driven to spend the night in a secluded country house. They were back at the airfield at first light and Bebb was told to set course for Tetuan in Spanish Morocco. General Franco was in uniform once more by the time Bebb flew over a parade

of the Spanish Foreign Legion drawn up on the airfield at
Tetuan. The legionnaires presented arms as the Rapide
landed near a group of senior officers and General Franco set
foot on Moroccan soil. There were the stiff salutes of military
protocol and then the officers made an emotional surge to
embrace their leader.

At that moment General Franco was merely one of the
leaders of the revolution. Another leader and the man most
widely expected to take over supreme command of the
revolution was General Sanjurjo, living in exile in Portugal.
The same day that Bebb's Rapide delivered Franco to
Tetuan another charter plane, a Puss Moth with a French
pilot, set off for Cascais, west of Lisbon, to take General
Sanjurjo to Burgos, in northern Spain, chosen as the capital
of the revolutionary government. The general boarded the
Puss Moth on the morning of July 20 and was killed when
the plane crashed into a tree on take-off. The pilot, trapped
in the wreckage and badly burned, was later flown to a
Spanish hospital at Burgos by a Rapide of British Airways,
piloted by R. H. McIntosh, known as "All Weather Mac"
from his experiences in the earliest days of commercial flying.

The crash at Cascais ensured that Bebb's passenger from
Las Palmas was the future ruler of all Spain. Several years
later the Spanish government was to buy the Rapide, GAC-YR,
as a museum piece and Bebb was to receive from Franco's
hands the Order of Merit. But on that July morning in 1936
Captain Cecil Bebb, of Olley Air Services, flew away from the
Foreign Legion parade at Tetuan and set off towards England
with no idea of the scale of events he had helped to set in
motion. The Spaniard who described it as a moment in history
for his country was unwittingly modest. The Spanish Civil
War would influence the history of the whole world—and,
not least, the history of aviation.

For some of the people due to be most directly involved
in all that followed the same July morning seemed like any
other.

Freddy Laker was at school in Canterbury, a 15-year-old

27

boy with a passion for motor cars. Harold Bamberg, at school in Hampstead, watched the air displays at nearby Hendon aerodrome with curiosity but little feeling. Another school-boy, Bill Bright, came from Marylebone to watch the same displays and stirred his ambition to become an electrical engineer with the first ideas of being a pilot instead. Living in Hendon was Bob Batt, working with his father in the building trade during the week but spending his weekends as an air frame fitter with 604 Squadron of the Auxiliary Air Force.

On the opposite side of London, Monique Agazarian, a schoolgirl at the Sacred Heart Convent, Roehampton, dreamed of becoming an actress after success in the school play. Alan Green was a pupil at Springfield Junior School, in Cheshire, the son of a gas inspector and mad about trains. Joe Viatkin, an engineering student, wore his khaki uniform as a Company Quartermaster Sergeant at an Army Cadet Force camp in the Isle of Wight, and secretly planned to emigrate to Australia and become a musician.

Dr. Graham Humby was taking two weeks leave from a London hospital to instruct other young glider pilots at the London Gliding Club he had helped to form on Dunstable Down two years before. Cliff Luxton, a wireless operator-air gunner with the R.A.F., had just returned to England after seven years in the Middle East. Captain Anthony Christopher Loraine was flying an Armstrong Whitworth Atlanta airliner between Karachi and Singapore on the Imperial Airways route to Australia where Don Ludbey was home from school on his father's farm in the Tasmanian bush.

And in the far west of Canada, Homer Cochrane, son of an M.P. who died when he might well have become Premier of British Columbia, listened to tales of the air battles of World War I told by a neighbour who was once a major in the Royal Flying Corps.

From such assortment of characters spread across the world was to emerge an Elizabethan age of aviation and a breed of far flying merchant venturers—gentlemen of fortune prepared to go anywhere, do anything; pilots willing to fly any kind of aircraft, carry any kind of payload; men and women eager for uncertainty, afraid only of the safe routine. They were to find their opportunity in the vast fleets of surplus aircraft at the end of the world war which so closely succeeded the civil war in Spain. They found the need in a a world made aware of exciting new possibilities in air travel and with the bomb damage left behind to emphasise its meaning.

There had been many charter pilots before Captain Bebb delivered General Franco to Morocco but out of all that followed came the fierce, fervent freemasonry of the sky tramps.

CHAPTER TWO

The Man from Moscow

MOST instinctive pilots reckon to fly by the seat of their pants. The romantics fly by the wings that grow from their shoulders. Others, like Harold Watkins, get swept aloft by a whirlwind of events and stay there, absorbed in the view.

Watkins never considered flying at all for the first twenty-four years of his life. The nearest he came to an aeroplane was watching a vintage biplane give pleasure flights from the beach at Southport in his native Lancashire. He saw it take off without the slightest swell of envy. He was happy enough with all that he could find to do on the ground— his work as a dental mechanic in Rochdale, his camping weekends as a Rover Scout, his games of Rugby League football, his singing with a dance band, his activities as a promoter of tennis tournaments.

The extra money from his singing and promotions was the reason why a young dental mechanic from Rochdale could afford to be enjoying the luxuries of Tenerife on a £1-a-day Canadian Pacific cruise when war broke out in September 1939. As the blacked-out liner sped back to England he decided that playing blind man's buff with U-boats was not his idea of enjoying anything as glamorous as a war. It meant the Royal Navy would have to manage without him. The Army was never even a faint possibility. Who could consider exchanging a crooner's tuxedo for an infantryman's khaki blouse? That left the Royal Air Force, and the more Watkins thought about it the more he liked the idea of becoming a top fighter ace. Now he saw himself at the controls of that biplane from the beach at Southport, but plunging instead into a startled flock of the enemy with a cool smile lurking behind his goggles and a silk scarf trailing in the slipstream. Harold Watkins' imagination had been well polished by the spotlights of his local dance halls. And even from this fringe of show business he recognised a good part in a big production when he saw it. The R.A.F. it would be for him. Within a week of getting home from the cruise he was volunteering for aircrew duties at a Manchester recruiting office.

"Go back home and get ready for a long wait," was the reply. "The training for aircrew isn't even under way yet. It might be nine months before we call you—if it lasts that long, of course." Harold Watkins (songs and guitar) walked out of the recruiting office as if it were an audition studio still ringing to the message: "Don't phone us, we'll phone you." Would it have to be the Navy or the Army? No, he could not settle for anything less than flying once he had glimpsed himself on his first leave as a fighter pilot. Ever since his first appearance on a bandstand he had always dressed with the care of a man with a public image to maintain. He knew that an R.A.F. officer's uniform would do him justice.

So Watkins worked and sang and strummed his guitar and played football and went cycling and waited for the call to wings. He was still waiting on November 30 when Russia invaded Finland and the newspapers—starved of any real news of Britain's war—eagerly paraded their columns of gallant little Finns being ravaged by the great big Russian bully. There was the same message in the posters decorating the Finnish Aid Bureau in London when Watkins was drawn there a few days before Christmas. This was just the sort of war to appeal to him. The big picture had already started and admission was free. He could see that old biplane swooping over the frozen wastes of Finland and hurling back the wicked invaders. He walked inside and signed on as a

volunteer for active service with the Finnish armed forces—
the air force, to be exact.

" How you fight will be decided in Finland," he was told.
" You must ask for the air force when you get there." Watkins
travelled with 300 other volunteers early in the New Year,
crossing from Leith to Bergen in a Norwegian pleasure
cruiser. The ship was kept waiting outside Bergen for two
days while a nervous Norwegian government tried to decide
whether its neutrality would be stained by the passing footprints of the volunteers. When they were allowed ashore,
a train hustled them out of the country and into an even
more grudging Sweden. On a slow, jerky rail journey to the
Finnish frontier Watkins saw several sidings full of R.A.F.
stores, dispatched unofficially by the British Government but
denied passage by the Swedes to the hard-pressed Finns.

At Tornio the volunteers got down out of the train, formed
themselves into some kind of column and marched across a
snow-packed river bridge into Finland. The muffled footfalls
seemed to throw up a sombre mood and men looked at each
other with an edge to their interest. Some were poor and
obviously running away from other people. Others were
wealthy and running away from themselves. Men with titles
marched with labourers and there was a heavy sprinkling of
Italians and Greeks—" the Soho International Bridge,"
thought Watkins.

The wealthy stepped out to meet a Finnish winter with
sheepskin lined coats and quilted ski trousers. Most of the
rest were further proof that Britain is never lacking in
maiden aunts to knit cardigans, mittens and balaclava
helmets for the world's lost causes. Watkins had chosen his
outfit to match the role of gentleman-of-fortune. Knee-length
riding boots and riding breeches gave him, he hoped, just
the right amount of swagger. The smartly tailored overcoat
he had bought in Rochdale only a few weeks before added
the necessary touch of casual elegance. Hidden underneath
was a bright blue sweater—knitted by his favourite aunt.

From Tornio the volunteers were transported south in lorries. Watkins travelled in the same lorry as two ex-R.A.F. sergeant-pilots he had made a point of befriending on the sea-crossing to Bergen. They had been flying Hurricanes before obtaining their release from the R.A.F. and, although Watkins had no idea what a Hurricane was, he was quick enough to be impressed and ask suitably vague questions about its performance. He was fascinated by their easy command of the jargon of aviation and set himself to learn it as if studying a foreign language. All the way across the North Sea he cross-examined them relentlessly about basic flying procedure, controls, instruments, and assessments of weather conditions. On the train through Norway and Sweden he harried them for airmen's views on the different types of aircraft they were likely to fly. And now, in the lorry taking them to war, he carefully observed the kind of slang they introduced into normal conversation.

" If you're so interested why don't you put down for the air force?" said one of the pilots as their interrogation ended with the lorries pulling into a military camp outside Lapua, in central Finland. " It's an idea," said Watkins, trying to avoid the complacency of a man of destiny. " I hadn't really thought of it before."

Three hundred other international volunteers, including a large contingent of Hungarians, were already installed in the camp and waiting impatiently for something to happen. The new arrivals caused a flurry of excitement and then there was more waiting until January 21 when the Volunteer Brigade was officially called into being. Kitting out began and Watkins was disgusted at having to replace his own dashing clothes with, of all things, an infantryman's khaki battledress and British Army boots. The addition of a Finnish ski cap with ear-flaps introduced a brighter, cosmopolitan flavour which the pitifully inadequate boots were soon to chill with drill parades and route marches through the snow. His romantic notions were finally frozen solid— from the feet upwards—during long Arctic nights of sentry duty listening to wild dogs howl and watching Northern Lights flash across the very skies he had come to fly.

The lights of battle were still more than 200 miles away to the east. The Russian advance, which had begun with brass bands playing and mobile cinemas to entertain the oppressed workers, plus free gifts for their womenfolk, had stumbled to a halt. Now the Finns were hitting back, encircling whole columns of ill-equipped Russians with sudden swoops by ski-troops almost invisible against the snow in their white cloaks.

Watkins heard tell of the massacre of the Russian 44th Division, surrounded at Raate. A break-out failed, with 1,000 prisoners and sixty guns in the hands of the Finns and 10,000 believed perished in a wilderness where snow froze so hard that a twelve-inch thickness of it would stop a bullet. A week after the battle a party of Russians were found hiding in the woods, living off the flesh of a dead horse. The fugitives were so horribly frost-bitten that some had their ears and strips of their scalp fall off when their hats were removed. None survived.

The excitement of Finns telling these stories only added to Watkins' frustration over the next two weeks of inaction at Lapua. Then a notice was posted inviting volunteers for the Finnish air force—"some flying experience necessary." The two ex-R.A.F. sergeant-pilots had quietly moved out a week before but Watkins was confident he had learned enough from them to play his chosen part. He went for an interview with a Finnish air force officer and recited all the aviation jargon he had so deliberately acquired over the past few weeks. He modestly claimed 200 hours of club flying in a friend's private plane, mentioned a few hours in Tiger Moths, explained he had been an officer with the Air Training Corps.

If the interviewing officer had any suspicions he did not press them. The Finnish air force, which began the war with only half of its 130 aircraft battle-worthy, was even more desperately understrength after more than two months of massive air attacks by the Russians. A few British Bristol Bull-dog fighters and some Blenheim bombers comprised the front-line element of the Finnish air force. British pilots for British machines was an attractive proposition. Harold Watkins and twenty other volunteers were accepted for the Finnish air force and moved to an air base near Jyvaskyla, a hundred miles nearer the front line.

Watkins made his first flight early in February 1940, and his Rochdale day dreams proved to have been remarkably accurate. He sat in the open cockpit of an aged biplane very similar to the flying machine of Southport Beach and pre-pared to meet the enemy with a World War I machine-gun mounted over the rear seat. The sensations of flying made an immediate appeal. The sportsman in him especially appreciated the sprinting surge of take-off, the pole-vaulter's feeling of pushing the earth far away beneath him, the long distance strides across the open skies with tingling fresh air to suck deeply into his lungs.

Watkins learned fast and easily which was a necessary qualification for a training course as hurried and pathetically equipped as this. The planes were parked and serviced in hangars formed by interwoven branches of trees covered with snow. The runway was a frozen lake. His first lesson in navigation was picking out his lake from the thousands of other lakes in Finland. One lake tends to look like any other lake when it is one more patch of white in a white land-scape. Lights from a Very pistol were the only approach aid in a mist or a sudden blizzard. Usually the pilot picked out the lake by some slight landmark and lined up on coloured markers across the ice as he let down over the surrounding trees. The Finnish groundstaff then displayed a flash of matador agility to help pilots facing the problem of landing on skids with no form of braking. As the plane approached the far end of the lake, with little loss of speed, two mechanics would run out from the trees, each grab a wing, and throw their weight against the forward movement of the plane. At the same time they altered the direction of the plane to run it off the lake and back to its hiding place under the trees. Several times Watkins crouched in his snow hangar and watched Russian bombers rumble overhead, looking for these airfields which were nowhere and everywhere. Watkins twice fled back to his lake from training flights when he caught sight of what might have been Russian planes in the distance. Tempted as he was to listen to the chatter of his venerable machine-gun, he knew the loss of a precious training aircraft would be a major blow to the Finns' supply of aircrew replacements.

The Russians had opened the war with air attacks on Helsinki (when one of the bombers they lost turned out to have had a woman pilot) and the raids had grown steadily heavier all over Finland. By the end of February Watkins found that he was navigating by the columns of smoke and heaps of blackened debris which littered the once clean tablecloth of snow. The wood-built town of Sortavala had been burnt down from end to end, leaving 17,000 people homeless. Russian losses averaged thirty-five planes a week but they could still afford to launch two hundred bombers at a single target. Finnish losses, though slight numerically, were disastrously heavy as a fraction of the total air strength they could summon.

Watkins finished his training during the second week in March and qualified for active service with an air force that now had more pilots than planes. At noon on March 13, the war ended without his firing a single shot at the enemy. The refusal of Norway and Sweden to allow the passage of Allied troops and equipment had finally forced the Finns to submit to Russia's territorial demands. Watkins read Field Marshal Mannerheim's last order of the day to the still-defiant Finnish people on March 14 and tried to find some consolation in the reminder that " 200,000 of the enemy now lie beneath the frozen snows or with sightless gaze contemplate our starry skies." One brand-new, unemployed pilot contemplated the same skies and wondered bitterly what he was supposed to do next. The Finns could offer no immediate suggestions. After sitting around their frozen airfield for a fortnight the volunteers were regrouped at Jyvaskyla in a lakeside holiday hotel to await repatriation.

Little more than a week later, the Germans began their invasion of Norway and Denmark and the route back to England was firmly closed for the rest of the war. The Finnish Government provided the compensation of unlimited hospitality at the hotel. Through the spring and summer Watkins and his comrades were able to wine, dine, swim, sail and ride at their hosts' expense. Local families pressed entertainment on them. Some of the volunteers fell in love with Finnish girls and stopped bothering about the problem of getting back home. Several men remembered the girls they had left behind and decided to make their own way back to England. Watkins never knew if they succeeded but he heard stories of stowaways being seized from American ships once outside Finnish waters, of Sweden turning back all illegal immigrants. His own inclination was to wait and see if the authorities could not come up with an official scheme for repatriation, perhaps organised by the Red Cross. By the end of August he was convinced such a scheme was not going to happen. Listening to BBC broadcasts about the Battle of Britain, he thrilled to an urge to be back in an aeroplane and fighting for his country. It was time to leave Finland.

Watkins set off for Helsinki with his best friend of the Volunteer Brigade, Frank Baxter, a small, dark, wiry ex-seaman was also about twenty-four. They stowed away on a Swedish ship but were discovered by the chief engineer while still at the quayside and returned to the shore. Next, they stole a twenty-foot yacht from its moorings in the outer harbour and set sail for the open sea with the wildly optimistic plan of sailing through the Baltic islands to reach Sweden, hugging the Swedish coast until they could slip through the Kattegat and Skagerrak and then cross the North Sea to England. Two days later they were back in Finland, run aground and minus all sail after being caught in a violent storm. Abandoning the yacht, they hiked back to the hotel at Jyvaskyla, covering a distance of 150 miles on foot. Then, while resting from these two unsuccessful attempts to get away, they evolved a third plan. They would take a boat and make the relatively easy fifty-mile crossing due south from Helsinki to Estonia. From there they would make their way overland through Russian-occupied Poland to Rumania where there was still a British consul. He would arrange for them to join the British forces in the Mediterranean.

This plan was worked out in face of the advice of everybody they consulted. The Finns warned them about venturing into Russian occupied territory. Their fellow volunteers insisted they could never cover such a vast distance on foot. Only Bob Francis, a middle-aged man who was once a Regular soldier in the British Army, was encouraging enough to offer to join them. The offer was accepted. Francis had also been a travel agent in Hamburg before the war. He knew Central Europe well and spoke several languages.

At the beginning of October, Watkins was back in Helsinki, prowling around the city's intricate waterway system in the middle of the night to find another escape boat. In the darkness, he spotted a yacht of about the same size as before. He called up his two companions and led them on board as it rocked at its moorings. Something seemed familiar in exploring the darkened cabin with an electric torch. He looked carefully at the curtains, the blankets, the brass fittings. This was the same yacht they had stolen for their first voyage. It must have been re-fitted and the hull repaired —just in time for the fugitives' next expedition. Watkins felt the twist of guilt, then chuckled to think of the owner deciding his boat really must be bewitched.

Once at sea, the yacht ran into the conditions which had hurled it back before. This time Baxter managed to hold the boat to some slight progress in face of high wind and fierce seas. The fifty-mile crossing took three whole days and they spent the last night with Watkins lashed to the mast, Baxter lashed to the wheel, and Francis collapsed exhausted in the bottom of the boat. Watkins woke at dawn and heard from Baxter how they had been almost run down by a steamer in the night while they rolled helplessly and showed no lights.

In the early daylight they could make out the Estonian coast ahead. Baxter and a revived Francis used blankets to improvise some extra sail as Watkins took over the wheel. At that moment, a wave as big and grey as an aircraft hangar swept over the yacht, plucking Watkins out of the cockpit and leaving him floundering in the wild sea, weighed down by the heavy ski boots he had chosen to wear for the trek across Poland. Then came another huge wave to lift the boat and place it carefully beside him. He grabbed the broken boom and pulled himself back on board. Baxter and Francis were baling out so furiously they scarcely hailed his safe return. The yacht was dangerously low in the water. Another wave could send her to the bottom. Watkins seized a bucket and began to bail, too.

They were hard at it when the Russian coastguard boat came alongside, bristling with rifles and grim faces. The yacht was taken in tow and led into the Estonian port of Tallin. An hour later the three men were in separate cells under armed guard. That night they were interrogated in turn by a Russian officer whose manner was that of dealing with self-confessed spies even when the Englishmen confessed nothing of the sort. Watkins thought it wiser not to explain about the Finnish air force. He said the war had found them working in Finland and they were merely trying to get back home to fight the Germans. The officer listened to his story with an implacable disinterest which chilled Watkins for the rest of the two days spent in the Tallin prison. From there, they were taken by train to Leningrad and then Moscow. Watkins began the journey with his confidence restored. Once in Moscow, he was sure, the British Embassy would have them free in no time. But he grew steadily more apprehensive as he looked out of the train window at the grey gloom of fear lying over recently occupied Estonia.

On Leningrad station Russian soldiers returning from service in Finland, clad in cheap, tattered uniforms, basket shoes wrapped in rags, and thin cotton gloves, rushed across the platform to stare in at the three prisoners. The Englishmen shrank back from the white faces with vacant eyes pressing towards the window. Then Baxter pointed out that the eyes were directed not at any hated foreigners but at a piece of bread left on the window sill after eating lunch in the compartment. The men returning from a war they had won were obviously starving.

Watkins was to learn all the foolish ecstasies of hunger in the months to follow. The three men were put in Moscow's elite Lubyanka prison (where U-2 pilot Gary Powers would also be imprisoned some twenty years later) and placed in separate cells once more. Watkins spent the next three weeks in solitary confinement on a diet of black bread and cabbage water. Then he was transferred to a larger cell and had to scramble each morning and evening with six or seven other prisoners for his share of the same diet. His cell-mates were of various mid-European nationalities with not a gleam of curiosity to brighten their despair when a brash young Englishman arrived in their midst. Watkins responded to every change of scene with nothing but optimism. He relished even this sort of human company after his solitary confinement and was soon assuring a Pole who spoke English that the British Embassy would have him released.

"And while I'm waiting," Watkins said, " I don't intend to curl up and die like this lot. I've come in here a fit man and I intend to keep in shape until the British Ambassador comes to collect me." The other prisoners watched blankly as he paced out the cell and calculated it was ten yards long by about ten feet wide. Their attitude changed to pity when he set himself the target of a ten-mile walk each day, pacing up and down the cell in his ski boots for two hours each morning and evening. The mood of the other prisoners changed again when Watkins rebelled against such prison routine as standing to attention for cell inspection or sleeping with both arms outside the blanket for the guard to see through his inspection grille. Now his cell-mates were uneasy, even hostile. They did not want anyone to cause trouble in case it meant trouble for them. Watkins ignored their protests. After all the fears and hopes of his first month in captivity he was angry with the Russians for all their stubborn suspicions about spying. To submit meekly would be an admission of guilt. Nobody was going to push him around.

He centred each day on the twenty minutes of exercise in a deep well of the prison with a tiny patch of sky far above. The days of flying high and free over Finland were far away but after the dank, sweaty atmosphere of the prison the breath of outside air seemed as fresh as that he tasted in his cockpit 5,000 feet towards heaven. He always joined the outer ring of brisk walkers to make the most of his exercise and one day was stimulated to whistle *Colonel Bogey* out loud as he strode out at the head of his file of prisoners. The effect was startling. The guards wheeled in his direction, levelled their rifles, clicked the safety catches and yelled for him to be silent. The prisoners shrank away from him, horrified by his temerity. Watkins didn't whistle again but he liked to think *Colonel Bogey* would long be remembered by all who heard him.

Another little gesture of defiance came on the way down the long iron steps leading to the exercise yard. The prisoners marched with hands on head, watched at every bend in the steps by an armed guard. Halfway down the steps Watkins came face to face with a guard who was an attractive Russian girl. She wore the same uniform as the men except for a blue skirt, displayed the same Red Star, carried the same kind of pistol. But the one-time crooning idol of Rochdale glimpsed a pretty face and long black hair swept back, and gave her a full-blooded wink from underneath the hands clasped on his head. Then he marched on his way, shaken by the stark terror which swept the girl's face before she turned to face the wall. She was still facing the wall when the column returned from exercise. Watkins lay on his bed that night and blamed himself for putting the girl in danger. No wonder she was terrified. If another guard had seen the wink she would never have convinced the authorities she was other than an accomplice of the foreign spy. A prisoner would not wink at a guard unless they were on intimate terms. Watkins shuddered at this robot logic and began to sympathise with the cell-mates he had been despising as docile cattle. Some of them were political prisoners, some were criminals, some did not know what they were prisoners for. All were suspicious and fearful because of the Soviet tradition of bribing one prisoner in each cell to be a secret informer.

The interrogation of Watkins continued relentlessly—always in the middle of the night when the prisoner was at his lowest ebb. He would be marched down long corridors with guards tapping with their keys on each door that had to be opened. The sound of metal tapping on metal was to feed his nightmares for many years to come. Questioning took place across a long green baize table in a dark room. Why did you come to our country? Who sent you to spy on us? Why not confess like your two friends who are going to be sent home? Do you want to be shot for refusing to tell the truth? One type of interrogator would be angry at Watkins' protests of innocence. Another kind showed no emotion at all. None believed him.

In February, some of the inmates of Lubyanka were transferred to another Moscow prison. Watkins went in one of a stream of small black vans and caught sight of big gates and a courtyard as they turned into his new home. He was pushed into a large room with fifty or sixty people inside and was elated to see Baxter and Francis in the middle of the crowd. His optimism soared again in the puppy-dog flurry of his reunion with them. Surely they would be released this time. His two friends seemed to think so and they pointed out something he had overlooked in his surprise at seeing them. A lot of the men in the room were in British Army and Royal

Navy uniforms. They had escaped from prisoner-of-war camps in Germany into Russian territory only to be charged with the inevitable espionage. Some of them were in a sad state of malnutrition and they told the three men from Finland of the primitive camps where they had been held. Unknown to them, their move to Moscow was part of a Russian change of policy which anticipated the need for better relations with Britain and the Western Allies should Hitler decide to invade Russia. Allied prisoners were to be given better treatment—and Watkins, Baxter and Francis shared in the extra rations, including half a glass of milk a day and soup which distinctly resembled soup.

' Looks like they're definitely fattening us up to send us home," Francis said happily towards the end of the third week of the new régime. That afternoon he was taken away for questioning. He came back several hours later with all the marks of a savage beating. He woke in the middle of the night, foaming at the mouth and screaming of black terrors. Guards came and carried him away. His comrades were never to see him again.

This was a great shock to Watkins' complacent dreams of home. Even worse, next day he and Baxter were moved to another part of the building on the grounds they were not in the same category as the British Servicemen. The two men managed to pass on their names and home addresses before being taken away to spend the next six months in the depths of the prison, deeper still in the misery that they were lost to the world for ever. It might have been some consolation to them that in far-off Rochdale Watkins' father was writing to the Foreign Office, telling them of a report from Finland which indicated his son might have been taken by the Russians in trying to return to England, urging some action to secure their release. But it was as well the two prisoners did not know the Russian Government would always deny their very existence.

At the end of August, Watkins and Baxter were taken before a cheerful young Russian officer who announced they had been sentenced to five years' detention for violating territorial waters and were being transferred to a labour camp in the Ural mountains. He suggested the Government had decided to be lenient. In fact, Moscow's prisons were being emptied for extra troops coming in to garrison Moscow in face of the advancing Germans. Watkins had heard prison rumours of the Germans invading Russia in June. Only when he and Baxter were taken with thousands of other prisoners to the railway station and could see the bomb damage and defence works did they really believe Russia was at war. Russian planes patrolled overhead. Watkins looked up and recognised them as the I 153 fighters he had been taught to identify back on that frozen airstrip in Finland when he was learning to fly.

The journey to the Urals took five day and six nights in cattle trucks packed with pale, gaunt men who became savages in the lurching, rattling blackness of night as they screamed and fought to find places on the wooden shelves which served as bunks. Watkins and Baxter were with a party dropped off at a camp which was a thousand kilometres east of Gorkiy. The camp was a collection of huts within double fences of barbed wire dominated by machine-gun towers. Floodlights swept the fences at night and guard dogs prowled between the wire. Conditions within the camp were calculated to ensure the release of a constant flow of prisoners—by death from starvation and exhaustion. The medical officer used a variety of powerful injections to make sure that disease did not complicate the system.

Watkins found himself having to get up at 3.30 a.m. to be marched ten kilometres to the woods where the work of tree felling to make railroad sleepers began at 5 a.m. and went on until 7 p.m., followed by a march back to the camp. The twelve-stone Rugby League player had lost weight steadily during the long months in Moscow's prisons. He was down to little more than six-stone within two weeks of arriving in the Urals and having to work 14 hours a day on black bread and cabbage water for breakfast and a bowl of soup for supper. He sprawled on his bed at night and tried to lose his hunger by singing to himself the words of the 200 popular songs he could remember from his crooning back in Lancashire.

Physically, the last glimmer of his old bandstand bounce disappeared within that labour camp. Gone was the proud rebel prepared to march ten miles a day within his cell. Instead, he learned the art of being idle and worked only when the guards were looking. He learned the more difficult art of watching cruelty and death without being moved to rage. He watched an 18-year-old German prisoner-of-war ordered to strip off his clothes and made to work in the blazing late summer sun until his body was one huge blister. He watched the boy being shot in the stomach as he stepped outside the permitted working area to get a drink of water. He watched him left to die in the sun—and almost envied his body the ride back to camp on a mule.

Watkins saw other prisoners make a bid for freedom without having the will to contemplate escape for himself. Yet he somehow never believed he would die or would stay there for ever. Not even when his shrivelled body was covered with sores and wounds and became so weak he could hardly walk from one side of the camp to the other when the administrator sent for him one afternoon in late September. Baxter was already there. If anything, he was in slightly better condition.

" You are both to go back to Moscow for further questioning," said the administrator. " Since you will be coming back here again do not take any more of your personal possessions than you need for the journey." Their return to Moscow was by passenger train and in a reserved compartment, escorted by two Russian officers. For the first three days the Russian officers said nothing and the two Englishmen wondered impassively what fresh fate was in store for them. Then one of the Russians permitted himself a smile and said: " Soon you will be back in England again." That was all he would say but the words brought a feverish flush of hope to two sunken faces. What, they wondered, had been going on?

The truth was that the personal details they gave to the Allied Servicemen they met in the Moscow prison had been passed on to the Foreign Office when the Servicemen were repatriated a few months afterwards as part of an Anglo-Russian trade deal. At last here was proof that Watkins and Baxter were in Russia. Sir Stafford Cripps personally asked for their release at one of his interviews with Stalin at the height of the German summer offensive. He raised the matter again in August after completing a further £10,000,000 aid agreement with the People's Commissar of Foreign Trade, Mr. Anastas Mikoyan. The Russians still denied all official knowledge of the three Britons. There was no explanation that Francis had been dead since February. But a devious course of action was begun by bringing Watkins and Baxter back to Moscow by train and ended with a taxi drawing up on the opposite side of the street to the British Embassy at daybreak on October 13, 1941. Two frail figures were pushed out on to the road and the taxi drove off.

Watkins and Baxter, a pair of scarecrows in dead men's clothes issued to them in a Moscow warehouse an hour before, ran across the street and into the Embassy. The sentry on the gate refused to notice their passing, the final Russian pretence that these were creatures who did not exist. An Embassy orderly admitted them with the more natural re-action of " Who the hell are you?" The formal welcome came from an officer of the British military mission. " So glad you turned up," he said. " We've been looking for you chaps for the best part of a year." Then came the sherry and the steak and chips and the vomiting and more steak and chips and brandy and more vomiting. Watkins and Baxter lay on their beds in a suite in the National Hotel and wallowed in the extravagance of eating food which would not stay in their stomachs. They listened to the advancing Germans' bombardment of Moscow and did not care to understand what it might mean. Two days later they joined the Embassy staff in the evacuation to the Volga and the emergency capital of Kuibishev. At one wayside station they saw Sir Stafford

Cripps take a wooden bowl and join the communal queue for soup.

From Kuibishev they were sent to Teheran, leaving Russia under diplomatic protection almost exactly a year after being arrested by Russian coastguards. The British military headquarters in Teheran offered them immediate commissions in Army Intelligence and the opportunity of employing their special knowledge of Russia. Watkins preferred to employ the brief experience of flying which had led to his ordeal. After those long months in captivity he wanted to go vaulting across the open skies again and breathe air which had never been filtered by prison bars. He joined the R.A.F. in Baghdad, moved to Rhodesia for training, and early in 1943 came home to Rochdale in the pilot's uniform he first chose as a replacement for his crooner's tuxedo.

Instead of the biplanes of Southport beach and the Finnish lake, he flew a Lancaster bomber of 9 Squadron on special operations, including the sinking of the *Tirpitz*. Frank Baxter also joined the R.A.F. in Teheran and went to Rhodesia for aircrew training. Eager to get home he volunteered as a rear-gunner, requiring only a three-month course. He returned to England in the spring of 1942 and was killed in action with a Lancaster squadron soon afterwards. That left only one survivor of the expedition which set sail from Helsinki in the stolen yacht.

Squadron Leader Harold Watkins, D.F.C., left the R.A.F. in 1947, unable to get a permanent commission. Joining British European Airways as a first officer, he resigned when he saw there was little chance of promotion. At a time when the State airlines had been given a monopoly of all scheduled services, there were no less than sixty-nine independent companies competing for charter work. Most charter companies were founded on ex-Service gratuities and sheer enthusiasm and were soon to founder through lack of business sense. They could find their aircraft from war surplus bombers, available by the hundred at a few hundred pounds each. But there were thousands of trained pilots looking for work and

Watkins joined the army of sky tramps, marching from one aerodrome to the next, willing to fly anything, anywhere for anyone. He found a job with the Lancashire Aircraft Corporation, and flew a converted Halifax bomber on passenger and freight charters throughout Europe, to Saigon and India.

Watkins moved on to a small charter company, World Air Freight, and the flair for survival which brought him out of Russia was put to the test again by a most ill-fated enterprise. One of World Air Freight's four aircraft crashed in the Isle of Man. A second crashed in the Russian zone of Germany during the Berlin Airlift, killing Watkins' crew and the pilot who had taken over the flight. A third crashed at Brindisi with Watkins on board as a passenger, wrecking the aircraft but injuring no one. The fourth and last of the fleet flew into the Alps and wiped out the whole crew. Watkins had already changed jobs by the time of the final disaster. He joined Harold Bamberg's Eagle Aviation and was so impressed by Bamberg's energetic good sense that he decided to make his career with Eagle. By 1953 he was chief pilot and flying into Communist Jugoslavia to inaugurate the first scheduled service to Belgrade.

In October 1955, the ex-prisoner of Lubyanka made his first return to Russian controlled territory when he flew the British Olympic football team to Sofia for their match with Bulgaria. Watkins' instinctive fears and suspicions vanished during four days of banquets and toasts of friendship. At one civic reception he was called forward and presented with a cigarette box and pipe. He took off from Sofia for the return flight feeling that his treatment while imprisoned by the Russians could well have been the result of war-time tensions, that perhaps the Communist mind had since mellowed its distrust of the foreigner.

At 5,000 feet, the air hostess hurried into the cockpit with the news that the aircraft appeared to be falling to pieces. Watkins went back to see the passengers, including F.A. officials, and several Fleet Street sports writers, protecting themselves against panels and brackets falling from the overhead luggage racks and from the ceiling. After a close examination, Watkins was able to return to his cockpit, reassuring the passengers that the aircraft had no structural weakness and that nothing else was likely to fall on top of them. During the Viking airliner's four-day stay at Sofia Airport, the security police had obviously dismantled the interior fittings in a search for sinister secrets which were not there, and had replaced some of the screws carelessly. Suddenly, the smell of his old prison cell reached to 5,000 feet and it lingered in Watkins' pillow for many nights to come.

CHAPTER THREE

Flight out of Africa

THE DC-3 airliner of Mercury Airways was forced down in
the desert mid-way between Wadi Halfa and Khartoum in
the early afternoon of October 12, 1948. A wandering lamp
in the cockpit, used for close inspection of individual pieces
of equipment, had fallen to the floor and caused an electrical
short-circuit on impact. The flash ignited hydraulic fluid
leaking from a small pipe almost beneath the feet of Captain
J. Scott, the pilot. In a matter of seconds, the cockpit was
alight. Scott's clothes began to smoulder as he stayed at the
controls and put the aircraft into an emergency dive. His
first officer warned the twenty-three passengers, English
families emigrating to South Africa, to fasten their seat belts
and prepare for a forced landing. A mother and her two
children, sitting in one of the forward seats, clung together
in terror as flames from the cockpit burst outside the fuselage
and began to lick back at the first passenger window.

Half-blinded by smoke and fumes, his hands and face
badly blistered by the heat, his trouser legs beginning to
burn, Scott made a perfect landing in the desert, ten miles
west of the Nile. He organised the evacuation of the plane
and led the passengers to a safe distance from the blazing
DC-3. His burns were then found to be severe and one of his
crew was also suffering from burns.

An Anson aircraft of the R.A.F. passing overhead
immediately afterwards reported the forced landing to Khar-

toum by radio and then turned to land beside the huddle of survivors. The two injured airmen, three women and two children were taken on board the Anson which flew them to Khartoum, returning later in the day to collect another eight women and children. A convoy of Army trucks then reached the scene and the rest of the passengers and crew began the 175-mile drive to Khartoum.

News of the DC-3's forced landing reached Bob Batt, flight engineer with Halifax ZS PTA of Alpha Airways, as he was working on an overhaul of his aircraft at Randfontein airfield, twenty miles west of Johannesburg. Capt. Dennis Parsons, pilot of the Halifax, took a telephone message and hurried out to the aircraft to tell Batt to abandon his servicing programme and prepare for take-off as soon as possible. "As you know, Bob, Mercury Airways are tied up with Alpha and they want us to dash off to Khartoum and pick up those stranded passengers."

Batt began his working life as a brick-layer in North London and retained the placid manner of a man who knows that the tallest building must still be built by placing one brick on top of another. He worked steadily into the night, reassembling an engine he had taken to pieces only that afternoon and then checking the whole aircraft for the flight north. The Halifax left Randfontein at 3.30 a.m. and called at Johannesburg International Airport to take on board a group of aviation officials who were to investigate the accident. The Halifax arrived at Khartoum at 8.20 the following morning, October 14.

While Batt prepared the plane for a prompt turn-round, Parsons was involved in a scene with the DC-3 passengers. Ten of them would have to wait for another plane as the Halifax could take only thirteen. He suggested that women and children should be given priority since none of them had been able to bring their belongings from the DC-3 and Khartoum was not the most pleasant place to be without any personal luggage or even a change of clothing. Tearful wives protested that they could not be separated from their husbands so soon after coming close to death. Husbands insisted that families should not be split up in the middle of a strange continent. Two or three men travelling alone claimed urgent appointments in Johannesburg.

Eventually the passengers agreed amongst themselves on the lucky thirteen—mostly women and children—and they went out to the aircraft. There were more complaints when they found themselves within the cramped confines of an ex-bomber after the more refined and spacious fuselage of the DC-3. Parsons took off from Khartoum at 10.15 on a morning of scorching heat and fierce turbulence. The flight to Entebbe on the shores of Lake Victoria was a series of bumps and lurches—to the alarm of thirteen people whose confidence in aeroplanes had been shaken by the forced landing. An overnight stop was made at Entebbe where the only form of hotel accommodation was a single hut at the side of the runway. Curtains, hanging from the roof, divided the hut into three sections. Women slept on straw mattresses at one end and the men slept at the other end. A long table enabled the middle section to serve as the dining room. Batt and the rest of the crew spent a restless night, punctuated by the sobbing of children from the far end of the hut and one hysterical outburst by a women passenger.

Next morning the Halifax pointed its nose at Lake Victoria and began its take-off along the runway stretching out into the lake, with water on three sides. Batt was in the flight engineer's seat, behind the pilot and facing aft. He watched the surface of the lake streaking past the side windows and then starting to fall away as the plane lifted off the runway. At an altitude of no more than twenty feet and with the wide expanse of Lake Victoria dead ahead there was the slightest tremor from the port wing. Batt looked out along the wing and saw that the reduction gear of the outer engine—contained within the propeller dome—was beginning to sag away from the rest of the engine. Oil was spurting in all directions and the whole engine seemed to be in the process of shaking itself clear of the wing.

Batt called out for Parsons to feather the propeller and close the engine. This was the most critical point of take-off and it would mean the plane losing a quarter of its power. But if the engine were to tear itself free it might take half the wing with it, meaning certain and total disaster. Parsons cut the engine, held the plane in a gentle climb, and then did a wide 180-degree turn to land back on the runway. The passengers first knew they had experienced another emergency only when they were returned to the airport hut and told there would be some delay. Batt propped a ladder against the wing and went up to examine the faulty engine. It was still all there although everything seemed to be hanging on to a few pieces of wire from the cowling. A thick smothering of oil could not hide that a major repair job was indicated. He walked back to the hut and began to prepare the passengers for the idea that it was going to be a rather long delay.

There were no Halifax spares available at Entebbe or anywhere else in Africa as far as he knew. He sent a cable to the company headquarters in London suggesting a replacement engine would be the simplest solution. He was not surprised when the reply ignored that suggestion and merely instructed him to carry out the necessary repairs on the spot. Batt was used to improvisation on Alpha Airways' tramping operations all over Africa and the Middle East but Entebbe was about the worst spot he could have picked for the biggest job he had faced so far.

The immediate need was for some lifting tackle to remove the reduction gear and propeller from the rest of the engine so he could see what damage had been done inside. Batt and Parsons went to see the airport commandant. He sent them into town to see the political agent. He referred them to a distant war surplus dump where they found a United States Army mobile crane which had been gently rusting away for the past two years. Batt spent most of one morning getting the engine of the crane to start, then drove it the ten miles to the airport at little more than walking pace. On the way, he called in at the local police station to get formal permission to drive an untaxed vehicle.

Once he could begin work, Batt took four complete days to overhaul the engine, helped by Capt. Parsons and the navigator. The radio operator, completely unmechanical, kept them supplied with food and drink as they hung from ladders leaning against the wing. Morning and afternoons were so hot the metal burnt their fingers. Each midday, every day, it rained so hard they were forced back to the hut. In the early evening every insect in the Lake Victoria area seemed to swarm to the attack.

The sagging of the reduction gear during take-off had torn or stretched most of the joints within the engine. Batt found he needed a new main gasket when no such thing was within several thousand miles. He cut a piece of brown paper from the wrappings of a parcel awaiting collection at the airport, pressed it against the open face of metal where the gasket was needed, and rubbed his dirty hands over the paper until the sharp edges of each hole in the metal showed up as distinct black lines amongst the general oily smudge. Then he placed the paper over a pointed piece of scrap metal and tapped gently with a hammer along the black lines until each hole was cut out to the required shape. A touch of grease was added to make it pliable and the brown paper gasket was ready for use.

Another problem was the need for a new seal at the point where oil was pumped through two spigots from the engine to the constant speed unit, which controlled the propeller speed. Batt sent the radio operator to the nearest native bazaar to buy a string of red rubber tap washers. He cut them to size, packed them around the spigots, bolted them tight— and there was not the slightest trace of an oil leak when the overhaul was finally completed and the engine was given its ground test.

By this time, the thirteen stranded passengers from the DC-3 had all been taken on by southbound planes of various airlines which passed through Entebbe and happened to have empty seats. Capt. Parsons sent a cable to London announcing the Halifax was able to leave and asking whether the plane should go to Johannesburg or return to England. He knew that Batt wanted the engine given a workshop overhaul as soon as possible. But Alpha Airways, like most other tramping companies of this era, could not afford the luxury of having a plane out of action for major servicing after five days of sitting on the runway at Entebbe. The return cable said: "Proceed to Jedda and collect load of pilgrims for Khartoum."

Batt's brown paper and tap washers were put to a seven-hour ten-minute air test across the mountains of Ethiopia and the Red Sea on the flight to Jedda in Saudi Arabia. A party of ragged pilgrims came on board, clutching their bottles of holy water, and were flown to Khartoum. It was an anxious flight for the men in the cockpit. The outer port engine behaved perfectly but three lots of engine instruments were not working at all and one of the starboard engines was beginning to play up. Batt went to examine the oil filter as soon as they landed and found traces of metal being shed from the bearings. There was nothing he could do but look at the filter after each flight from then on. Each time he found more metal. He told Parsons and the captain decided the plane should begin to work its way in the general direction of England. "Let's make sure we go all the way home this time," said Batt. "That starboard engine won't last much longer and there's no point in handing this one on to the other crew."

A month before, Parson's crew had been flying back to England in an Alpha Airways Halifax which was based at Bovingdon. This plane went to and from Dar es Salaam on a regular Government charter, carrying personnel and equipment for the Overseas Food Corporation's ground-nut scheme. The round trip normally took ten days but the company's policy was to divert the plane in all directions on the return journey to make short hauls of whatever passengers and freight its local agents could provide. These were lucrative payloads even if the agents had to quote almost cost price to get the business. Since the Government charter allowed for an empty flight home, all the revenue accumulated on the way back was extra profit. That was why a flight from Uganda to England could take in Kenya, Saudi Arabia, Israel, Cyprus, and Greece on charters involving cattle hides, aircraft engines, army boots, bananas, bulldozer parts, and pilgrims' water bottles.

Parsons' Halifax had got as far north as Malta on September 20, returning from Dar es Salaam, when he received a radio call from Halifax ZS PTA, flying over the Mediterranean at 5,000 feet about three hundred miles to the east. This was another Alpha Airways plane, based at Randfontein in South Africa, and its regular run was taking immigrants to Johannesburg from Paris, Rome and Athens. Once again, the return flight to Europe was given over to tramping operations to make sure the aircraft flew empty as little as possible.

" We haven't got nearer home than Paris for weeks," said the message from ZS PTA. " Running out of money, laundry, and razor blades. How about it if we meet up at Rome tonight and swop planes?"

This sort of conversation had taken place between captains of Alpha aircraft all over Africa and Europe. Parsons had made the same sort of request himself when he had been too long at the Randfontein end of things. The two planes would rendezvous at the nearest airport, catch up with each other's news and gossip and the fresher crew would take over the African plane to give the opposite crew the chance to get back to Bovingdon. That was what happened at Rome in September, and, in taking over ZS PTA Parsons' crew let themselves in for the events which stranded them at Entebbe.

After Batt's warning at Khartoum about the starboard engine, Parsons realised the Halifax must get back as quickly as possible for some major servicing. Even so, the economics of tramp flying meant that it should not go back empty. He found a load of food parcels from South Africa to take to

Israel. From there he took on oranges for Malta. On October 25 the Halifax landed at Bovingdon.

This was where Batt first became a flight engineer six months before. He began in aviation as an air frame fitter with the Royal Air Force during the war and then joined London Aero Motor Services as an engine fitter early in 1946. LAMS was an unusual organisation founded by the most un-likely personality in post-war aviation—Dr. Graham Humby, a plastic surgeon who interspersed his medical career with spells as a ship's steward, as a dancer understudying Fred Astaire, as a pioneer glider pilot, and as operator of the most ambitious charter company of its day.

Humby's ideas for a world-wide tramping organisation, which won him the title of the " Drake of the Air," were inspired by his experiences in the improvised hospital on board an aircraft carrier in the Pacific at the end of the war. The carrier was collecting Australian prisoners-of-war from their Japanese camps. Humby worked day and night to save emaciated figures in advanced stages of tuberculosis, malaria, malnutrition, and suffering from a grotesque assort-ment of tropical skin diseases. He came back to England in 1946, horrified by the futility of war and inspired by a vision of returned warriors banding together for the common good. His appeal was directed towards airmen because they seemed to be finding special difficulty in applying their flying skills to civilian life.

Humby started a flying club at Elstree aerodrome to pro-vide half-a-dozen unemployed ex-R.A.F. pilots with jobs as instructors. Then he bought a war surplus Halifax bomber for £500 and engaged ex-R.A.F. engineers, Bob Batt in-cluded, to convert it into a civilian freighter by adding a cargo pannier. When the conversion was completed, Humby and his men watched the Halifax make a ceremonial take-off along Elstree's single 700-yard runway. They saw the old bomber fail to get off the ground in that distance, slide off the runway and crash into the control tower. Batt and the other engineers showed the disappointment of directors watching their company lose its major asset. A system of profit-sharing made every LAMS man a director, and the teaboy was very often the managing director. Fitters working through the night to prepare a flight would have mugs of tea brought to them by Humby himself.

The loss of the first Halifax only heightened the doctor's ambitions. He moved to a larger airfield at Stansted, in Essex, a disused U.S. bomber base, and bought forty-three more Halifaxes in all over the next two years. The staff built up to 250, including an ambitious young flight engineer by the name of Freddy Laker who dabbled in second hand cars and insisted on wearing the dark blue uniform he brought out of the Air Transport Auxiliary on demobilisation. Ten of the Halifaxes were always on active operations, comprising the largest air freight fleet in the world at that time. LAMS flew to southern France, Italy, Africa, and the Middle East carrying potatoes, mimosa, cherries, peaches, tractor spares, outboard motors, plumbers' tools, typewriters, sunglasses and anti-mosquito ointment. One Halifax took a consignment of silk stockings to Norway, another took seven tons of opium from Teheran to Madrid for hospital drugs. Smaller aircraft from the original flying club, Austers and Proctors, did passenger charters to Paris, Dublin and Brussels. The dismembered body of Stanley Setty was dropped into the Thames Estuary from one of the Austers on charter to Donald Hume, who later claimed to have committed the perfect murder.

In 1947, Humby took one of the Halifaxes on a flight round the world to find overseas bases for his fleet. His first stop was at Lydda airport in Palestine where leaders of the provisional Israeli government made a long-term agreement for LAMS aircraft to be serviced and re-fuelled at Lydda airport in return for reciprocal facilities at Stansted when Israel came to operate its own aircraft. He flew to South Africa and formed LAMS (South Africa) Ltd., to work a similar arrangement with the company operating Alpha Airways from Randfontein. Humby's next call was Australia where he arranged to take over a disused airfield near Sydney as base for LAMS (Australia) Ltd. Finally, he visited Pan American Airways in New York and secured servicing facilities there against Pan American's use of Stansted. That completed Humby's world-wide tramping empire. With bases in five continents, his aircraft could operate abroad indefinitely and avoid the high overheads of having to fly home empty from each long-distance charter. To prove his point, Humby returned from his world tour with seven tons of butter which he delivered to Dr. Edith Summerskill, Parliamentary Secretary to the Ministry of Food, on behalf of the people of Australia.

Later that year he went to Seattle to place an advance order for a Boeing Stratocruiser. It was a moment of triumph to be one of the first customers for the most advanced aircraft in civil aviation, a far extreme to the old bomber which crashed at Elstree. Humby began to feel ill during his talks at the Boeing works. He went back to his hotel room and lay on the bed, too weak to do anything but drink black coffee through the night. Next day he flew to Washington and went to a hospital for an X-ray examination. Dr. Humby's own tests had told him he was a very sick man. The X-ray plates showed him to be desperately near to death. He was in the last stages of tuberculosis. Returning to London for an operation, he lost one complete lung and nine ribs. He was to spend four years in hospital.

Within nine months, LAMS was bankrupt, Humby's proud empire fallen. Robbed of his forceful leadership, the profit-sharing team became a quarrelsome rabble and the enterprise could not continue. Humby lay in his hospital bed, tragically disappointed but consoling himself with the thought that LAMS had led the way for others to follow, that the ex-R.A.F. men he had saved from unemployment were now eagerly courted by other airlines. The hardest fact to accept was the hospital verdict that the tuberculosis which wrecked his dream was contracted from the men who inspired it on the mercy ship of the Pacific.

Batt was thrown out of work by the collapse of LAMS, and the prospect of earning three times as much in the air as he had been earning on the ground persuaded him to become a flight engineer with Alpha Airways, which operated one Halifax from England and another from South Africa.

Batt's previous experience of flying was brief and confined to light aircraft. As a flight engineer on long distance tramping operations he came to enjoy flying for its fresh perspective rather than any thrill of moving in an extra dimension. Until then, while loving the shape and power and sound of the aircraft he tended on the ground, he regarded the sky as a man walking along a river bank looks at the water. It was all the same. But once in the air he could watch a never-ending scene as if he were a man in a boat studying the unfolding world of the river bank. On his first flight south over Africa he gazed down at the majestic monotony of the deserts and the potted plants that were oases, came across the Nile like a half-buried mirror with the silvering cracked off, saw the scrubland turn to the dense green of jungles with curling rivers and islands tiny as canoes. Then came vast plains which finally crumpled into hills, then mountains and gaunt escarpments, and finally the South African veldt. All this in one continent which was his to fly over hour after hour.

At night in the tropics, the aircraft would sometimes be ringed with the blue fire of electricity. Huge sparks jumped across the propeller tips so that Catherine wheels were spinning along the length of the wings while blue flickers of light ran round the cockpit like a school of gremlins. Batt learned not to be frightened and to appreciate the spectacle. But, like all flying men, he was instinctively frightened of cumulonimbus air currents which can go up and down in opposition to each other within the breadth of an aircraft's wing span. A violent updraught might be pushing under one wing while a down-draught tugs in the opposite direction. Within the aircraft the sensation is of two giant hands trying to tear the machine apart.

Batt was in a Halifax returning from one of his first

African trips when it ran into cumulonimbus over Sardinia. The plane wallowed heavily between being thrown up and down three or four hundred feet at a time. Then a fast rising column of air began to lift the Halifax at the rate of 1,000 feet a minute. Even with the power throttled right back and the nose down, the plane continued to rise. Batt didn't need to look out of the window to know the extent the aircraft was icing up. Ice was flying off the propellers in great lumps and banging against the fuselage. Even more disturbing, he knew the engines' oil coolers would soon go solid as the plane was hurled far above the Halifax's normal ceiling of 9,000 feet. He looked at the pilot sitting at his useless controls and saw the same sort of expression as a man experiencing a front-wheel skid with his car. The man's face said: "This is ridiculous—I'm pointing this way and I'm going the other way . . . Or is my mind playing me tricks and I've lost my sense of direction? Is left really right, and perhaps down is up?"

At that moment the Halifax ran clear of the cumulonimbus. The pilot descended to 5,000 feet, the icing cleared and Batt had learned one very important explanation for the apparently inexplicable disasters of the sky.

Within eleven days of returning to Bovingdon from the Entebbe incident he was Africa-bound once more. Parsons' crew had been transferred back to the English-registered Halifax. They left for Dar es Salaam on the ground-nut charter in a blaze of bonfires and fireworks. It was November 5th and Batt was gazing back at the beacons of England long after they had faded from sight. From Dar es Salaam, the Halifax moved to Johannesburg and then flew a party of Greek immigrants, a load of food parcels and some aircraft spares into Israel. This was 1948 and the newly established Jewish state was besieged by its Arab neighbours. The British Government had not yet recognised Israel and so Alpha Airways allowed Capt. Parsons the privilege of refusing the proposition put to him when the plane was directed to Rome.

Jews anxious to reach the Promised Land were willing to pay high prices for planes to take them into Israel. The company would pay each member of the crew £25 per trip if they would agree to accept the business. There was nothing illegal about the flights themselves—not even when thirty-five passengers were crammed into an aircraft which normally carried thirteen. Parsons could have refused on the grounds that it would be politically embarrassing for a British aircraft to take part or physically too dangerous to face Arab fighters and anti-aircraft guns. He talked it over with his crew and they ruled out both possible objections. The company was at least half South African and South Africa did recognise Israel. As for the danger of being shot down, they felt there were very good odds on getting through, especially at £25 per trip.

The Jews who joined the Halifax at Rome were mostly young German married couples. These were not illegal emigrants because their passports were checked by the Italian authorities before they were allowed on board. Batt thought they were unemotional for people leaving behind the terrors of Europe for a new life in the land of their ancestors. The Jews quietly allowed themselves to be packed into an aircraft which had been stripped of all its seats to make use of every square inch. There were people hanging on to the roof in the forward turret, standing behind the pilot, squatting in the engineer's compartment, squashed along the whole length of the fuselage. Pieces of rope were threaded through the plane to give the passengers some sort of support in the event of bad weather or sudden evasive action to avoid Arab fighters.

Take-off was carefully timed for nine o'clock in the evening so that the Mediterranean was crossed under cover of darkness and the plane could land at first light. For the passengers there were six hours and fifteen minutes of uncomfortable air travel and the uncertainty of ever getting there. Batt took part in a dozen such flights. Egyptian fighters came to intercept them only twice and were easily avoided. Fighting was going on in the hills around an old R.A.F. aerodrome where they landed. Batt thought the Arab forces' flak was sparse and ineffective. Light machine guns mounted in jeeps would blaze away as the Halifax swept in but the few scattered bullet holes which appeared in the wings were obviously from the rifles of infantrymen in trenches along the hilltops. Much more dangerous to Batt's mind were the antiquated re-fuelling facilities of the Israelites. There were no filters on the petrol bowsers, and he had visions of the engines clogging up with sand on the way back across the Mediterranean. Whenever possible he tried to take on extra fuel and oil at Rome so that the Halifax could make an immediate turn-round and drop in at Nicosia, in Cyprus, for re-fuelling in a civilised manner.

After the Israel operation, it was back to tramping with flights to El Adem, Marseilles, Ndola, Salisbury, and Khartoum. Batt first began to suspect something was wrong with the company when the Halifax reached Johannesburg on January 21, 1949, and by mid-February was still there, with no instructions from London, no hint of charters from the local agent. There was a suggestion that the seating which had been replaced after the immigration flights should be permanently removed in favour of two long benches on either side of the fuselage. The plane could then concentrate on pilgrim traffic, the so-called *hajj* flights. But Batt pointed out firmly that the Halifax was British registered and the crew were operating on British licences. The interior could not be stripped in this way without the approval of the proper authorities. He realised this attitude might be considered fussy after the loads carried on the Israel run but he had an uneasy vision of being doomed to an eternal shuffle to and from Jedda, a flying Dutchman at 5,000 feet.

Towards the end of February, Parsons had a cable from the captain of the South African-registered Halifax, still awaiting its major overhaul in England. "What's happening your end?" said the cable. "We've been sitting here for months and no sign of action. Talk of aircraft being seized by airport people for non-payment of parking fees." Pilots passing through Johannesburg brought more disquieting news. Mercury Airways, an associate of Alpha, had lost one of its two remaining DC-2's in flight. The other one was remaining in England and there was no indication it would ever be returning to Africa. Finally, a man from Alpha Airways' Johannesburg office called round at the hotel and asked Parsons for the Halifax's journey log book and registration papers. It might have been a perfectly innocent request but the captain refused to hand over the papers.

" You're so right," said Batt when the crew held a meeting to consider the situation. " I'm not saying they would do such a thing but if the company is in real financial difficulties they might be tempted to sell the plane from underneath us. That would mean we'd be stranded in the middle of Africa, probably without a cent to get home. As long as we hang on to the Halifax we can always pull out of here and somebody will have to pay us up to get the plane back."

Parsons pointed out that the plane was not Alpha's to sell. It was on hire to the company from Freddy Laker's Aviation Traders Ltd. Parsons knew Laker from when they both worked with Batt for LAMS. He sent a cable to Laker saying: " Might be in danger of losing an aeroplane. Send carnet for fuel and will deliver Halifax to Southend." Laker diplomatically sent the carnet without comment, and the crew began to make secret plans for a flight back to England. Parsons still insisted they find a payload to cover landing fees and overnight stops on the way home. " I'm holding several hundred pounds of revenue from the tramping we've done so far on this trip," he explained. " The more of that I can take back home the bigger the kitty when we get the company to settle up with us."

Preparations for the flight had to be made with great care as the hotel where the crew stayed was owned by the South African end of the company. The four of them split up and set off on a round of shipping agents and hotel bars to see if they could find anyone or anything wanting a quick trip to

England. One of the crew found a businessman wanting to re-export a paper pulping plant he had bought from a London firm twenty-five years before. Parsons picked up four white South African passengers. Batt ran across nine coloured Merchant Navy men who had left their British ship in Capetown, travelled as far as Johannesburg by rail and then been stranded by South Africa's colour bar. They found themselves banned from bars and hotels and unable to buy tickets for scheduled airliners because all seats were reserved for white passengers. Batt met the seamen on the fringe of the native quarter where they had found some consolation in being easily the wealthiest, best-dressed, most sophisticated coloured people in the city. They were wearing brightly coloured zoot suits, the latest creations from London's Euston Road, with a glimpse of gold-plated key rings dangling beneath almost knee-length jackets. Most of them appeared to have at least two native girls hanging on each arm.

"We got plenty of money," said the leader of the seamen. "We drew all our pay at Capetown and the shipping company will settle for the air tickets. It's their responsibility to get us home but until you turned up we looked like having to walk all the way."

On the afternoon of March 4, Batt had the Halifax re-fuelled and checked-out under cover of what appeared to be routine maintenance work. At two o'clock the following morning the crew slipped out of the hotel and went to the airfield which was deserted except for the two groups of passengers waiting in the darkness. The navigator and radio operator helped Batt load the three tons of cast iron cogs, wheels, rollers and struts which were the paper pulping plant. Parts of it went in the freight pannier slung beneath the aircraft. Other pieces went in the forward turret and were balanced by still more pieces in the tail of the fuselage.

Parsons collected the fares from the thirteen passengers and then faced an embarrassing scene when the white South Africans were introduced to the seamen. "But these men are coloured," complained one of the white passengers.

" They can't possibly travel with us." Parsons explained that the South Africans would be sitting in a small passenger compartment in the centre of the aircraft where the crew bunks used to be in war-time Halifaxes. The seamen would sit in the completely separate main compartment to the rear.

The South Africans became noisy in their indignant refusals to travel on the same plane as coloured people. The seamen, grown tired of being treated like natives, were getting openly hostile at this last minute threat to returning home to London. Parsons knew the last thing he could afford was a protracted argument ending in a brawl which might bring in the police and ruin all his plans for a discreet departure. He told the seamen to go out to the plane and invited the South Africans to follow. When they refused he climbed on board and ordered Batt to prepare for an immediate take-off. The Halifax left at 3.55 on the eleven-hour flight to Entebbe. Parsons landed there the following afternoon with the intention of stopping for only one hour to re-fuel. The seamen would not be allowed in the airport hut if a single white South African chose to object. Luckily, the place was deserted and the manager, an Indian, agreed to let the seamen sleep for the night in a section of the hut. Parsons was rationing his cash carefully and apologised to his passengers for a meagre supper of fruit, biscuits and lemonade.

Next day the Halifax flew on to Khartoum and after a brief stop to take on fuel began the long desert crossing to El Adem. This was where things began to go wrong. Both air speed indicators were behaving wildly, suggesting to Batt that water had got into the instruments while the plane stood idle for six weeks at Johannesburg. Parsons switched on the automatic pilot and slipped away from the controls to let Batt take over his seat. While the Halifax flew itself across the sky, the engineer methodically dismantled the instrument panel to take out the two faulty air speed indicators and replace them with two more. He re-assembled the panel, got up from the seat, and allowed Parsons to take charge of the plane once more. The Halifax behaved perfectly while Batt worked, yet when Parsons wanted to take a rest two hours later the automatic pilot device was no longer functioning.

Once again Batt took over the pilot's seat. This time to "drive" the Halifax while his captain relaxed. Batt often did this. He learned to fly with Auster light aircraft two years before he became a flight engineer and always relished the personal power of handling the controls of an aeroplane. On calm, cloudless evenings such as this high above the desert he felt the temptation to throw the plane about the empty skies in great swirling dives and rolls. It was a temptation he could not resist in an Auster. But there were only twinges of it when he was flying a four-engined ex-bomber, especially when three tons of cast iron were scattered through the aircraft.

Batt saw an oil gauge begin to flicker and looked out at the starboard wing to see one of the engines vibrating in its mounting and giving out a fine black spray. In front of him, the instruments showed the oil temperature to be rising steeply, together with a dramatic fall in oil pressure. The situation required more than a "driver" at the controls. Batt called Parsons to take over and the captain was in time to feather the propeller before the engine could seize up.

There was a special compartment of the 22-gallon oil tank which contained a further two gallons reserved for feathering. On reaching El Adem, Batt was to discover the main tank was empty. The spray he saw was the last of twenty-two gallons being blown out of the engine. A few seconds later and the engine would have seized into a solid mass with the most expensive noise in the business.

Coming in to land at El Adem on three engines Batt suffered the classic frustration of a flight engineer. He was looking out at an engine he could almost touch and he had a good idea what was wrong with it. But until the plane was on the ground he must remain a helpless spectator. Parsons touched down perfectly and within ten minutes Batt was at work. As he suspected, there was a leak in the oil-cooler.

This was very similar to the honeycombed radiator of a car and there was the same tendency for the tiny passages within the cooler to become blocked with age. The hydraulic pressure of oil being pumped into the cooler from the engine and then obstructed by such a blockage was sufficient to burst the soldering at each end of the cooler. A temporary repair could be made with a rod long enough to run the length of the cooler and take a washer at each end which could then be screwed hard against the two faces of the honeycomb. All that Batt needed was a suitable rod and the necessary washers.

He went over to an R.A.F. workshop at El Adem and begged a piece of welding wire, ran a thread on each end and found two nuts of the same thread. He had two East African pennies in his pocket. They might have been designed as emergency washers with a small hole in the middle of the coin. But they would need some kind of leather seal to fit tightly enough to withstand the pressure of the oil being pumped back into the cooler. Batt spotted an old bicycle standing at the back of the workshop. He bought the saddle from an R.A.F. corporal for half-a-crown, cut out two pieces of leather, and assured an anxious Parsons that they were in business again. Although he was merely returning the aircraft to its rightful owners the captain was worried whether he might run into trouble from his immediate employers, Alpha Airways, once they discovered the Halifax had left Johannesburg for an unknown destination. If they guessed the plane would be making an unauthorised return to England, they could have asked airport authorities en route to seize the Halifax in the company's name. Even when nothing was said by the airport commandant at El Adem, Parsons waited for Batt to repair the oil cooler in constant dread of a cable catching up with them from Johannesburg and a summons to the commandant's office.

Parsons would have liked to press on for Malta without further delay but it was midnight before Batt finished and so the crew and their remarkably good-natured, patient passengers spent the night at El Adem, sleeping on Army cots without mattresses or sheets. Take-off was at first glimmer of dawn and Parsons relaxed for the first time in days once the Mediterranean appeared beneath the wings. He felt they were over the top of the hill now, and coasting home. Landings at Malta and Marseilles passed without incident and GA HDO touched down at Bovingdon at 5.45 p.m., on March 7. That evening the crew visited the home of the managing director of Alpha Airways' British operations, handed over the tramping revenue, and took back their outstanding pay and expenses. They left a profit of £100 on the managing director's dining table at the end of a company meeting which had been conducted entirely by the employees.

The Halifax was flown to Southend next morning and presented to Freddy Laker. Batt had asked Laker for a job once before and been turned down when he asked for £9 a week. "That's more than I make," said Laker. Now Batt asked again and this time felt he was in a stronger position. He had acquired better engineering qualifications and considerable flying experience, he and Laker had been co-partners in the LAMS enterprise, and he had helped to rescue one of Laker's aircraft from Africa. The Lancashire Aircraft Corporation approached Batt as soon as he landed at Bovingdon with the offer of £16 a week as chief flight engineer so he had a good idea of his own market value. "All right," said Laker, "you've got yourself a job. I want you to come as my chief inspector—and I'll go as high as £8 a week." Batt accepted from sheer exasperation. Within nine years he had a seat in the boardroom and his tramping days were done.

CHAPTER FOUR

. . . and Hay for the General's Charger

THE teleprinter message issued by the Soviet News Agency in the early hours of June 24, 1948, proved to be the formal invitation to an international convention of sky tramps. The message said that "as a result of a technical hitch" the Russian military administration would be compelled to close the railway line between Berlin and Western Germany. It was a technical hitch which inspired the technical miracle of the Berlin Airlift and brought together charter pilots from all over the world. One of them was Joseph Viatkin, a powerful man with a slow, almost sleepy manner and the quick, sensitive mind of his Russian-Dutch-Scottish ancestry. He was an ex-R.A.F. test pilot who had been earning a living by flying fruit from the Mediterranean and milk from Northern Ireland until the land blockade of Berlin offered something more dramatic at rather better rates of pay.

The memory of Viatkin's father, a lieutenant-commander in the Imperial Russian Navy who died in exile after fleeing from the 1917 revolution, was with him on every crossing over Communist territory. Shortly before one mid-morning flight to Tempelhof airport in the American zone of Berlin. he was warned by the American control centre to postpone his trip. The Russians were staging one of their periodic frictions and had announced a practice drop of paratroopers would be taking place in the northern air corridor between 11 and 11.30 a.m. "Am I clear as far as you are concerned?"

asked Viatkin. " The flight is fine by us," said the American voice from the control centre. " We just don't see any point in getting tangled up with those paratroopers for the sake of half-an-hour."

Viatkin saw the situation rather differently. The Russian interference with the air corridor at the very time he was due to fly to Berlin became a Communist challenge to the family honour which had to be met in the name of the late Lieut.-Commander Viatkin. There was the broader principle of the freedom of the skies. There was also, from his R.A.F. war-time service, the Bomber Command tradition of reaching an objective in face of all opposition. Finally, there was the 30s. to be earned by making the flight and a further £3 to come from two more flights that same day if the first one could be completed on time.

" If I'm clear by control," said Viatkin, " I'm going and the paratroopers can keep out of my way." His four-engined York took off from Hamburg at 10.40 and the troop-carrying aircraft were spotted by Viatkin's co-pilot halfway along the corridor. The Russian planes were flying at right angles to the York, about 2,000 feet above its path, and the first paratroopers began to tumble into sight as the co-pilot spoke to Viatkin. " They look as if they are going to spray right across our path," he said. " Shall we try and go up over them or change course for the northern edge of the corridor? We might just squeeze past, then." Viatkin spoke softly and sleepily as ever. " Keep her just where she is," he said. " We'll let them take the avoiding action."

The York flew on towards the unfolding curtain of parachutes across the sky. At closer range, Viatkin could see the Russian paratroopers and their garlands of equipment. The York drew closer still. Fists were waved at the approaching airliner and then the same fists clawed at canopy strings to spill air from the parachutes in an effort to get out of the way. Viatkin studied the transformation from grim, hostile fighting men, elegantly poised in mid-air, into jerking puppets. He flew the York through the falling parachutes as if they

were wisps of cloud. He showed no reaction when a paratrooper passed so close to the outer starboard engine he nearly
lost his feet in the propeller arc. The port wing brushed the
dome of one parachute and left it bobbing wildly in the slipstream. Another paratrooper collapsed his parachute when
about to be struck by the nose of the aeroplane, and plunged
out of sight.

Then the York was clear of the Russian exercise and
Viatkin flew on to Berlin with the impassive contentment of
a cat emerged safely from a dog-fight. At Tempelhof he con-
founded a U.S.A.F. officer, apprehensive about Russian
reaction to the incident and eager to apologise, by insisting
that a formal protest be lodged against a civil aircraft being
endangered by falling paratroopers. "Aeroplanes were never
designed to avoid pedestrians," he said. "Those Russian
soldiers should know better than to cross a busy road when
the traffic travels at 185 m.p.h. and is in no mood to stop."
There were no more parachute drops during the airlift.
Viatkin scored it as a defeat of the Red Army on behalf of
the Imperial Russian Navy—3,500 feet above Germany.

The Berlin airlift was in two distinct phases and in two
different directions. A military blockade of the city led to a
West-East flow of supplies by air. An economic blockade
brought about an East-West flow of exports by air and produced Viatkin's parachute incident. To have been on the
Lift at all remains the most common and also the most exclusive order of charter flying's freemasonry, certainly the
most acceptable excuse for late nights and heavy drinks and
long stories which now suggest the whole operation was some
kind of aerial Monte Carlo Rally undertaken by the organisers
of a wild university rag on their way to find sanctuary in a
Foreign Legion recruiting office.

Two of Viatkin's friends, a pilot and a navigator, arrived
at Lubeck station at eleven o'clock one night and demanded
a train to their airfield, a few miles away. When told the last
train had gone, they referred to the train standing at the
platform. "That is an international express about to leave

for Sweden," the station master explained. "It does not go anywhere near your airfield." "Well it does to-night," said the pilot, the arrogance acquired in a tour of local night clubs stiffened by the knowledge that his navigator was a pre-war engine driver. The two fliers climbed into the cab where the pilot seized a shovel and held off the driver and fireman while the navigator put the train into motion.

Confusion raged along the platform as the express pulled out of Lubeck five minutes early, couples being torn apart from farewell embraces, businessmen arrived with time to spare having to sprint to pull themselves on board, the station staff blowing whistles and waving lanterns in protest. Even so, most passengers were already in bed in their sleeping compartments or dozing in the carriages. They slept and dozed on without knowing the train was no longer bound for Sweden but in the hands of two British airmen determined to get to their own beds by the shortest possible route.

The navigator was never able to explain how he proposed to navigate a main line train to the particular local station serving the airfield. He soon discovered that trains can be stopped and started by two desperate men armed with a shovel but they can go only where the man in the next signal box wants them to go. The station master telephoned the first signal box out of the station and the runaway express was simply diverted into a siding. The navigator was driving at less than 20 m.p.h. while familiarising himself with the controls of the train and he saw the set of buffers ahead in time to slam on the brakes. There was a minor collision but no one was hurt and the front of the engine was not badly damaged.

Dropping his shovel in the jolt of hitting the buffers, the pilot formally surrendered the stolen train to its rightful crew. He and the navigator were arrested by a large force of police dispatched to the siding and only high-level intervention by the British military authorities in Germany saved the two airmen from heavy prison sentences. They were presented as two heroes of the great airlift, suffering from

3*

acute exhaustion through their labours on behalf of the gallant people of West Berlin. The German authorities chose to accept the excuse but insisted the pilot and navigator must leave the country within twenty-four hours and cease all connection with the airlift. The official figure of forty British aircrew lost during the Berlin operation does not include the two victims of the Lubeck train robbery although Viatkin still mourns their loss to the buccaneering mood of the airlift. Like most charter pilots he admired the fantastic business efficiency which built up throughout the airlift without wanting to be identified with this factory routine which had aircraft landing day and night with a tolerance of only 15 seconds, plus or minus, between one arrival and the next. It was as if the sky tramps answered the call to adventure and found themselves tending a conveyor belt.

Gatow, in the British sector of Berlin, became the world's busiest airport with up to 1,000 movements a day. On no single day throughout the severe winter of 1948-49 was there a complete breakdown of flying. A lighting approach system developed by the Royal Aircraft Establishment for landings in poor visibility, especially in fog, was tried out at Gatow and later adopted for London Airport. The technique of blind approaches by instruments was perfected by a British system of Ground Controlled Approach which took charge of incoming aircraft while still 150 miles from the airport, compared with a range of less than thirty miles possible before. The new system was approved for world-wide use by the Council of the International Civil Aviation Organisation. The handling of 335 aircraft of thirteen different types at six levels of altitude along the three corridors to Berlin was the most advanced demonstration of air traffic control in the history of aviation and became the model for the world's busiest airports.

Yet the airlift began on June 28, 1948, as nothing more than a temporary improvisation. The crews of the thirteen Dakotas which flew forty-four tons of flour on the first day had been moved to Germany with personal luggage for a stay of ten days. No one thought the 2,100,000 people of West Berlin could be supplied indefinitely from the air. One newspaper predicted an insuperable obstacle: " Coal cannot be flown in." But coal was soon being flown into Berlin in such quantities that coal sacks were worn out at the rate of half-a-million a month and Army kitbags had to be pressed into service. Along with the coal went flour, cereals, dehydrated vegetables, oil, petrol, medicines, newsprint, and raw materials to keep West Berlin's factories working. More specialised freight included a steam roller, the regimental goat of the 1st Battalion of the Royal Welch Fusiliers, a fire engine, a consignment of latrine buckets, and supplies of hay for a general's charger.

One problem was the city's need for thirty-eight tons of salt a day—a commodity the human body must have, as ancient man first established. But salt is poison to aircraft in that it will alway manage to escape from its package, find its way into the controls and corrode all metal in its path. Flying boats, built to resist salt water, were the answer until their landing place on the Havel Lake froze up in midwinter. Then converted Halifax bombers were used, carrying the salt in panniers suspended beneath the fuselage.

The airlift began as an R.A.F. operation under the codename of Carter Paterson—soon changed to Operation Plainfare when Russian propaganda broadcasts suggested Berlin was to be evacuated by pointing out that Carter Paterson was the name of a company which specialised in *removals*. Within a month the charter companies were called in and they provided an invaluable reinforcement with Tudors and Lancastrians converted into air-tankers. These aircraft carried Berlin's supplies of liquid fuel, certainly the most dangerous cargo on the airlift.

Civilian operators were paid by results and led the way in achieving higher and higher payloads. The previous capacity of the Halifax bomber was regarded as six tons. They proved it could carry eight-and-a-half tons. The payload of the Lancastrian (the civilian version of the Lancaster bomber) was steadily increased from four-and-three-quarter tons to eight tons. Skyways loaded 20,000 lb. of cargo into their York airliners compared with the 17,000 lb. managed by the R.A.F. when using the same aircraft. These increases were mainly achieved by a ruthless slashing of refinements. In one case a saving of 400 lb. was the result of stripping several coats of paint from a heavily camouflaged ex-bomber. Air Vice-Marshal " Pathfinder " Bennett, who personally made 300 flights to Berlin in the Tudors of his Airflight company, sometimes carried over 20,000 lb., a better performance than the U.S.A.F. Skymaster transport planes which contributed most of the American effort. The British air fleet, drawn from twenty-three charter companies, incorporated pretty well anything that could fly, from Dakotas to Bristol freighters, from Handley Page Hastings to war-time Sunderland flying boats. The Texan pilot of a Skymaster approaching Berlin in a general stream of traffic saw an aircraft of unfamiliar shape. He called up the control tower at Gatow and said: " What's this coming in now, fella?" Over his crackling radio came the explanation that it was a British freighter, a Bristol Wayfarer. " Did you say Mayflower?" said the Texan. " You guys are sure throwing in everything you've got."

Viatkin took off from snow-covered Gatow on a March afternoon in 1949 in the ex-Alpha Airways Halifax which Bob Batt had helped to escape from South Africa earlier that month. Viatkin had just delivered a load of dehydrated potatoes and the 30s. per trip on top of a basic salary of £65 a month made him eager to get back to Wunstorf for his third flight of the day. At 1,000 feet above Gatow and at the start of a dog-leg turn to get on course, he felt a drag on the tail and the whole plane began to shudder. The boost gauge showing the supercharger pressure within No. 3 engine was fluctuating and he looked outside to see black smoke was pouring from the engine cowling. Viatkin knew the aircraft had been worked hard on its jungle tramping with Alpha Airways. The smoke could merely indicate a well-worn engine burning a spot of oil. But if the flickering boost gauge meant a supercharger failure he was about to have a blow-lamp burning on petrol where No. 3 engine used to be. The main spar of the starboard wing would be burnt through in a matter of minutes. He feathered No. 3 propeller and cut the engine, leaving the Halifax to continue its climb and fly back to West Germany on three engines, thankfully without the eight-and-a-half tons of potatoes which it took into Berlin.

There was no provision for returning to Gatow because of the engine failure. Viatkin was travelling the airlift conveyor belt and a single aeroplane which tried to go into reverse would disrupt the whole flow of traffic. The Halifax was fitted with a replacement engine at Wunstorf but a few weeks later ran into a construction trench while taxi-ing at Tegel airport, in the French zone of Berlin. It met the same fate as all other threats to smooth progress and was pushed out of the way of other aircraft by a bulldozer to be cut up for scrap at the side of the runway.

Viatkin was flying with Bond Air Services and their aircraft were supplied by Freddy Laker's Aviation Traders. Laker was a shopkeeper's son who trained as an aircraft engineer, learned to fly and became a leading figure in civil aviation, but remained basically a dealer. Like all dealers, he would trade in anything which showed a profit. The man who admired his car would always be invited to name a price for it. Aviation Traders, formed in 1947 to buy and sell aircraft and spare parts, also dealt in lorries, Army uniforms and ex-R.A.F. radio equipment. Years later, as managing director of Britain's largest independent airline, Laker interrupted his return from a business meeting in East Africa to buy a pile of ships' chains rusting in Naples harbour and then sell them by telephone to a scrap dealer in Canada.

The young engineer began business with a capital of £240, built up from the £40 gratuity he received at the end of his war service with the Air Transport Auxiliary. Within three weeks his capital had gone and he was having to borrow money. Within six months he was able to attend a war surplus sale and buy 99 Halifax bombers at £100 each, plus £5 for spare engines. He bought the Halifaxes to break up for scrap. "I wouldn't dream of trying to operate them," he said to his chief engineer, Jack Wiseman, who joined Aviation Traders after being stranded in Australia on the death of LAMS' world-wide tramping organisation. "The Halifax is the wrong shape, the wrong size to make money. I left Dr. Humby before the end because I could see those old bombers would kill the business more effectively than his tuberculosis. I'll buy and sell them but I'll never fly them."

Laker would not change his mind even when the Berlin airlift began soon after he bought from B.O.A.C. a fleet of twelve Haltons, the civilian version of the Halifax, and a hangarful of spares. He sold six and leased the other six to Bond Air Services. From his scrap heap he could produce 6,000 aeroplane engines of all types and a mountain of spare parts. Aviation Traders became general factors for most of the companies on the airlift, making money out of flying by resolutely staying on the ground.

Harold Bamberg, founder of Eagle Aviation and Laker's principal rival over the next seventeen years, reported only a modest profit after operating three Halifaxes throughout the first airlift. He started Eagle Aviation at about the same time as Aviation Traders with a single Halifax he bought for £500. He had to borrow £3,500 to construct a freight pannier underneath the old bomb bay and to make other civilian modifications. Early charter work concentrated on flying peaches, apricots and cherries from Italy and Spain. Then came the airlift and the Treasury's offer of £85 per flying hour for Halifaxes persuaded Bamberg to buy two more. One of his planes had the honour of making the last flight of the airlift.

Laker and Bamberg made an interesting comparison— Laker chirpily aggressive, the hint of a bright-eyed schoolboy with a drawerful of bargaining treasures never properly hidden in the image of a brisk executive which might have been borrowed from a careers supplement; Bamberg tall and fair, moving elegantly through the world of the sky tramps with his eyes raised in search of greater things. Laker remains happiest with dirt on his hands whether it's helping to sweep snow from the runway outside his office at Gatwick Airport or climbing a ladder to tinker with the engine of a VC-10 airliner when a fault developed during proving trials in Africa. Bamberg, who learned to fly as a transport pilot with the R.A.F., gave up his place in the cockpit as soon as he became an employer and prefers the highly pressurised atmosphere of boardrooms and penthouse conferences.

The two men reacted very differently to the shattering slump in charter work which followed the ending of the first airlift in August, 1949. If Laker enjoys doing business by a dealer's furtive nod from the back of the crowd, Bamberg is much more the professional gambler who sits down at the centre of the table and plays a series of big, dramatic gestures.

When the other operators who managed to stay in business were intent on cutting their losses, Bamberg went out and bought ten York airliners. They were cheap because nobody else was buying at the time. He used them on Far Eastern charters and long-distance tramping. One of the Yorks, under the command of Captain Storm Clark, flew the equivalent of one-and-a-half times round the world on a single mission which carried a variety of cargoes between Britain, Japan, the Middle East, Africa and South America. In 1952 he sold his entire fleet of Yorks, including four to Freddy Laker and five to Skyways, as a personal protest against the continuing monopoly of scheduled services by B.E.A. and B.O.A.C., and prepared to give up aviation altogether. The same year, when the new Conservative Government offered greater opportunities for private airlines, Bamberg arranged the necessary overdraft with his bank manager and bought fourteen twin-engined Viking airliners from B.E.A. for £420,000. He had them drawn up for his inspection at Blackbushe Airport, then went home to think up some work for them. He found work for all fourteen, and another seven Vikings he bought later, by developing scheduled services to Jugoslavia, Sweden, Luxembourg, Brittany and Jersey, by winning trooping contracts, by taking part in the Suez evacuation and the Hungarian refugee airlift.

When Thomas Cook's were not interested in Bamberg's plans for package holidays by air, he borrowed another £50,000 from his ever trusting bank manager and bought up Sir Henry Lunn's travel agency to provide his own passengers for his own aeroplanes. Lunn's was an old-established firm in need of new ideas. Bamberg dreamed up inclusive tours to Pisa and San Sebastian with titles like "Treasures of Italy" and "Castles in Spain". The agency prospered to the extent of opening 45 branches and handling so many tours each summer that it had to employ most of Eagle's competitors as well.

One happy coincidence about Bamberg's entry into the travel business was Lunn's association with winter sports, through Sir Arnold Lunn's role as the father of British ski-ing. Flights of ski-ing enthusiasts to Innsbruck and other winter resorts kept Eagle aircraft busy during the usual seasonal slump in holiday travel. By an unhappy coincidence it was at Innsbruck in February 1964 that Analiese Hausman, Bamberg's orphaned niece and a girl he had brought up as his own daughter, died with eighty-two other people when one of Eagle's Britannias crashed into an Austrian mountainside. "The hardest blow of my life," said Bamberg.

Laker survived the aftermath of the first airlift by following his instincts as a dealer. His aircraft engineers at Southend airport—then a grass field with Ministry of Food flour stored at one end of the solitary hangar—had no work so he had them build a brick-lined tank, 8 feet long by 5 feet wide, with a gas burner at the bottom. Into "The Pot", as the tank became known over the next twelve months, went the broken pieces of hundreds of war surplus Halifaxes and Lancasters which Laker bought from the Ministry of Supply at £100 each. Remembering these aircraft were built

The first charter flights were made in converted bombers — World War I — like this Handley Page 0/400 of 1919. It could carry fourteen passengers over a range of 500 miles, cruising at 75 m.p.h.

By 1928, cruising speed had increased to 100 m.p.h but flying was still leisurely enough for passengers on board the Handley Page W airliner of Imperial Airways to hold a traditional party mid-air.

Sir Alan Cobham's air circus brought a spectacular form of flying to the public during the 1930's by staging aerobatic displays from farmers' fields and factory sports grounds.

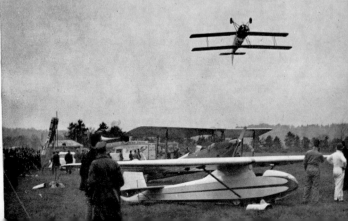

Air Vice-Marshal D. C. T. Bennett, founder of the R.A.F.'s wartime "Pathfinder" force and a controversial charter operator in post-war years, staked his career on the ill-starred Tudor airliner.

Capt. A. C. Loraine, of B.O.A.C., and the Short flying boat in which he made his epic flight to the Congo on the secret mission which brought French Equatorial Africa into the war on the side of the Allies.

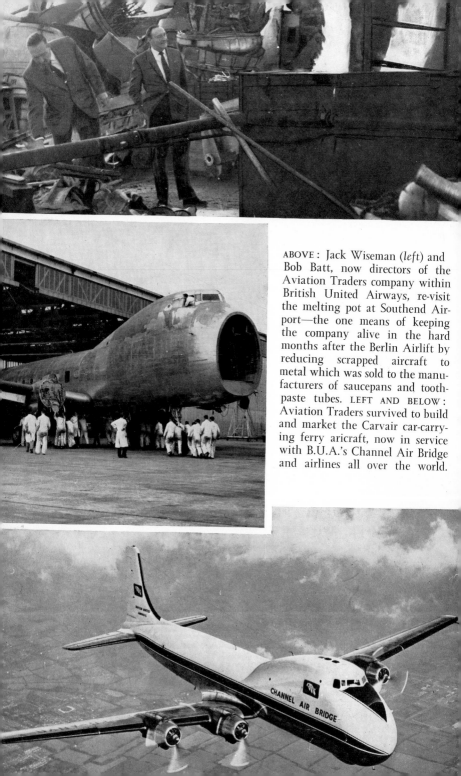

ABOVE: Jack Wiseman (*left*) and Bob Batt, now directors of the Aviation Traders company within British United Airways, re-visit the melting pot at Southend Airport—the one means of keeping the company alive in the hard months after the Berlin Airlift by reducing scrapped aircraft to metal which was sold to the manufacturers of saucepans and toothpaste tubes. LEFT AND BELOW: Aviation Traders survived to build and market the Carvair car-carrying ferry aricraft, now in service with B.U.A.'s Channel Air Bridge and airlines all over the world.

CHANNEL AIR BRIDGE

when housewives were being asked to surrender old saucepans and toothpaste tubes to the war effort, he neatly completed the circle by selling the metal which was melted within The Pot to the manufacturers of saucepans and toothpaste tubes. The profit was big enough to keep the Aviation Traders organisation intact for opportunities to do its real business. Engineers were called away from The Pot to work on the three ex-B.E.A. Vikings which Laker picked up cheaply from the Ministry of Supply between scrap metal negotiations. The three Vikings were renovated so efficiently at Southend that he was able to sell them to B.O.A.C., making an excellent profit on restoring nationalised aircraft to a nationalised airline.

In 1950, Laker went to the Ministry of Supply again and bought a selection of Yorks and Lancasters which had been involved in accidents. One of them was Churchill's personal war-time aircraft. Pieces from nine Yorks and three Lancasters were cannibalised to make three Yorks in first-class condition. One took to the air made up of parts from eight different aircraft as well as components created in the workshop at Southend. The three Yorks were ready for Laker to make his reluctant beginning as an operator, under the name Air Charter, when the second Berlin airlift was called into being, in August 1951, by the economic blockade of the city. The Soviet authorities began interfering with the flow of exports from West Berlin factories and air freight was the obvious way of moving goods without submitting to checkpoints. Air Charter's aircraft were to dominate the second airlift as much as Aviation Traders' spare parts sustained the first.

At this time Laker appeared to his rivals to be behaving like the only man in the Stock Exchange who does not know the market has collapsed. He was systematically buying up every available Tudor airliner, the one type of aircraft nobody wanted after its record of mysterious disasters. Two Tudors disappeared without trace on flights to and from Bermuda for British South American Airways and led to its absorption in B.O.A.C. Air Vice-Marshal Bennett, who was dismissed from his post as chairman of B.S.A.A. at the height of the Tudor controversy, kept faith with the aircraft when he formed his own charter company, Airflight. He flew Tudors on the Berlin airlift, including one which had its controls jam during take-off in West Germany. Bennett continued the flight to Berlin, using only the trimming tabs and variations in engine power to handle the aircraft. He landed safely in Berlin, his cargo undamaged.

After the airlift, Bennett took his aircraft to the Middle East and specialised in *hajj* flights to Jedda. One of his passengers was a dying girl who wanted to meet her death in Mecca. Bennett went back to see the girl during the flight and had to dissuade her companions from cooking over an open fire on the floor of the aircraft. Bennett's airline also ferried a desperately oppressed community of Yemenite Jews from Aden to Israel. They were tiny, wizened people, so thin that they slipped out of their safety belts during take-off and landing. Bennett afterwards preached the cause of the Tudor with the added conviction of a pilot whose passengers fell on their knees and worshipped him at the first sight of Israel, quoting one of their ancient prophets: " Ye shall be carried to the Promised Land on the wings of an angel." But on March 20, 1950, one of Airflight's Tudors, carrying a party of Welsh Rugby supporters back to the land of their fathers from an international match in Dublin, crashed at Llandow with the loss of eighty lives. Bennett sold out and retired from charter flying. The company was acquired by Laker who found himself the owner of Airflight's surviving Tudor. He read the reports on the Tudor disasters, he talked to pilots who had flown Tudors, he examined the plane from end to end to consider a theory that the type had a misplaced centre of gravity, he flew as an observer on a series of test flights. Then he bought eleven more Tudors at clearance sale prices and set out to produce a freight aircraft to higher standards of air worthiness than the transatlantic airliner was designed for originally. The suspect pressurisation system

was removed, the hydraulic system renewed. Mark IV noses
were grafted on to Mark I fuselages. A cargo door was cut
into the side of the aircraft. Ministry of Aviation inspectors
were so impressed by the aircraft's complete change of
personality they allowed Laker to put it into service on
the airlift under a new name—the Avro Supertrader. Before
long the Supertraders won a Government contract for carrying space age freight to the Woomera rocket range in Australia. Laker had to buy more Yorks when Air Charter was
awarded Mediterranean trooping contracts as well. And in
Europe the second airlift was to prove a lucrative charter
lasting six years.

Laker was already the head of a sizeable airline when he
went aboard one of his Yorks, GAM George Love, at Southend on the afternoon of March 11, 1952. The aircraft was
returning to service on the airlift after a routine overhaul.
Sitting at the controls was Joe Viatkin, back on the Berlin
conveyor belt once more. At the end of the first airlift he
returned to general charter work with Gordon Olley, still
operating from Croydon thirteen years after sending Cecil
Bebb to collect Franco from the Canary Islands. Laker went
to Croydon to see Viatkin when the second airlift began.
" You know the run backwards," he said. " I'll pay you
more than you're getting here to come and fly for me."

Viatkin agreed to go. His attitude to flying was an odd
mixture of business and romanticism. He joined the R.A.F.
and became a pilot because he had fallen in love with a girl
and wanted to impress her. But he always insisted he did
it only for the money and described the great moment of his
first flight as " Horrible—just like going up and down in a
lift." He complained of boredom during his hazardous war-
time work as a test pilot, flying crashed bombers and fighters
which had been put together again. The one-time engineering student took over a rebuilt bomber in which two other
pilots had found themselves flying backwards before reaching
the end of the runway, and saved himself and the aircraft
from disaster by diagnosing that the rudder controls had

been connected the opposite way round. Viatkin became a charter pilot because he said he could not think of an easier way to earn a living. At the end of the most spectacular flight, he would emerge from his cockpit grumbling that the sound of aeroplane engines always gave him a headache. Yet the same man could say this of sunrise over the Mediterranean: "You've been flying all through the night and then everything starts lighting up on one side of you although the other side stays black. Then the sun appears, a deep, deep red, and you feel there are just the two of you alone in the sky. The aeroplane, the crew, the passengers—they aren't there any more. Just you flying along and the sun coming up to meet you. It's a strange feeling and everytime has been the first time in all my years of flying."

There was no magic about Viatkin's departure from Southend for his return to the airlift routine. The York left at 2.15 p.m. on a dull winter's day and Viatkin preferred to talk about a trip to Singapore on an R.A.F. charter he had been promised for the following week as a change from the Berlin shuttle service. Travelling with Laker as passengers were Jack Wiseman, his chief engineer, and ten fitters being transferred from Southend to the airlift base at Hamburg. In command of the aircraft, with Viatkin as co-pilot, was Captain Norman Jennings.

Jennings was a veteran of airlifts on both sides of the world. In the autumn of 1947 he flew on the India and Pakistan refugee airlifts, the greatest evacuation of civilian population ever attempted by air. In the space of eight weeks, twenty-three B.O.A.C. and private charter aircraft, mainly Dakotas, carried 43,500 people over a total distance of more than a million miles. They were 43,500 people lifted out of the massacres which followed the partition of India. Jennings, a pilot with Scottish Airlines at the time, saw from both sides of the new border the terror of Moslems seeking escape from India and of Hindus stranded in Pakistan.

The first airlift was Operation Pakistan, a fairly orderly movement of 7,000 Pakistan government servants and their

families from Delhi to Karachi and the repatriation of 1,500
Indians from Karachi. But mob violence was building up
throughout the three weeks of the airlift and Jennings flew
over burning villages and columns of refugees attended by
hovering vultures. One pilot had the macabre experience of
a vulture shattering his windscreen and spraying the cockpit
with bloodstained glass.

By early October, uncontrolled civil war was raging in
both countries and the Indian government called for a
further airlift, Operation India. This was a much more
ambitious project, with aircraft ranging from Delhi to
Peshawar, Rawalpindi, Quetta and Lahore as well as remote,
overgrown airstrips abandoned by the R.A.F. at the end of
the war with Japan. The refugees were usually waiting on
the runway and would scatter at the sound of aircraft engines,
leaving the Dakota to land amongst a litter of sleeping rolls,
cooking pots and other personal belongings. A child's cane
chair, an elderly parrot, a tea urn, an electric fan, a grand-
father clock, a primitive radio complete with spare batteries
—these were some of the objects submitted to the 44 lb.
personal luggage allowance by people trying to take some
fragment of their old life to the strange land which was
proclaimed to be their new home.

The refugees surged back on to the runway before each
arriving aircraft came to rest. Jennings often had his Dakota
so closely besieged that it became something of a brawl to
open the doors and unload the incoming load of refugees
from the other side of the border. Once the doors were
opened and the departing passengers had struggled clear,
the people at the front of the mob waiting on the runway
tended to hurl their luggage ahead of them into the empty
aircraft to stake a claim for a seat. Others used heavy metal
trunks as battering rams to try and gain a place on board.
Sometimes a Dakota would become so packed to the roof
with this advance luggage that there was no room for a single
passenger and the crew could not find a way through to the
flight deck.

Jennings and his colleagues worked with great patience to disentangle the panic, always remembering these were not normal passengers but men, women and children who could be brutally murdered within an hour of being left behind. Dakotas, built to carry fifty-six passengers, were stripped of their seats and crammed in up to eighty-six. A Bristol Wayfarer of Silver City achieved a record load of 119. But always there were hundreds more clamouring to be taken as well. Pilots had to start their port engines—on the door side of the aircraft—to disperse the crowd with propeller blast before being clear to taxi for take-off. Even then, the mob would give chase and Jennings once waited to land while another Dakota zig-zagged up and down the airstrip to dislodge a group of refugees sitting on the tailplane.

Captain Marian Kozubski, a Polish charter pilot, landed at an aerodrome in Pakistan a few minutes after several hundred Hindu refugees had been attacked by a larger number of local Moslems. His plane came to a halt within a swirling hand-to-hand battle. All he could do was open the Dakota's door, allow the nearest eighty people to swirl inside, and then take off as soon as possible. The groans of combat accompanied him on the flight back to Delhi. Kozubski took a brief look at his passengers and saw he had picked up forty Moslems and forty Hindus. They were still fighting when the Dakota landed at Delhi and riot police were called to separate them. No one was found to be seriously wounded, thereby preserving the airlift's record of transporting its passengers in 100 per cent. safety—including the young refugee girl who gave birth to a baby at 6,000 feet.

Unfortunately, the dead and dying among those le behind steadily mounted and the skies around each landing ground became clouded with vultures and hawks. Another aircraft had its windscreen shattered by a bird of prey, injuring the co-pilot. A third had an engine put out of action by a hawk flying into the air intake. The engine had to be changed on a primitively equipped airstrip lacking any form of lifting tackle. Engineers dug long, sloping trenches in front of the landing wheels and the aircraft was rolled down the incline until the engine nacelle was within easy reach from ground level.

When Operation India came to an end on November 30, 1947, Jennings shared the professional pride in a historic demonstration of air transport. But he brought back to Europe the picture of a small Indian child chasing after a Dakota beginning its take-off. She was weeping bitterly and her sobs were lost on the slipstream. In the clamour for a place on the aircraft her parents had fought their way on board and left her behind. The little girl who didn't go was to be Jennings' lasting memory of the airlift which saved so many.

For Viatkin, sitting at Jennings' right during the flight to Hamburg, the second Berlin airlift was becoming a blur of monotony. His clash with the paratroopers had yet to come and he saw little service to humanity in the manufactured goods, copper ingots, and scrap metal he brought out of the blockaded city, or the few aircraft spare parts the York was now bringing to Hamburg. The monotony snapped at 4.43 p.m. on the final approach to Hamburg airport. Wiseman had come forward to watch the landing and was sitting behind Viatkin. Laker, standing between the two pilots' seats, performed his old job as flight engineer. At 600 feet the York had flaps and landing wheels down. Speed was 165 m.p.h. Then both port engines cut out at the same time and the aircraft swung 70 degrees off course to the left. Jennings was trying to correct the course with the remaining two engines when they failed in the same mysterious way. Then first two fired again briefly followed by a short burst the starboard pair. When all four engines were dead, the York was 90 degrees off course, losing height fast and heading straight for a large cemetery. There was no trace of smoke from the engines and Viatkin could only imagine a drastic fuel leak had developed during the flight and that the engines were starved of fuel.

Laker reached for the controls in the roof panel and retracted the undercarriage, normal procedure for the situation. He also lifted the wing flaps, an unlikely move since it raised the aircraft's stalling speed. Jennings and Viatkin felt the controls become heavy and they kicked hard on the rudder to fight the York's tendency to roll on to its back. But they appreciated that Laker lifted the flaps in a desperate effort to flatten their angle of descent and get the York over the big square mass of a crematorium standing directly in their path at the far end of the cemetery.

Viatkin watched the tall, ornate tombstones crowding up towards the cockpit window and cursed the Germans for erecting such solid monuments to their ancestors. He was convinced the York would never even reach the crematorium and that he would be impaled on the stone wings of an angel. While Jennings and Viatkin were physically engrossed in holding the plane's nose up and stopping her from rolling over, Laker was mentally checking the fuel system of the Merlin engines fitted to the York. He remembered there was an accelerator pump between the throttles and the carburettors. He reasoned that there would be a small amount of petrol left within the pump after the engines stopped through the failure of the main fuel supply. It was an engineer's reaction to a situation which was already hopeless from a pilot's point of view.

With the steeply sloping roof of the crematorium filling the view ahead, Laker started to push the throttle levers to and fro. The accelerator pump responded by squirting its small content of petrol into the carburettors, the engin burst into life for a few seconds, and the pilots felt a dist check to the plane's fall. Laker pumped the throttles a to squeeze the last ounces of petrol from the acceler Again the engines fired briefly, the York cleared t crematorium with inches to spare, and snapped aside a stretch of power lines beyond. The engines were finally dead now. Jennings and Viatkin could only hold on to the controls as the York went into its final descent. They glided the whole length of a school playground and glimpsed terrified children running for cover. The nose skimmed the roof of a small house and the tail actually hit the house and removed the roof. Viatkin covered his head with his hands and never saw the allotment until after the plane came to rest with its nose buried five feet in the soft earth.

The impact was no more dramatic than a sports car slamming on its brakes at high speed. The four men in the cockpit ended in a heap with Laker sprawled on top. Jennings was bruised about the face and Wiseman had broken his nose. The fitters travelling in the rear were unhurt. Viatkin forced open a side window, pushed away the soil heaped against the side of the York, and pulled himself out into the allotment. There he was greeted by the owner of the house which had lost its roof. The owner was a cheerful, grinning man who seemed delighted at finding someone crawling from a wrecked aircraft half-buried in his allotment. He turned out to be a deaf-mute who heard nothing of the York removing his roof but felt the building tremble, followed by a shaking of the ground outside. His smiles for Viatkin and the other figures emerging from the aircraft were for what the deaf-mute thought to be his fellow survivors of an earthquake.

Viatkin, Jennings and Wiseman were well aware they survived at all only because Laker's engineering mind produced the two extra bursts of power which avoided a head-on collision with the crematorium. Jennings stayed with Laker to become Flight Manager of Operations for British United Airways, and Wiseman is now Technical Director of Aviation Traders within the B.U.A. group. Viatkin went his independent way from one charter company to another over the following years but carried with him Laker's first words on realising they were all still alive when the shattered cockpit of the York finally came to rest: "Will you kindly take your bloody arm out of your managing director's face?"

CHAPTER FIVE

Taxi to Venice

BUYING a twin-engined aeroplane to take his family and friends on a touring holiday across Europe was an extravagance Ernie Taylor could well afford. He was rich enough from various rag trade and publishing enterprises to have retired for life at 45. He called the aeroplane Pickles III after his 18-year-old son, a gangling youth who impassively answered to the name of Pickles. The family motor cars were already named Pickles I and Pickles II. But Ernie Taylor really bought the aeroplane for his wife, Elsie. " This holiday will be whatever you want it to be," he told her. " We can fly anywhere you want to go, do anything you want to do."

The Taylors chose to live in a surprisingly modest semi-detached house in Epsom. Mrs. Taylor matched this homely image rather better than the far-flying spectacle of travel by personal aircraft. She was a thin, neat woman with a hearing aid showing through her greying hair, pleased that a local garage owner and his wife were going to come along on the holiday. Mrs. Taylor was also pleased that the plane, a 10-seater Rapide, was going to be flown by someone she considered another friend of the family, Monique Agazarian. One of the few women to make a career in charter flying, Monique had flown the Taylors on all their previous travels by air. Until this holiday they travelled in a Rapide belonging to her company, Island Air Services, one of more than fifty small charter operators struggling to exist at Croydon

Airport during the late 1940's. Taylor bought his own
Rapide to give an extra pride of luxury to what was going
to be his wife's last holiday. Doctors had told him she had
only two or three months to live. " Of course, she doesn't
know," he told Monique, " and she must never know."

Mrs. Taylor was suffering from cancer. A major operation
and deep-ray treatment failed to check the disease although
she claimed to feel well and dismissed the darkest pains as
lightly as wasps intruding on a family picnic. She had a
determined capacity for enjoyment of whatever was offered
her to enjoy. Her husband announced the special treat of a
holiday in their own aeroplane and she climbed on board
Pickles III with the due delight of a woman who could wish
for nothing more. Monique, studying the ever-patient smile,
decided Mrs. Taylor would have been equally delighted
doing anything else her husband wanted her to do.

Pickles III took off from Croydon and flew to Cannes airport where Pierre was waiting with his aged Mercedes taxi.
This was the taxi which happened to pick up the Taylors on
their first visit to Cannes, by train several years before, and
they had insisted on reserving it as their chauffeur-driven
hire car for all subsequent visits. Pierre, a large, heavy
Frenchman of about 50, greeted them with the eager defer-
ence of a family retainer welcoming his employers home,
and drove into Cannes by way of Ernie Taylor's two favourite
bars. In each there were fond welcomes, drinks and jokes.
Monique noted Mrs. Taylor's modest acknowledgment of
the reception while her husband plunged in as heartily as a
British Tommy revisiting an old foreign billet. The garage
owner and his wife were pleasantly gay. Pickles, an apprentice
engineer, discussed the Mercedes gearbox with Pierre.

The party was booked into a small hotel in the centre of
Cannes, the place where the Taylors always stayed. That
evening they all went out for dinner at the Taylors' favourite
restaurant. Next morning, Pierre called to take them on their
usual drive through the hills, stopping at the usual spot to
enjoy the view and take the air. Mrs. Taylor enjoyed her

hotel room, the meal, the ride, the view and the air. The following morning Monique flew them on a day-trip to Ajaccio in Corsica and Mrs. Taylor found the mountain scenery " absolutely gorgeous."

A few weeks before, Monique had postponed a charter flight because of those same mountains. She was just about to leave Nice on a night flight to Ajaccio when the pilot of an incoming airliner warned her that a power failure at Ajaccio had cut off the warning lights on the mountain sides surrounding the airport. The lack of power meant there would be no radio warning from Ajaccio and she might well have run into the mountains while still waiting for the first sight of the airport lights. The flight was to rescue the chairman of a rival charter firm from his creditors. Monique did not consider the mission noble enough to grope her way into Ajaccio and she abandoned the take-off until next morning.

There was no problem when she flew the Taylors there. The sun was high in a clear sky when they landed and so hot they soon took a taxi into the hills to get cool. The driver posed as a local celebrity. His brother had been executed as a bandit only the week before and he saw no reason to be modest about such family fame. Ernie Taylor, wearing the Bermudan beach shirt he wore as part of his Mediterranean uniform, offered the man his sympathy, his congratulations, his admiration, and any drink he cared to name. Mrs. Taylor switched off her hearing aid at the first mention of bandits.

From Ajaccio, Monique flew them back to Cannes and then on to Pisa. She hinted at a visit to Venice instead of Pisa, never having been to Venice herself, but Taylor insisted it was his wife's holiday, and suggested she would want to go to Pisa. Mrs. Taylor cheerfully agreed that she did want to go to Pisa and that was where Pickles III went, landing at an Italian air force base outside the town. Monique and her passengers spent that night interned in a hotel, trying to convince the policemen who arrested them as they left the plane that they were unaware of regulations which required five days' advance permission for such a flight.

Monique had heard of such regulations but the airways of Europe were far from strictly prescribed at this time—much more a maze of ill-defined aerial tracks—and she hoped to escape attention by following the Italian coast from the north as far as the mouth of the River Arno before making a short, sharp turn into Pisa. When there were policemen waiting for them, she argued that she was in business as an air-taxi and it was unreasonable to expect her to wait five days each time she picked up a fare wanting to go into Italy. The policemen insisted an offence had been committed, relenting only to the extent of allowing the party to choose which hotel they wished to be interned in, and of driving them to the hotel by way of the Leaning Tower so that Pickles could buy postcards for his friends back in Epsom.

The airport commandant finally rescued the lady pilot in distress by gallantly insisting she was a victim of a navigational error and did not intend to land in Italy at all. This explanation was accepted by the police and the visitors were returned to the air force base for an immediate flight back to Cannes. Pickles III flew into Pisa again the following day and this time the commandant greeted the party instead of the policemen. Monique had at last persuaded the Taylors they should see Venice and she telephoned the commandant from Cannes for his advice on how not to be arrested when they got there.

"Come to Pisa immediately," he said, "and I will have everything arranged for you. There will be no more trouble with the regulations." The only threat of trouble at Pisa was the bad weather hanging over the mountains between there and Venice. The commandant insisted on joining the flight to afford his personal protection but climbed on board the Rapide with obvious apprehensions about the weather ahead. During an uncomfortable passage across the Apennines, Monique's radio operator was kept very busy. "I've never heard anything like it," he told her. "It sounds as if every radio station in Italy is working us—as if somebody wants to make extra sure we get safely to Venice." The commandant, hunched tightly in his seat as the plane rocked and lurched above the mountains, gave a pale but inscrutable smile. There were certain precautions a man would take whether he was being flown by a woman or not.

The weather cleared beyond the Apennines and Monique thrilled to see Venice for the first time in bright sunshine, tilted towards her at a more dramatic angle than Canaletto ever saw. Mrs. Taylor and the garage owner's wife said they were surprised there was quite so much water. Monique landed at the Lido and stayed behind with the commandant to fasten the aircraft down for the night while the Taylors and their friends went on by launch to book the whole party into the Danieli Royal Excelsior hotel, once a Venetian palace. Monique and the commandant joined them there in time for dinner, followed by a gondola tour of the city's canals. This was charter flying at its most attractive, Monique decided, reclining in a gondola.

Back at Croydon, nearly a hundred aircraft were standing idle during a drastic collapse of charter business. Operators who could find customers were having to demand cash-on-landing to pay the next night's hangar fee. While here she was sharing the Taylors' holiday across Europe and being paid for it, too. The party spent the next three days sight-seeing in Venice, with Monique the most excited tourist of them all. Then she had to take off in the Rapide and head back to England, leaving the Taylors and friends to spend another three weeks on holiday. She flew out of the Lido with a strange mixture of emotions.

Ernie Taylor had been talking about the extravagance of buying Pickles III for a family holiday. It came when Monique was persuading him to let her company use the Rapide on charter work whenever he had no use for it. That way he would still have a personal aircraft but it would be earning him money for most of the year. The idea appealed to Taylor and a formal arrangement was eventually completed. But first he sat in a bar overlooking a Venetian canal and said: "I bought that plane to make sure Elsie had a

real good last fling. And I think it's been worth every penny.
Of course, Elsie doesn't know she hasn't got long to go and
she will never know. I want her to feel she can fly right round
the world as often as she likes."

All the way back to England, Monique was thinking of
the little, self-made man from that semi-detached house in
Epsom going out to buy an aeroplane as a last treat for his
wife. Monique was also picturing Elsie Taylor and the gentle
smile she carried through Cannes and Nice and Ajaccio and
Pisa and Venice, sipping a drink in Ernie's favourite bars,
dancing a foxtrot in a strange nightclub, eating a small meal
in an expensive restaurant, admiring scenery which reminded
her of the postcards she had already sent home. Then there
was the afternoon her husband took her to watch the Venetian
glass blowers at work and she went away with a spectacular
chandelier for her sitting room, choosing it as a child reaches
for pieces of pretty glass while Ernie Taylor was happy to
pay £100 for the privilege of making her happy. Remembering Mrs. Taylor's fond expression as she watched her husband
buy the chandelier, Monique was suddenly quite sure this
woman had known all along the real reason for Pickles III.
She was not supposed to know she was dying but the only
secret between the Taylors had been Ernie not knowing that
Elsie did know. And Mrs. Taylor was so devoted to her
husband she responded to their farewell holiday as she knew
he would want her to respond, determined not to deny him
the pleasure of planning these last surprises.

It was a secret Mrs. Taylor observed longer than Ernie
Taylor ever expected to maintain it himself. She lived for
four years after returning from Venice. Two years after her
death, Ernie Taylor was also dead, the sturdy little man who
claimed never to have had a day's illness in his life being
struck down by a heart attack. By this time Pickles III had
already been sold to Island Air Services and changed its name
to the more workaday Baker-Baker.

The Taylors, extraordinary in their wealthy ordinariness,
remained Monique's favourite passengers from all the varied

people she flew on charter trips throughout Europe—film stars, millionaires, international playboys, jockeys, and business executives. She had girlish ambitions of becoming a film star herself and was studying at the Royal Academy of Dramatic Art in 1939 when she became a V.A.D. nurse on the outbreak of war. Three of her brothers joined the R.A.F. and it was from one of them that she first had the idea of taking up flying.

Pilot Officer Noel Agazarian, a Battle of Britain hero whose name is on the Spitfire preserved in the Imperial War Museum, told her about girls training as ferry pilots. Monique applied immediately but it was not until 1943, two years after Noel was killed in North Africa, that she was accepted for training. She passed her medical examination only by learning in advance from an R.A.F. doctor that a minimum height of 5 ft. 5 ins. was required. She was not quite 5 ft. 4 ins. but knew as a nurse that it was possible to gain an inch for a few seconds by lying flat on her back until immediately before her height was measured. The examining doctor came into the room to find her lying on the floor. "Would you mind taking my height straight away?" she asked, then jumped to her feet and stood against the wall. "Not quite 5 ft. 5 ins.," said the doctor. Monique went to get back on the floor. "Just a minute," she said, "I can do better than that." The doctor said he was prepared to believe her and that it would not be necessary to repeat the gymnastics. She passed the rest of the medical without effort.

Monique did her training and soloed in a Miles Magister. She shrieked with delight all through her first flight and afterwards explained to her instructor: "I suppose I have always really wanted to do this. After seeing *Peter Pan* as a little girl I kept trying to fly by jumping off the bed although I must admit I was never keen enough to try it out of the window." Her flight training began in the autumn and Monique took a woman's delight in the gold and brown colour scheme which unfolded beneath her. She liked, too, the feeling of rising away from dirt and dust so that every flight became a long, luxurious bath in sensations of cleanliness and freshness. Her first ferrying was with Tiger Moth and Swordfish biplanes, then progressed to Harvards, Spitfires, Mustangs, Typhoons and Hellcats. She enjoyed the sports car temperament of the fighters and was disappointed that the end of the war brought only a return to RADA.

Mary Guthrie, a fellow student there in 1939, had also been a ferry pilot. The two girls went together to see Sir Kenneth Barnes, Principal of the Academy, and persuaded him to telephone Sir Alexander Korda and recommend them for film work. While waiting for the call to come through, Sir Kenneth read through the pre-war records on their acting and an account of their war-time activities. " I have two young ladies here," he told Korda, eventually, " whom I would recommend unreservedly should you ever find a need for a pair of female stunt pilots."

Both girls accepted the hint to forget acting as a career. Mary Guthrie joined British South American Airways as Britain's first air hostess. Monique applied at the same time but the reply was addressed to Miss M. Agazarian and regretted that foreigners were not being employed. Her mother was French but it was an unfortunate reason to give a girl whose father fled to this country from Armenia when he was only fourteen, and became a naturalised Englishman in time to lose two sons in the war.

Rejected as an air hostess, Monique took out a commercial flying licence and began to look for a job as a pilot. Like so many war-time fliers, she was incredibly naive about civil aviation. One of the R.A.F.'s most experienced bomber pilots turned down the chance of a job with T.W.A. because he thought the London staff were being awkward in wanting to send him to New York for an interview. He had no idea that Trans World Airlines was an American company. In Monique's case she wrote the same letter to every air charter company she found in a classified directory, assuring them all she was very interested in making maps and charts—presumably by aerial photography. She received only five replies and no offers.

An optimistic visit to Elstree aerodrome did eventually lead to Monique becoming the London manager, at £5 a week, of Island Air Services. The company had two Proctors. One operated a service between the Scilly Isles and Land's End, piloted personally by the owner of the company, Daughley Hills-Grove-Hills. The other Proctor was leased to another charter firm, based at Elstree. By early 1947, Island Air Services had moved into Croydon Airport and Monique was flying the second Proctor herself. Hills-Grove-Hills, a wealthy young man who had learned to fly since the war, was persuaded to let Monique develop the Croydon end of the business while he concentrated on the Scilly Isles. Croydon was busier than at any time in its history and that was as long as civil aviation itself. The big corporations, particularly B.E.A. and Air France were slow in establishing their passenger routes throughout Europe after the war, and the nationalisation of ten leading independent companies to become part of B.E.A. in 1946 left the domestic scene sparsely provided for. At the same time the potential passenger traffic was greater than ever before. Small charter companies rushed to meet the need, able to fly their customers direct to their individual destinations at whatever times the customers found most convenient. It was the air-taxi competing with an infrequent yet expensive bus service and more than 100 operators could keep busy from Croydon alone.

Monique was determined to prove there was room for one more operator. In a single day she flew a businessman to Southampton, flew a football manager and two directors to Leeds, took a party of holidaymakers to Cowes in the Isle of Wight, brought a group of people back to Fairoaks, near Woking, and returned to Croydon in time to squeeze in two pleasure flights for members of the public visiting the airport. Next day she flew to Birmingham to pick up a couple of business executives for a day-trip to Hamburg. The following morning she flew a family to the Scilly Isles, and found time to remind Hills-Grove-Hills that she was still being paid only £5 a week as manager of the London office. He agreed it was time she was paid as a pilot. The extra money was welcome but not important. At last it was recognised that flying was her business. Monique Agazarian, the gay, attractive girl who once wanted to be an actress, could claim a place in the brotherhood of the sky tramps as a pilot ready and eager to fly anywhere with anyone or anything that needed to be flown.

When Hills-Grove-Hills was sick, she took over the entire freight service of cut-flowers between the Scilly Isles and Lands End. Seven times a day she helped the engineer load fifty boxes of flowers into a Proctor stripped of its seats. Seven times she helped a B.E.A. man take them out again at the other end of the flight. There were seven take-offs from the Scilly Isles' hump-backed airfield with a 110 ft. sheer drop into the sea beyond. There were seven return landings with the Proctor being lifted over the edge of that same cliff and set down upon a 1-in-4 gradient.

The following summer she was doing two or three holiday flights a day between Croydon and Jersey, flying a larger, more sophisticated Rapide but still crudely equipped for landing in the Channel Islands' notorious fog. Sometimes she would fly to Jersey and have to return to Croydon without ever seeing the island. More often, she would let down through the fog to 200 feet and approach over the sea with her radio operator calling out her course on bearings he calculated from signals on the W.T. equipment. The Rapide had no blind-flying instruments, no automatic " fixing " device for navigation, and the basic handicap of its wireless telegraphy was the delay involved in transmitting and receiving only by Morse code. A sudden emergency allowed no time to discuss the situation with ground control, such as it was, or even query their instructions.

Monique ran into filthy weather when taking a flight from Paris to Nice on May 20, 1949. She landed at Dijon and re-fuelled in torrential rain, holding an umbrella over the petrol intake to keep water out of the tanks. From Dijon, she was cleared to over-fly Lyon and proceed down the Rhone Valley to Nice, at an altitude of 5,000 feet. She was warned that the freezing level was 6,000 feet. The weather was reported to have cleared beyond Avignon. Monique took off and climbed through dense cloud to 5,000 feet. Nearing Lyon, she received a W.T. message from her radio operator to increase height to 7,000 feet. " Surely they know there's ice up there," she said ."Ask if we can't let her down instead." The operator sent off the request in Morse and translated the reply when it came: " Negative. Climb to 7,000 feet." Monique began to climb. A simple argument became a ponderous debate by Morse and she presumed Lyon wanted her at a higher altitude because there were other aircraft ahead at 5,000 feet.

The ice, when it came, formed with spectacular speed, building up to a thickness of two feet inboard of the engines and spreading out along the wings as she watched. At the same time the controls became stubbornly sluggish. In what seemed a matter of seconds the Rapide was no longer a flying machine but an almost uncontrollable heap of ice. Monique went to put the nose down but the control surfaces hardly moved. Air speed had fallen to within a few miles per hour of stalling so that the Rapide was on the point of dropping out of the sky. She pushed harder on the controls and the nose did go down slightly, beginning a long, laborious descent through cloud as thick and dirty as a winter puddle, with Monique beginning to worry about the mountainside which might be waiting at the bottom. She was keeping to the centre of the valley when the icing happened but could now be well off course. The aircraft was still on the point of stalling and if it did stall she preferred to be well clear of the mountains.

" Tell Lyon I'm having to let down," she said to the radio operator, " and get me something to aim at."

He took a back bearing from Lyon, now some miles behind

them, and a front bearing from Montelimar. Monique let down on this deadline. The ice had gone at 5,000 feet and she emerged into clear weather directly over Montelimar airport. Her passengers, three Wolverhampton businessmen, began the flight from Paris stressing the urgency of their appointment in Nice. After the experience of being buried in ice at 7,000 feet they were happy to stay overnight at Montelimar. Their pilot went to bed convinced she had been within ten seconds of having the Rapide fall from under her. The aircraft was of pre-war design—a type first produced in 1934 when air mail took ten days to reach Australia—and flying remained a primitive business.

Monique was by now managing director and chief pilot of her own charter company, Island Air Services (London) Ltd. Hills-Grove-Hills agreed to her taking over the London operations which she had built up, and his original company continued to work from the Scilly Isles. She set up in business with two pilot friends, Ray Rendall and John Helps. They could raise £5,000 between them as capital and she borrowed a further £1,500 from the same bank manager who backed Harold Bamberg in his £420,000 purchase of the fourteen Vikings to establish Eagle throughout Europe. Island Air Services was more modest. A second Rapide was bought from B.E.A. on hire purchase, and Ernie Taylor's Rapide was also available whenever he was not needing it.

The company's first two summers were most successful, especially holiday flights to Jersey. But by early 1950 Monique was admitting that she had started her own business in time to meet the biggest slump that the small charter operators were ever to know. The usual seasonal decline in work was particularly severe that winter. Even worse, B.E.A. and Air France were beginning to win back passengers from the air-taxi operators by offering a considerable increase and improvement in their scheduled services. Monique had one charter all winter. That was one more than many of her rivals. Rather than stand idle, a large proportion of the charter pilots at Croydon pooled their money and flew their own families to Switzerland for a communal holiday of winter sports. When they flew home the problem of unemployment was still there.

Monique, now married to Rendall, one of her business partners, put an advertisement in a London newspaper: " Madame Monique, just returned from Paris "—where she made a landing on the way from Switzerland—" would be pleased to hear from clients old and new." To an embarrassed counter clerk, she added: " That's for the ' Dress Making ' column." The advertisement appeared when the New Look had out-dated all previous fashion. The French name and the mention of Paris brought an immediate rush of business although Monique had no previous experience of dress-making and could work only from simple cut-out patterns. She was soon making a profit of £20 a week but that was little towards the overheads and heavy depreciation of aircraft parked in a hangar.

In March, 1950, Monique persuaded her partners that the company should spend what remaining cash it had on buying her some new clothes and sending her to France. The clothes were to boost her morale. The trip to France was to talk the owner of the casino at Deauville into the idea of establishing a regular air service for British gamblers wanting to play at his tables. The casino owner was impressed by her detailed forecasts of the traffic he could expect, the seasonal peaks for passengers, and the costs of operating such a service. Monique proposed he should pay full charter rate for a daily service by Rapide between Shoreham, in Sussex, and Deauville, and look after all publicity in France. Island Air Services would pay him 75 per cent. of all ticket revenue and publicise the service in England. If the service flew regularly with a full load of passengers the 75 per cent. of ticket sales would more than cover the casino's cost of chartering the plane, leaving a 25 per cent. profit for the operators. They were the kind of odds which appealed to the casino proprietor.

Island Air Services duly moved into the league of inter-national scheduled services, operating in association with

B.E.A. (a licensing requirement) and charging fares laid down by I.A.T.A. The Mayor of Brighton and the Mayor of Hove travelled on the inaugural flight. The Mayor of Deauville, French aviation officials, and the casino executives were assembled to meet them. Monique flew as a passenger and led the way out of the aircraft in her capacity as managing director of the company establishing a link between the two countries. The dignity of the occasion was shattered when two of the French ground staff, waiting in oil-stained overalls to re-fuel the Rapide, recognised her from working flights into the airport. They ran forward to embrace her with cries of " Madame Monique, how lovely to see you again." The reception committee discreetly ignored the oil smudge on the tip of her nose when it was their turn to greet the airline's managing director.

On subsequent flights to Deauville as pilot, Monique became the first woman ever to captain an airliner flying on an international scheduled service. She also established the Deauville service as a complete success, achieving 100 per cent. regularity and carrying many stage and TV personalities on its flights to and from the gambling tables. A very different kind of passenger was being provided for by another operation being developed by Monique at the same time. First at Croydon and also at Northolt she found an eager demand for pleasure flights from members of the public visiting the airport to watch aeroplanes come and go. The opportunity to go up in one of those aeroplanes gave most airport spectators an active interest in aviation for the first time. Flying became something real and personal instead of a distant view of complicated machinery. A fear of flying was usually a fear of the unknown and Monique saw a profitable business in demonstrating that flying was fun.

The big chance came when she won the concession for pleasure flights from London Airport when it was still in its first stages of development. Her base was an ex-R.A.F. caravan near a public exposure which was little more than an open space, and pleasure flying was restricted to Sundays. But by the early 1950's she had four Rapides making 100 flights a day for six whole months of the year. A shift system of pilots, including two more women pilots, Veronica Volkersz and Susanne Chapman, ensured a continuous sequence of flying from 10 a.m. until early evening. White-uniformed marshals formed the ever-present queue into groups of nine people ready to board each Rapide as it completed one flight and started the next without stopping its engines. The turn-round averaged thirty seconds and at peak periods the four Rapides would be landing, loading and taking off side by side. Becoming airborne in such a relatively short distance the Rapides could take off across one of the main runways, passing at right angles to the airport traffic like ferry boats on a busy river. The turbulence created by the passage of large airliners, hanging over a runway for as long as sixty seconds on a calm day, posed the same sort of problem as the wake of a large boat.

Whenever possible, Monique tried to time her aircraft's movements for them to pass in front of oncoming traffic and so miss the turbulence altogether. Knowing that the very presence of Rapides flying at right angles had the same neurotic effect on four-engined airliners as mice frisking around an elephant's feet, the airport control took great care the pleasure aircraft were never actually on the runway within sight of approaching traffic. If Monique was taking a pilot's shift, she would lead the other three Rapides along special taxiing routes to whatever runway the control specified. All her aircraft had duplicated radio equipment covering all frequencies in use at the airport to ensure constant contact with the control staff. Monique was aware that pleasure flying at an international airport was considered a dangerous nuisance in some quarters and laid great emphasis on her pilots knowing what movements were taking place about them and obeying all instructions from control.

On reaching the edge of the specified runway the four Rapides would take up a loose box formation. The formal message to control at this stage was: " Ready immediate

take-off." Over the years, this became " The Shower's ready
to go." Then the four planes would take off across the runway in the same loose formation, climb to 1,000 feet, make a
five-minute circuit of the airport, request permission to land,
touch down one behind the other, and turn off the runway
at four different intersections, almost while their tails were
still in the air. As a variation on this procedure, there was a
longer flight, costing 22s. per head instead of 11s., which
offered a conducted tour of London at 1,500 feet. Pilots
averaged six airport circuits an hour or three of the tours.
The public still queued for more whatever the hour.

Monique catered for the widest range of customers. There
was the 96-year-old woman who arrived wearing a shawl and
elastic-sided boots and went on her first flight to celebrate
being up and about again after eleven years confined to her
bed. There was the pre-1914 pilot, himself one of the earliest
pioneers of pleasure flying, who travelled from his home in
the Cotswolds to judge how well this young woman was
handling his old job. There were women's institutes, factory
outings, polio victims, and always a steady stream of blind
people who seemed to find in flying an exquisite sensation
of their own. When Elizabeth Taylor was expecting her first
baby she had an urge to fly low over London and see her flat
from the air. Michael Wilding, her husband of the time,
brought her to Monique and the wish was granted. While the
two film stars were smuggled out of the airport afterwards in
an old Austin 12, Monique was happily signing autographs
as a celebrity in her own right. She always appreciated the
publicity value of being a woman airline chief and encour-
aged her other two women pilots to glamorise the job as much
as possible. An 82-year-old Uxbridge man saved from his
pension for a pleasure flight once a year, insisting that it was
with Monique. When he died he left her a pile of newspaper
cuttings about her career. They were dedicated to " his "
pilot.

With this sort of following, Island Air Services built up to
a level of profitability which few airlines have ever equalled.

4*

Even after paying £3,000 cash in advance to the airport authorities for each season's flying concession and being charged landing fees and parking fees, the company could make 20 per cent. profit on the operation. The airport flights were also an effective advertisement for holiday charters to Jersey. Monique recorded a clear profit of £10,000 during six months of 1955—plus the prestige of chartering two fifty-seater Elizabethan airliners from B.E.A. to cope with a sudden surge of business.

Then, in 1956, pleasure flying at London Airport was brought to an end. Monique carried her protests to the House of Commons and was assured the decision was taken on operational grounds. She was told of fears of an increased accident risk with airport traffic reaching new peaks and the prospect of the big jets to come. Monique preferred to believe, as she still does, that her little fleet was made a scapegoat for local residents' complaints about noise. A routine protest, made soon after her concession was withdrawn, brought a Parliamentary assurance that movements in and out of the airport had been reduced by 100 flights a day. The banning of the small Rapides presumably lessened the noise made by four-engined transatlantic airliners.

Monique looked for somewhere else to carry on the pleasure flying and tried a season at Ramsgate airport. But the absence of international flights by large aircraft meant there was no captive audience in the public enclosure to be tempted into the Rapides. Takings were low and her enthusiasm began to sink to the same level. Her domestic commitments were mounting. She now had three children and her husband had taken a job as a pilot with B.E.A., looking for more home life between flights than he did as a business partner. The turning point came when one of the Rapides crashed and broke its back at the very end of the Ramsgate season. This was the first Rapide the company ever owned, call sign Uncle Fox (unless Monique was at the controls and then it was known as Auntie Fox). The death of faithful Uncle Fox, built for the R.A.F. during the war by a firm of piano makers and nine years in service with Island Air Services (London) Ltd., seemed sadly symbolic. Monique sold the remaining aircraft, and retired to the life of a housewife and mother, brooding over all that might have been had Uncle Fox and the other Rapides been allowed to stay on at London Airport.

The only accident to have happened there also had a strong personal significance. A Rapide was caught in the slipstream of a Stratocruiser and crashed at the side of the runway, badly injuring the pilot but with the passengers unharmed in their safety belts. The aeroplane crumpled in the grass at London Airport was Baker-Baker, alias Pickles III. For Monique Agazarian it was the end of a strange road which began at Ernie Taylor's semi-detached in Epsom.

CHAPTER SIX

Monsoon, Elephants and Bandits

THE two elephants only a few feet away from the tip of the DC-3's port wing were distinctly worrying Capt. Donald Ludbey. His nerves were not fully composed from the manner of his landing on this rain soaked airstrip in the far north of Burma. The DC-3 had broken dense monsoon cloud immediately above 100-foot-high bamboo surrounding the airstrip, made its approach across a stretch of rice paddy, and put down on a runway neatly marked out with rows of white markers. Ludbey lost control of the aircraft the moment its wheels touched the ground and skidded in mud so soft that it might have been an extension of the paddy field. With brakes full on, the DC-3 began to slide sideways towards the edge of the runway. At close range the neat line of markers revealed themselves as whitewashed Himalayan boulders, each capable of wrecking the plane. Ludbey could only watch the boulders approach and shrink from the impending moment of impact. Disaster was averted when the wheels reached a stretch of firmer ground, the brakes were able to bite, and Ludbey could swing the DC-3 back towards the centre of the runway.

The landing was watched with cheerful interest by a crowd of two hundred people, including two timber workers who had arrived by elephant to witness the excitement of the last scheduled flight of the monsoon season. Headed by the elephants, the crowd trailed behind the DC-3 as it finally slithered to a standstill at the furthest end of the runway and turned round into its take-off position. There was a high-spirited reception for Ludbey's fifteen passengers as they emerged, clutching the pots, pans, chairs, tables and bicycles which were typical of the hand baggage accepted by the Union of Burma Airways. Then the outgoing passengers climbed on board with their own junkshop clutter of personal effects and the crowd pressed close with their goodbyes, delivered with the beaming optimism which bestows the glow of a honeymoon departure on every Burmese farewell.

Ludbey, a squat, dark-haired Australian, glowered at the happy scene. The two elephants were making him nervous, the way they were drawing nearer and nearer the aircraft. "Get those bloody animals out of here," he shouted from the cockpit. "They're not particular where they stick their big feet—and I don't reckon being marooned here for the rest of the monsoon with a broken wing. Get them out of here, will you?"

The timber workers smiled back at the pilot who was obviously admiring their fine beasts. They began to edge the elephants even closer to the plane's wing tip. "Right, you pair of bright boys," said Ludbey, a man whose quiet manner disguised a temper well sharpened by the ritual of Saturday night brawls in the cattle towns of Queensland. "I'll just have to fix you before you trample all over this bloody aeroplane."

Ludbey started the port engine and threw open the throttle. This sudden din at the range of a few yards sent the elephants rearing in panic while the crowd fled from under their feet. Ludbey started the other engine with a further flourish of noise. The elephants turned and galloped away. To the Australian's concern he saw them heading for a small village about two hundred yards from where the plane was standing at the end of the runway. "Oh, no," he said to himself. "Let's get out of here." He gave a last backward glance before the DC-3 began to roll into its take-off. The elephants were trampling through the cluster of bamboo *bashas,* the native huts. Their riders were hanging on to the elephants' ears. Younger members of the crowd were still running for their lives. Old people had collapsed in heaps of cowed despair. Then the DC-3 showed its tail to the scene and Ludbey rose thankfully into the cloud. By the time the monsoon was over, he hoped the Burmese villagers, basically a happy people, would have forgotten all about the stampede.

Ludbey was one of several British and Commonwealth pilots recruited by the Union of Burma Airways from 1948 onwards to operate the newly independent country's air services and to train Burmese air crew in the process. It was the sort of job which has appealed to the pioneering instinct of the sky tramps since 1921 when British charter pilots went to Holland to establish the K.L.M. airline. From then on, they and their successors colonised the airways of the world. While German, French, Dutch and Italian fliers helped to pioneer the great inter-continental routes, it was largely British pilots who took the first aeroplanes into the far corners of Africa and Asia, stayed to build up regular local services in face of the most difficult conditions, and taught their keenest native customers to fly aircraft for themselves. Most of these colonies in the sky have achieved independence in recent years but the Sudan, Iraq and Sierra Leone still operate their internal services under British supervision.

Burma summoned Ludbey and his like to the rescue when the country was disintegrating in the first years of independence. Government forces had lost control of large areas to Communist insurgents, Karen rebels, and Chinese Nationalist troops seeking a new home by right of conquest. Between these areas, local populations were terrorised by bandits. Roads were blocked, railways bridges destroyed, river traffic attacked. A desperate Government realised air communications were the only means of holding the nation together and U.B.A. came into being as the scaffolding from which Burma was to be re-built.

The repairs were far from complete when Ludbey first arrived in Rangoon in 1953 to join the operations being supervised by a fellow Australian, Alan Gifford. On one of Ludbey's first flights he picked up passengers at Thaton while armoured cars held rebels away from the airstrip. Warren Wilson, yet another Australian pilot, returned from the next flight to Thaton with the news that this time there were no armoured cars, no fighting. " But it's about time you fired the local agent there," he told the Burmese traffic manager. " He never showed up with any passengers or freight. I hung around for half-an-hour, then shut the door and flew back home." The manager was horrified. " Surely you did not land at Thaton," he said. " It has fallen to the rebels. The agent and most of the local people are reported massacred. You were waiting for passengers in the middle of enemy territory."

Ludbey and Wilson both joined U.B.A. at the height of the monsoon season and were too engrossed with the hazards of flying over unfamiliar terrain in terrible weather to make a full acquaintance of the political situation as well. Wilson claimed that he did not find a single break in cloud during his first three months in Burma.

Low cloud over the surrounding hills made Ludbey turn back three times on a flight to Kengtung in North-East Burma. At last he flew through the hills by following the course of a steep ravine. He landed at Kengtung to discover that he had flown two hundred feet beneath the headquarters of exiled troops of the Chinese National Army who were blockading the airport with a heavy calibre anti-aircraft gun.

Ludbey had some experience of monsoon flying. As an R.A.F. pilot he flew over parts of Burma and Malaya on bomber raids against the Japanese. After the war he volunteered for Australian National Airways' " flying ambulance " service in North Queensland and had to make many emergency flights in full face of the Wet, the Australian equivalent of the monsoon. It was towards the end of the Wet of 1949 that Ludbey was called from his base at Cairns to collect a seven-year-old boy, Kevin Callaghan, from a cattle station 150 miles to the north-east, at Palmerville. The boy's mother reported his symptoms by a portable telephone plugged into the overland telegraph wire passing through the station. The diagnosis was suspected peritonitis. A flying ambulance was to be sent rather than an aircraft of the flying doctor service because on-the-spot treatment was out of the question in such a case. The child needed to be rushed into Cairns hospital for tests and a possible operation.

All Ludbey knew of Palmerville was that only one house now stood in an area where some 30,000 Chinamen were living seventy to eighty years before—at the time of the Queensland gold rush, in the days when the politicians had not invented the tradition of " White Australia ". Ludbey telephoned Tom McDonald, a Cairns jeweller who had flown a Fox Moth biplane around the territory until ten years before. " Yes, I remember the house at Palmerville," said McDonald. " This boy must be there. It's got a bit of a field in front of the house but the overland telegraph runs across one end of the field and there are some big trees at the other end. I always used to go underneath the wires to give myself most room for a landing." Ludbey went out to his twin-engined de Havilland Dragon and tried to imagine an aircraft of this size landing beneath the telegraph wires. Four of the Dragon's six seats had been replaced by two stretchers for ambulance work. Mr. L. N. Howard, the Cairns Ambulance deputy superintendent, was Ludbey's only crew.

The flight to Palmerville took an hour. Ludbey looked down on scrubby hills splashed with bright green from the Wet and lined by fat brown rivers. When he came to look down at the cattle station he saw that heavy rains had caused a wash-out at the telegraph line end of the field. A large patch of soil had been washed away and all that remained was a deep, water-logged crater. That meant there was no chance of landing the McDonald way. As two or three figures emerged from the house and waved, Ludbey circled low and tried to work out an alternative approach. He saw the trees McDonald mentioned. They were gum trees, about fifty feet high and standing on a slight ridge. He decided to go in over the trees. The Dragon touched down almost half-way along the field and within another hundred yards he had thrown the plane into a 180-degrees turn to avoid plunging into the wash-out.

While Howard took the sick child on board, Ludbey went for a walk to find his best line of take-off. He soon realised he would have to go back over the trees. If he tried the other way he would have to approach the wash-out up a gradient and he would never have enough speed to clear the telegraph wires beyond. Setting off from the wash-out towards the trees he would have the advantage of the gradient. He paced out 400 yards before a stretch of stony ground rising to the trees. Behind these the ground fell away again into a gully. Ludbey calculated that once over the trees he could drop down into the gully to gather air-speed and then climb away.

What bothered him was the height of the trees and the angle of take-off he was going to need to get over them at all. He went to the house and suggested to the boy's father and brother that it would be safer to lop off the top branches of the trees. The two men went to an outhouse and came back with the news that there wasn't an axe on the place. Ludbey's face could not conceal his disgust for a cattle station which could not produce an axe in an emergency. Back at the aeroplane, he was further upset to find the patient's mother installed as an extra passenger. Every pound of weight was going to count when he tried to lift off over the trees and here was a fully grown woman coming along for the ride. He was about to insist she stay behind when he noticed the boy on the stretcher, puffed with fever and writhing in agony. Perhaps a mother's soothing touch was going to be needed on the flight back to Cairns. The boy seemed to be very ill.

Ludbey started the Dragon's engines and began his run down the field. At 65 m.p.h. and with the trees looming ahead he lifted off. The speed began to fall away as he had to climb sharply. There was an added complication. It was early evening and the Dragon was losing lift because of a downward flow of cool air from a hillside adjoining the field. Ludbey saw the first row of smaller trees pass underneath but he was conscious of the machine squashing forward into the big trees at the top of the ridge. He was aware, too, of the plane's fabric-covered fuselage and had visions of being speared by a splintered tree trunk. Then everything disappeared around him and he found himself at ground level with only a bruised back to prove he had been flying the tattered wreck now embracing the foot of a gum tree. The boy was lying near Ludbey, still strapped in his stretcher and uninjured even if more feverish than ever. His mother and the ambulance man stirred from among the wreckage with the glazed calm of people tasting immortality. Then the men from the house were on the scene and the boy was carried back to his sick bed.

The crash was reported to Cairns by telephone and the only other available plane, a Tiger Moth, was promised for early next morning. It could not reach the cattle station before darkness. " Even a Moth is going to make hard work of getting over those trees," said Ludbey. " We chopped the top of some of them with the old Dragon, but the rest could do with some lopping." He gazed with almost comic disbelief when the boy's brother produced three axes. " We found these just as you got into the plane back there. It was too late to stop you going." Ludbey groaned with each blow of the axes as he and the two cattlemen worked for several hours to reduce the height of the trees. The boy spent a restless night but appeared no worse next morning when the Tiger Moth duly arrived and he was installed in the front cockpit on Ludbey's knee. Halfway across the field the Tiger Moth pilot abandoned his first take-off attempt and went back to the edge of the wash-out for another try. This time Ludbey felt the plane lift off, then the nose began to dip, the propeller dug into the ground, and the Moth fluttered over on to its back. Ludbey was hanging upside down in the cockpit, his head about three feet from the ground and little Kevin Callaghan clinging tightly in his arms. He lowered the boy to the ground and watched this desperately sick child run across the field to his mother like a sprinter at the school sports. Ludbey released himself from the cockpit and helped to free the pilot. Once again no one was injured.

"Well, one thing's for sure," said Ludbey. "Nobody's going to put another aeroplane in here. This is the strip of no return. But if that kid has got peritonitis and we don't get him to hospital soon he's not going to live."

"There's only one way out of here," said the father. "This is black soil country and it's just like porridge from the Wet. We'll have to take the horses and head for Laura. That's sixty-five miles away but it's the nearest town and they might put a plane in there."

Ludbey grew up on his father's farm in the Tasmanian bush and was no newcomer to a saddle. But he had never known a ride like that facing the cavalcade which set off from the cattle station. The father led the way, his boy sharing the saddle, hunched there pale and silent in his jogging misery. The boy's brother followed, then came Ludbey and finally Howard, the ambulance man. They moved across the stubborn landscape like flies testing their strength against a strip of last year's fly-paper. Thick black mud tugged at the horses' legs and all the hot, sweet stickiness of the Wet enveloped the riders. They covered less than twenty miles before nightfall and made camp in a tent left at the side of the trail by a passing stockman. "The kid is standing up to it bloody well," Howard told Ludbey. "I don't know how much more he can take, though."

The ride continued next morning. Two rivers, the George and Palmer, bloated by the rains, made progress difficult. The father rode straight into whatever blocked his path and sat erect with the boy in his arms while the horse struggled to the other side. Ludbey allowed his horse to swim without his weight on its back, preferring to hang on to its tail and take a tow. Towards the end of the second day the party met up with a truck driven from Laura by Police Constable V.

Booth and an aborigine tracker. The child's brother agreed to follow with the horses while the others pressed on by the truck. Progress proved almost as slow and much more difficult. The truck had to wallow through twenty miles of almost continuous bogland. Ludbey and the ambulance man were felling trees every mile of the way to make pathways of logs for blindly spinning wheels. The truck would find some kind of grip and slither onwards, sinking the logs deep into the bog under its weight. Ludbey and the ambulance man would swing their axes yet again to get more logs for the next quagmire.

At noon the following day, after an overnight stop in a telegraph station at Fairview, the horses caught up with the truck and the party from the cattle station were happy to go back into the saddle. They reached Laura during the afternoon and were picked up by a plane diverted there from a routine flight into Cairns. Crowds were waiting at Cairns airport to witness the sick child's dramatic arrival and an ambulance rushed him to hospital. Ludbey reported to Mr. L. Clarke, the Ambulance Superintendent, with the shame-faced humility of a pilot who had wrecked his own aeroplane and taken another with him.

' Don't worry, Don," said Clarke. " You don't know it but you've become heroes while you've been struggling through the bush. The papers and radio are full of nothing else. People have been sending in thousands of poundsworth of donations for a new ambulance plane. We look like getting enough money to buy three new planes, not one. And nobody blames you for not getting out of that field. It would have been a tight squeeze in a helicopter from what I've heard about it."

This was some balm for Ludbey's grudge about those misplaced axes which had nagged like a saddle sore all the way from Palmerville. It even balanced the anti-climax of discovering from the hospital that the boy was suffering from nothing more serious than an attack of colic. " It sounded like peritonitis from how the parents described it," a doctor explained. "The symptoms are similar and they weren't to know one from the other, anyhow. You had to fly in there because the boy could have been desperately ill. That's the trouble of diagnosis by telephone or radio. The patient always looks bad to the people at the other end and we can't afford to take any chances."

Ludbey was not complaining. It was the uncertainty of flying ambulance work which appealed to him after the domestic routine of the inter-city services along Australia's eastern coast. While operating in the Queensland outback he met and talked flying with Nevil Shute, an aircraft engineer before becoming a world famous novelist. Shute had an aeroplane of his own and saved Ludbey several ambulance flights by picking up sick and injured people on his travels around the area. They talked on the verandah at the home of Jimmy Edwards, a friend of Ludbey's and the man on whom Shute based his character, Joe Harman, in *A Town Like Alice*.

Cairns was a town like bedlam each Saturday night, full of cattlemen celebrating pay-day and looking for spectacular fist fights as their favourite form of amusement. Pilots were rated as foreigners and offered each brawl the glitter of an international championship. Whenever Ludbey flew into Cairns at a weekend he was deliberately provoked into a pre-arranged contest. The quiet young man from a Tasmanian farm discovered and perfected a vicious right hook as a social asset. Unfortunately the same right hook was at his command when he had a row with an official at the airport. The man's jaw was broken with a single punch. Ludbey, demoted to first officer and transferred to domestic duties at Brisbane, felt the urge for happier landings. When Warren Wilson, another pilot, announced he was taking up the Union of Burma Airways' offer of jobs for all at £8 a week, Ludbey followed close behind. Burma's atmosphere of intrigue, corruption and violence promised even more colourful excitement than Saturday night in Cairns.

Ludbey never tried to conceal his sympathy for the Karen rebels. He remembered them as the most pro-British of the Burmese peoples from his war service in the area. They were a proud race, fighting for the independence which they claimed had been promised them by the British. Ludbey's assessment of a complex political situation was summarised in many a Rangoon bar: " The Karens have had a bloody raw deal." He agreed to meet two representatives of the rebels and listened with interest to their proposition. They wanted him to fly his U.B.A. plane off its scheduled route, land on a disused Japanese airstrip, take on two bombs, and then drop them over Rangoon. They guaranteed he would be safely smuggled into Thailand after the raid and that money would be placed to his account in any bank he cared to nominate outside Burma. " I admire your nerve," said Ludbey, " but I'm never interested in anything less than worthwhile. A couple of bombs on Rangoon isn't going to do anybody any good. You can count me out of this one."

There were many other propositions for the U.B.A. pilots when they were building up the company's international services. Ludbey arrived in Singapore with a letter of introduction to an Armenian solicitor. The first meeting was merely a courtesy visit, and so was the next. On the third occasion the solicitor received Ludbey with a dozen sinister Chinese in attendance. " We want you to join us in our import-export business," said the Armenian. " You will import opium into Singapore from Rangoon and export cocaine from here to Rangoon. Our organisation at each end will arrange that the consignments are securely hidden on board your aircraft for take-off. The drugs are to be dropped in the sea just short of your destination and they will be collected by luggers. Needless to say, you will be well rewarded." Ludbey was not easily frightened but this plot had the taste of a knife in his back. He indicated a vague willingness as long as he was in the room. Once out of the door, he fled to his hotel and took care never to meet the solicitor again.

Opium-smoking was widespread in the northern areas of Burma. Warren Wilson saw a shop in Lashio displaying the sign " Licensed Victualler and Opium Dealer ". The main street of Kengtung had an obvious opium den, a dark shack littered with coolies smoking long pipes and dreaming dark dreams. Wilson went inside briefly and met a smell as sweet as incense, as exotic as a Turkish cigarette, as insistent as burning fat. A young Burmese aristocrat who showed Wilson the opium den explained: " Like labourers the world over, these men need some kind of consolation and escape. They find it in a pipe. Your people find it in a bottle of beer."

The aristocrat was educated in Australia and once invited Ludbey to dinner in his large Western-style house in Kengtung. " I hated Australian food when I was at school," said the Burmese. " It is the food of savages. Tonight you will eat our special delicacies." Ludbey thought most of the dishes distinctly repulsive, especially fried hornets and fried sparrows—complete with heads and eyes. He struggled to keep up with his host and observed local etiquette. The hornets were chewed and swallowed whole, giving off a strong gingery taste. The sparrows were picked up and gnawed, ignoring the head.

Ludbey found the Burmese the happiest of people. As aircrew, they learned fast and worked reliably to rule. The best of the first officers made excellent pilots but were inclined to be excitable when faced with any kind of emergency not included in the flight training programme. This was a disadvantage on services where the unexpected had to be expected, where passengers were issued with boiled sweets on take-off in return for the surrender of their personal firearms until touch-down.

Captain Alec Hare, an English pilot with U.B.A., was fifteen minutes out of Rangoon on June 26, 1954, when one of his fourteen passengers entered the cockpit of his Dakota and produced a revolver. Hare's Burmese co-pilot went to take the gun, thinking the man had forgotten to hand it in on take-off. The passenger jumped back to the cockpit door, took a Mills bomb from his pocket, pulled the pin out with his teeth, and then handed the first officer a note written in Burmese: "Dear Pilot, We are sworn enemies of the Union of Burma government and wish you to land at the place indicated on a map drawn on the other side of this paper. We mean no harm to you and your passengers. After landing you will be transported to the nearest town by elephant." Two other men appeared from the passenger compartment, also armed.

Hare had no idea which kind of rebels had joined his flight but he knew exactly what they wanted. The Dakota's freight consisted of fourteen cases of Government currency, about £200,000 in all. He heard the first officer translate the note a second time and was tempted to hurl the plane into a steep dive. The rebels would be thrown off balance and there was a chance he could reach a gun before they recovered. The man with the grenade sensed Hare's attitude and declared: "Land where we say or I blow us all up. I am not afraid to die." Hare had a look at the sketch map on the back of the note and set course for a point on the coast to the west of Rangoon. The rebels wanted him to put down on a beach there but he flew over the landing site twice and then told them, through the first officer, that the surface was dangerously rough. He offered to find a better stretch of beach and politely suggested that the pin should go back in the grenade. It was going to be a bumpy landing, anyhow. The rebels agreed to his suggestions and Hare put the Dakota down on a beach about three miles from the original spot. "This place is good enough for me to take off again when you've finished with us," he said. "That will save you making fresh arrangements for the elephants."

Once again the rebels were agreeable. But first, Hare and the passengers had to help unload the cases of money. The rebels noticed 20 lb. of paludrine, used in the treatment of malaria, and took that as well. Then they allowed the Dakota to go on its way. Hare's last glimpse was of them waiting amidst the money and drugs for a party of their comrades to arrive from the other beach. He heard afterwards that a party of local villagers arrived first, murdered the three men, and stole the money. A week later that village was burnt down in a reprisal raid by a large force of rebels and the money recovered.

Ludbey was himself involved in a rather different form of hold-up. Six members of one of the several rival bands of Communist rebels, who fought amongst themselves as well as plotting to overthrow the Government, joined a ship sailing from Rangoon to Moulmein, disguised as Buddhist monks. During the journey they produced sub-machine guns from beneath their saffron robes and captured the ship. The hundred passengers were robbed of their personal belongings and put ashore on a small island south of the mainland. The ship then went into hiding among the mass of rivers in the Rangoon Delta. A U.B.A. aeroplane was chartered by the ship's owner to go in search of the missing vessel and Ludbey was allocated to the flight because he knew the area well from the air. For three hours he flew over the coastal fringes of the Delta and then caught sight of the ship, anchored beyond the bend of a small river.

" Now we go back and tell the military," said the ship's owner, a nervous middle-aged businessman. " Sure, we'll do that," said Ludbey, " but those jokers down there will know we've seen 'em and who knows the ship will be here by the time the military arrive? I think a spot of dive-bombing is called for." The owner was horrified. " But we have no bombs, no weapons of any kind," he said. " They will open fire if we get too close."

" Don't worry," said Ludbey. " You've chartered the aeroplane and it's my job to look after you. But the Burmese air force have been bombing and machine-gunning these Communists and I reckon it's worth trying to give them a fright. They won't know a dive bomber from a Dakota." The ship owner moved to the rear of the plane and closed his eyes when Ludbey swooped down towards the ship. Even as he began the dive, he saw brown specks running across the deck, jumping over the side and swimming for the bank. By the time he flashed overhead at mast height the ship had been completely abandoned. Great moans of fear were coming from the back of the plane. " You can come out now," said Ludbey. " Your ship is nice and empty and all ready to be collected. I'll give it another couple of goings-over to show we mean business just in case anybody is tempted to come back. Then we'll go and tell the military where it is." The ship was deserted when Burmese para-troopers were dropped in the area next morning. It was back on the Moulmein service within the week.

Ludbey and his friend, Warren Wilson, had each put in more than 1,500 flying hours in less than a year when they resigned from U.B.A. in 1954. They left as a protest against a progressive system of income tax which meant that most of their pay for the last three months of the year went to the Government. In any case, the two Australians wanted to fly in Europe. For Wilson there was six months' unemployment in England before free-lancing with Dan-Air. In 1956, he joined the staff of Dan-Air and became chief pilot during eight years with the company. Then, wearying of the desk work demanded of a chief pilot, he moved from one end of Gatwick Airport to the other and returned to active flying with Lloyd International, a charter company specialising in Far Eastern operations for shipping companies. Wilson found himself ferrying spare parts and replacement crews to ships stranded in far distant ports. As a change, he flew parties of Chinese waiters from Soho on holiday visits to their families in Hong Kong. He was happy to leave the desk work to the Director of Operations—his old comrade, Don Ludbey, who came to Lloyd International after flying on general charter work for B.K.S.

Sitting in his map-lined office at Gatwick, Ludbey now professes to enjoy the mental exercise of arranging other people's travels. " The only trouble," he says, " is that the better I do my job the quieter it gets. I sometimes walk through the airport and get irritated by the smug way that things are always just so, with the aircraft all neatly lined up as if we are expecting a parade or something. Then I think to myself: What this place needs to liven itself up is for just a couple of elephants to come wandering in off the Brighton Road . . ."

CHAPTER SEVEN

The Desert Fliers

THE early morning flight to Baghdad was cancelled. Captain Homer Cochrane, a large, softly rounded Canadian, arrived at Kirkuk airfield in north-east Iraq to find the seats being removed from his de Havilland Dove and a stretcher fitted into position. An official of the Iraq Petroleum Company, to which Cochrane was on permanent charter, explained: " I'm not going to make that conference in Baghdad after all. Dr. Faud has telephoned from Ain Zalah to say they've had a serious accident. He doesn't panic easily like some of the locals so it must be pretty bad."

Cochrane was airborne within five minutes and setting course towards the Turkish frontier. Ain Zalah, near the banks of the River Tigris, was in the area of Iraq's first oil concessions, negotiated before the First World War by a one-time bank messenger named Calouste Gulbenkian who became the legendary Mr. Five Per Cent, one of the richest men on earth. Cochrane headed for Ain Zalah with the early sun reaching for his starboard wing and reflected that by the next dawn the Gulbenkian family's five per cent. of Iraq's oil would have produced yet another £10,000. The following dawn would ring up further £10,000 and so it seemed destined to continue for many more dawns than the story tellers of Baghdad could imagine when they told of a thousand and one nights. Cochrane did not know what emergency awaited him but the doctor's message indicated that the price of this day's oil was being paid by some unknown workman's pain and suffering at Ain Zalah.

The Dove landed on an airfield which was 1,500 feet above sea level and yet still some 400 feet below the oil company station, sitting elegantly on top of a hill like a summer retreat. An ambulance was racing down the hill before Cochrane completed his approach. The ambulance men had the back doors open as the aircraft taxied alongside. Cochrane got out and an ambulance man said: " It's a bad one. Some stupid Englishman tried to cut his throat."

Dr. Faud, a studious Iraqi in his early thirties, supervised the transfer of his patient from the ambulance to the aeroplane. Cochrane looked down at the man on the stretcher and shuddered to see, amid the gaudy profusion of blood, an open wound from side to side of the throat, with one fat vein clearly exposed. " He didn't know how to commit suicide properly," said Faud with that doctor's briskness which often sounds like heartiness. " You can see that he missed the jugular completely. This is how you should cut your throat." He gave a vivid demonstration. Cochrane hurried back to the cockpit and tried not to think of the man with the grinning throat, lashed to the stretcher only a few feet behind him and bleeding his life on to the cabin floor.

The man was a mechanical engineer with the oil company, Cochrane established later. He was awakened that morning as usual by an Arab boy who brought him tea in bed. The boy came back for the pots half-an-hour later and found him on the bathroom floor with his throat cut. There seemed no motive for suicide. The only explanation was the man's nerves had broken under the strain of the oppressive isolation known to all oil stations amidst the sand and rocks of the Middle East. " It's like living in a lighthouse where even the sea has run away and left you," a veteran oilman once admitted to Cochrane.

A hundred and twenty miles of sand and rocks now separated Dr. Faud's patient and the hospital at Kirkuk. Cochrane began his take-off and immediately saw he would have to vary the usual line of flight. The airfield at Ain Zalah was in a hollow and planes had to lift over a small ridge beyond, having a line of oil rigs on top. This day, the rig in the very centre of the ridge was out of control and gushing oil 2,000 feet in the air. A single spark from a passing aircraft engine could explode it into a gigantic sheet of flame. Otherwise, the thick column of greasy smog would remain in the sky for two or three weeks after the gushing stopped, visible for forty miles.

Cochrane took off in a steeper climb than normal to give him the extra altitude he needed to bank to the left of the gushing oil and clear the ridge at the same time. There was a yell from the doctor at the back of the plane. " Get lower, get lower. The higher you go, the less atmospheric pressure, the more this man bleeds." Cochrane swung clear of the oil, dipped down beyond the ridge and levelled off at about 150 feet above ground level. " Lower still," cried the doctor. " Every foot counts. This country's so hilly you're at a decent altitude with your wheels on the ground."

The Dove dropped to no more than fifty feet and stayed there for as much of the flight as possible, cutting between hills and following dried-up river beds to minimise altitude. Faud was improvising a blood transfusion. There was no sound from the patient. Cochrane wondered if a man could speak or even moan with his throat cut.

Out of the brown, drab landscape came the greyish sprawl of the walls of Nineveh with the great Assyrian bulls standing guard on the northern gates. This claimed to be the longest inhabited town known to man and the thought of people living in this place since the civilised world began seemed to the mild-mannered Canadian to put such things as suicide attempts into proper perspective. He enjoyed reading his history from the cockpit of an aeroplane. Soon he would catch a glimpse of Salavadin, one of the many birthplaces of Saladin, the man who led the armies of the East against the Crusaders. Not far away to the south was Nimrud, where Agatha Christie sometimes joined her husband at his archaelogical diggings. To the east was the Raunanduz gorge and the spectacular road built by the British during the 1914-18 war.

The Dove came to land at Kirkuk shortly after 8.30. Doctors and nurses were waiting with an ambulance to rush the patient to the oil company's own first-class hospital. There he was operated on by a surgeon who normally practised on the local population with the zeal of a medical missionary. He would remove up to thirty appendixes from Iraqi Arabs in the course of a single session with an efficiency which had his fellow doctors laying bets amongst themselves as to which patient would have the smallest operation scar. In the case of the engineer, his life was saved as a further demonstration of the surgeon's skill but the scar was huge. The engineer was returned discreetly to England, no longer employed by the company. A year later he was seen in London by an Iraq Petroleum Company executive, home on leave. The attempted suicide of Ain Zalah looked fully recovered but a jagged mark across his throat was visible from the other side of the street.

As one of a dozen pilots operating along the 500 miles of pipelines between the oilfields and the Mediterranean tanker terminals, Cochrane was always in the position of relieving the desert lighthouses. The hardship of loneliness and boredom was something he only visited for a few hours of the time, and left behind with every take-off. Even his routine flights suggested a social diary compiled for a restless playboy—breakfast in Tripoli, lunch in Baghdad, afternoon tennis on the shores of the Persian Gulf, and back to Kirkuk for an evening game of bridge.

Cochrane was once flying from Tripoli to Kirkuk when an emergency call on his radio gave instructions to land beside the pipeline at T 1, the first pumping station into Iraq from the Lebanon. The pipeline superintendent, George Robinson, was waiting at T 1. He wanted the Dove's eight passengers to leave the plane. "There's a panic on," he said. "A bad fire has broken out on the line between Kirkuk and

K 2 station. I'm going to need this aircraft. We can either come back for you or try and get another plane out."

There was an embarrassed silence. None of the passengers offered to move. " Why not come and sit up front with me?" said Cochrane. " You'll get there hardly any sooner by turning these people off. And we've all got a rather urgent appointment in Kirkuk." The superintendent relented and the Dove resumed its flight along the pipeline. They saw the fire, a familiar black smudge in the sky, from forty miles away. Cochrane dropped to a hundred feet when he reached the outbreak and circled for the superintendent to study the flames sprouting from a shattered stretch of line. The men of a maintenance gang were scattered at a cautious distance from the blaze. A spark from a cutting torch had ignited oil seeping from a section of pipeline due for repairs.

"You can go back and drop me at K 2 station," said the superintendent. " It's only twenty miles down the line and I'll take a car from there." Having delivered Robinson to K 2, Cochrane flew on to Kirkuk and changed from his uniform into white shirt and shorts to join his passengers for their urgent appointment—a tennis match between the Tripoli and Kirkuk sections of the oil company. The Canadian was relaxing over an iced drink after winning his game when the tennis club telephone rang and he was ordered back to K 2. Cochrane put on his khaki and epaulettes once more, drove to the airfield, and took off for the pumping station beyond the Tigris. Passing well clear of the outbreak, now busily littered with fire-fighting equipment, Cochrane saw a long string of camels heading for the scene. Bedouins were always attracted by the prospect of oil leaking on to the desert. When the oil evaporated it left behind a shallow pool of water and the camels would drink this with great relish. Cochrane counted nearly a hundred Arabs on the move with their animals and tents. He called up K 2 to report the movement, a routine requirement on all flights along the pipeline. Pumping stations liked to know the whereabouts of these nomads. Sometimes a report of Arabs converging on the pipeline was the first indication of an oil leak. Always there was the risk that Arabs with thirsty camels might be tempted to create a leak for the magical water which appeared afterwards. In this case, the Arabs were merely hoping that all the oil would not go up in flames before the line was restored.

Cochrane was at K 2 within twenty-five minutes of leaving the tennis club. There was an ambulance parked at the side of the airfield. Inside the ambulance was an Iraqi labourer, almost every inch of his swarthy skin burnt away so that his body was a bright plastic red. An Iraqi doctor, applying lotion to the burns, looked up at Cochrane and shook his head. The labourer had taken the full blast of a further explosion at the scene of the outbreak. His clothes went up in flames and the man, screaming with panic, ran away across the desert, burning like a torch. He was in a desperate condition when other workmen caught him and smothered the flames with sand. Brought into the pumping station by truck, the labourer was still conscious. He was heavily doped by the doctor before being put into the Dove and flown to Kirkuk for hospital treatment. The oil company's policy ensured he was given the same attention as the highest paid European executive but the Iraqi was too badly burned to survive. " He died within an hour of your bringing him in," a hospital doctor told Cochrane at a party held that night to mark the Tripoli-Kirkuk tennis match. " He never had a chance from the beginning and we knew you were called out there on a hopeless case. But we've got the aeroplanes and it's always worth a try."

Discussing the labourer's death in an air-conditioned cocktail bar was typical of the extreme contrasts which Cochrane found in thirteen years of flying along the desert pipelines. The contract with I.P.C. was held by Airwork, Britain's longest surviving aviation company. Founded in 1928, Airwork bought and built one of London's original airports at Heston, and operated it for twenty years. This experience enabled Airwork to take part in the establishment of two major national airlines before the war—Egypt's Misrair and

5

Indian National Airways—and to help found Sudan Airways in 1947.

Cochrane was offered a post in the Sudan when he joined Airwork in December 1946. He preferred an assignment to the Iraq pipelines, a charter dating back to before the war. His wife, of French and English descent, was born in neighbouring Turkey. He served with the R.A.F. in that part of the Middle East, and as a squadron leader out of a job he liked oil company rates of pay—£800-a-year plus five shillings an hour flying time. Cochrane had been sorry to leave the R.A.F., would have liked to make it his career. If he had to become a sky tramp, he demanded a decent roof over his head, and a comfortable bed at the end of each day's tramping. As a family man, he enjoyed variety in his work but preferred stability. Airwork could offer both qualities. Its policy of building up long-term contracts for many different kinds of operations throughout the world avoided the week-to-week uncertainties of most charter companies. Airwork was also to lead the way for private operators taking over air-trooping and establishing their own international scheduled services during the early 1950's—notably the " coach-class " routes to East, West and Central Africa. This all helped to make independent flying at least a predictable gamble instead of a wild, blind lottery.

The Arab-Israel conflict was at its fiercest when Cochrane went to Iraq. The pre-war pipeline to Haifa was closed as a political move and work began on a new and larger pipeline to Tripoli in the Lebanon, followed by an even bigger line to Banias in Syria. Cochrane flew above native labour gangs, digging ditches across this fierce, empty land and pursued by the " Mighty Antar ", an enormous pipe-carrying transporter named after a legendary Arab warrior of immense strength. The oil company's mechanical warrior brandished nine 93-foot lengths of 30-inch steel pipe on its advance across the desert. The labourers were not so impressed when their more mechanically minded workmates demonstrated that Mighty Antar could be rendered helpless by a few handsful of sand in the gearbox. Sabotage of all forms of transport reached a peak each time the new lines came to cross a frontier. The Lebanese government insisted on Lebanese labourers being employed for the work carried out in the Lebanon, the Syrian Government demanded the same principle for work in Syria, and only Iraqi labourers were tolerated in Iraq. The result was that each nationality was dedicated to prolonging the construction work within his own country. Strikes, go-slows and sabotage became a form of Customs formality to be endured at each frontier.

Cochrane and the other Airwork pilots never feared any interference with their fleet of Doves and Rapides. The workmen very obviously appreciated the value of the aeroplanes in taking casualties to hospital from remote areas where sickness and injury rates tended to be highest. Even more important, the aircraft also delivered their pay packets, landing by the side of a construction camp with as much as £60,000 on board. A favourite theoretical exercise for the pilots was a cocktail bar competition to produce the perfect plan for disposing of the paymaster, who was the only passenger on such flights, and for getting the money as far away from Iraq as possible.

Highest paid of the construction workers were the European specialists, mainly riveters and welders from the Clyde shipyards. They were allowed to use the social facilities of the nearest pumping station, in effect a miniature town with its own swimming pool, cinema, library, laundry, shop, billiard room, and bar. Cochrane called in at the stations regularly on his flights along the pipeline and was always impressed by the colonial etiquette which created a quiet purpose from utter boredom. As a Canadian he was also amused by the Wild West atmosphere which took over when the riveters and welders arrived to celebrate pay-day. Fist fights were soon replacing small talk, bottles were emptied and then hurled across the room, followed by convenient pieces of furniture. The thick breath of Glasgow on a Saturday night hung on

the desert air long after the construction men went back to
their camp.

Violence on a larger scale was never far away in the Middle
East. The Suez invasion in the autumn of 1956 brought open
hostility towards the European-operated Iraq Petroleum
Company. Two pipelines were blown up near the Lebanon-
Syria border. Syrian Army units seized three pumping stations
in midnight raids, handcuffed the British personnel and
marched them off into the desert while engineers wrecked the
pumping machinery. Cochrane and the other pilots were
based at Tripoli at the time. The first signs of trouble at the
airport were strikes and demonstrations by Lebanese ground
staff. Then bombs were exploded on the runway one night
and the hangar wrecked. Cochrane took a car to drive out to
the airfield and see what was happening to the aircraft. The
car stopped suddenly before reaching the outskirts of Tripoli.
"What's the matter?" he asked the driver. The man pointed
down the road. A tank of the Government forces and a tank
captured by pro-Nasser rebels were blasting at each other
from point-blank range. Cochrane agreed with the driver it
would be a good idea to abandon the car. He took cover
round a street corner and, in the best tradition of Middle
Eastern revolutions, slipped into a barber's shop for a haircut
until the battle had passed by.

From Baghdad came the order for the I.P.C. aircraft to
move base to Kirkuk. None of the aircraft had been damaged
by the bombs at the airfield and the runway was still operational. Cochrane and the other pilots prepared the Doves for
an airlift of their families while vapour streams in the sky
caused ominous rumours. Some suggested they were Russian
bombers about to attack the American Sixth Fleet. Others
claimed they were British reconnaissance planes from Cyprus
off to see if there were any troop movements from the Russian
border towards the Kurdish mountains. All the rumours
agreed the Russians were certainly coming one way or another. Two of the aircraft engineers listened to this talk and
refused to be transferred to Kirkuk, less than 250 miles from

the Russian border. The engineers were left behind, the Russians never came, and the Airwork community settled with now-accustomed luxury into their new home.

Cochrane never flew into K 3, the largest of the pumping stations, without marvelling at the way a garden suburb had been created in the middle of the desert. There were bungalows set amongst lawns grown from special grass flown in from East Africa, and exotic birds sang in the trees of the superintendent's garden. The superintendent was Jimmy Smith, an Irishman with an Iraqi wife. Cochrane was to see Smith's understanding of the natives and command of their language put to the test during a visit to K 3 in June 1958. It was not long after the attempted suicide at Ain Zalah and the assistant-superintendent was discussing the incident as he drove Cochrane back to the airstrip on the far side of the station's golf course. " I can understand the poor devil doing it," said the oil man. He nodded towards the European quarters, drowsily still and silent in the first hour of the afternoon. " You can go mad waiting for something to happen out here."

The last statement was qualified within a few hundred yards when the assistant-superintendent stopped the car and turned about to drive back to the station at high speed. Coming up the road from the direction of the airstrip was a mob of 200 Iraqi workers, carrying banners and brandishing sticks. Cochrane could not read the slogans but the mob's mood made the message international. The Canadian translated it as " Less Work. More Pay. Down with the Bosses."

Jimmy Smith was sitting in his garden among his trees and birds when the assistant-superintendent arrived with the news of the trouble fast approaching. It was a rest day and Smith was well aware that most of the Europeans would be sitting at home with their families, not suspecting anything was wrong, totally unprepared for the standard emergency drill of evacuating to the administration centre. This was deliberately built like a desert fort so that the grocery store and laundry stood side by side with quarters for a garrison of twenty Iraqi soldiers and four or five I.P.C. security officers. Smith doubted if there was time to move the families before the mob penetrated the station. If he tried to move them and was too late some of the women and children might be caught in the open. It could tempt the mob to attack and that would bring the Iraqi soldiers charging out of their quarters. The outcome of such an explosive situation was only too easy to imagine.

From a window of the station's clubhouse, Cochrane watched the little Irishman deal with the problem in his own way. He walked out of his house and stood alone in the middle of the road which would lead the workers into the residential area. He took up his position when they had marched to within a hundred yards of that point. The mob faltered at the sight of the superintendent, then came on again at the cry of the obvious agitators carrying the banners. Smith called out when they were within twenty yards of him and the unruly column checked smartly as if the front rank had been struck by a volley. He called out again when the men with the banners tried to resume the advance. Cochrane watched a group of workmen, armed with shovels, start to edge round to Smith's left. This looked very serious. If they were prepared to attack their superintendent, a man they knew and normally respected, they were in a mood to attack everybody.

Smith turned his head slightly, and held the flanking group with his stern expression. Then he began to talk to them all in their own language, firmly at first and then gradually his tone softened so that the atmosphere seemed to soften, too. The angry interruptions when he started became reasonable statements which in turn became almost apologies for disturbing his day of rest. Smith talked and talked and talked. He told the men he understood they had a grievance about working conditions. He promised to discuss possible improvements if they would form a proper deputation and see him at a proper time. He inferred that professional agitators from Baghdad had infiltrated into the camp and were trying to cause trouble for political reasons. He suggested they could trust him to look after their real interests. Smith talked for half-an-hour. During that time most of the European families managed to slip discreetly into the administration centre or the clubhouse. The Iraqi soldiers were alerted by their officer and prepared for action. Smith's speech would have been highly successful even if at the end he was swept aside by the mob. Instead, the workmen made a sheepish retreat.

Cochrane waited for another two hours and was then driven out to his aircraft without meeting any interference. He did not know it then but the incident at K 3 was a symptom of unrest and intrigue soon to burst into the bloodiest revolution of all the thirteen years he spent in a part of the world prone to political earthquakes. Within six weeks he was back at K 3, taking part in an emergency airlift to remove the women and children from the threat of mob violence too great for even Jimmy Smith to turn away. The evacuees were delivered to the relative safety of the I.P.C. compound at Kirkuk while 120 people died in the Iraqi quarter of the town in a pitched battle between rebels and troops. The King had been murdered and the whole country was reacting hysterically.

On the evening of July 13, 1958, 23-year-old King Feisal was talking of the charter flight he planned to make to Istanbul and then on to England where he went to school at Harrow and where he would meet his schoolgirl fiancee. On the morning of July 14 he was seized by revolutionary forces and machine-gunned with other members of the Royal Family under a pepper tree in the Palace gardens. His prime minister, Nuri Es-Said, was impaled on a spear and displayed to the mob.

One of the Airwork pilots brought the news to Kirkuk, taking off from Baghdad while Royalist supporters and revolutionary troops fought a pitched battle on the edge of the airport. Cochrane flew into Kirkuk from Ain Zalah and joined the airlift of families from the pumping stations. That night he and his neighbours in the oil community stood guard with shotguns and pistols on the flat roofs of their homes. They watched Iraqi soldiers move into position around them, completely isolating the compound. Then followed a fortnight of uneasy stalemate. Nuri Es-Said, the murdered prime minister, had personally conducted many of the negotiations with the I.P.C. over oil royalties and there were fears that the rebels would regard this as an excuse to nationalise the industry and drive out the Europeans. But General Kassem, who emerged as leader of the new Republican Government, contemplated the £80,000,000 a year being paid by the oil company, his country's major source of income, and decided to leave things as they were. While the British and American embassies in Baghdad were in a state of siege, while Western businessmen continued under house arrest, work in the oilfields was allowed to resume as usual. Cochrane made his routine flights along the pipeline, and bridge parties returned to the Kirkuk compound. Even when an anti-Government rising took place in the area of the northern oilfields and a British engineer operated the rebels' wireless transmitter, Kassem took care to quell the rising without harming I.P.C. personnel or installations. He accepted the explanation that the engineer handled the transmitter at bayonet point, and normal working continued throughout the oilfields.

Another kind of revolution was taking place in Britain, several thousand miles away from Cochrane's desert patrols but of close importance to his career as a charter pilot. At the time that young King Feisal was dragged from his throne to be murdered by his own troops, Freddy Laker chose to surrender the business empire he had been building up for eleven years and which now included the successful Channel Air Bridge car ferry as well as Aviation Traders and Air Charter. He sold out to Airwork, Cochrane's employers. It was the hardest decision of Laker's life, a dealer offering himself for sale. But he had come to believe that independent airlines must merge into larger, more efficient units if they were to survive into the jet age. The price of a single turbo-prop airliner was more than he had paid for all the aircraft in his own fleet put together. Pure jets were going to cost a million pounds each, enough to have bought the whole of Bomber Command when he toured the war surplus auctions. His own business could never raise that sort of capital.

Airwork already had the financial backing of two major shipping companies, Furness Withy and the Blue Star Line. Similarly, P. & O. had a controlling interest in Silver City Airways, and the Clan Line was in partnership with Hunting-Clan Transport. When Hunting-Clan and Silver City eventually followed Laker into the Airwork group, forming British United Airways, the total result was Britain's largest independent airline, operating with the financial support and world-wide influence of the country's leading shipping interests. In many ways, the arrangement was as unlikely as British Railways buying shares in the British Motor Corporation, and the new board of directors were soon to find that experience of sea transport, based on the ancient principle of freedom of the seas, had disappointingly little in common with the tightly fettered world of civil aviation. But the presence of the shipping companies brought new strength and respectability to the business, a source of comfort to a family man like Cochrane who survived four Middle Eastern rebellions in thirteen years with an increasing hunger for social security.

By mid-1959, Iraq was at peace with itself again and wandering Bedouins with thirsty camels were once more the only threat to the pipelines. Cochrane had now been a desert pilot for most of twenty years, beginning with Gladiator biplanes of the R.A.F. in Egypt in 1939 and later progressing to Spitfires. He did not care for big aeroplanes. A Dakota was the largest plane he ever flew. The eight-passenger, twin-engined Doves he piloted to and from the oilfields were small enough to give him a sense of intimacy with the desert. He could stand on one wing and turn aside for anything that caught his eye, climb over mountains, explore the deepest valleys, embrace an Arabian sunset. Cochrane felt that he rode through this country in his Dove. Anything bigger would have merely passed overhead.

Sandstorms were the constant uncertainty of desert weather, developing suddenly, travelling fast, and changing direction with the wind. One of Cochrane's "milk run" flights along the pipeline was interrupted to organise a search for another of the company's aircraft which had disappeared in a sandstorm. The other plane was a Rapide, having very elementary instruments and no provision for blind flying. The pilot radioed he was in trouble and that was the last heard of him. His message placed him near the road between two pumping stations, a desert track repeatedly smothered with oil to make a smooth surface. The road made a bold line across the desert and the Rapide would have been following it home when he ran into the sandstorm. By the same principle, the first airliners to cross the Iraqi desert in the 1920's used to navigate by following a furrow made and maintained by R.A.F. ground patrols towing a plough along the whole length of the route to Baghdad.

Cochrane set off for the Rapide's last reported position, somewhere in the middle of the black mass of the sandstorm, 12,000 feet high and several miles wide. His Dove was equipped to fly through the sandstorm but visibility would be nil and there was always the hazard of the other plane, possibly flying round in circles inside and trying to get out. He began to fly alongside the sandstorm to gauge its speed and direction. The starboard wing of the Dove was in clear air and the other was touching the smooth wall of sand heading east at between forty and fifty m.p.h. Cochrane was sure the Rapide could not have stayed aloft in these conditions. The place to look was on the ground.

Flying to the nearest pumping station, K 3, Cochrane borrowed a car and set off along the glistening desert road towards the sandstorm. The centre of the storm was now swinging to the south and only the fringes of it swept the road as he approached. Visibility had improved to the brown gloom of a London smog. He saw the Rapide lying on its back at the side of the road. The pilot had tried to land on the oil-polished surface and the plane overturned. He and his one passenger were unhurt, squatting at the side of the Rapide to shelter from the stinging spray of sand. The two men got into the car and Cochrane hurried back to K 3. He could see the centre of the storm was changing direction again, heading straight for the pumping station. The car narrowly won the race. Two minutes later the air was black outside hastily shuttered windows. A column of sand 12,000 feet high trampled over K 3. The superintendent's East African lawn was going to need digging out next morning.

In 1960, Homer Cochrane was transferred to Morton Air Services within the British United Airways group, and placed on charter to the Burmah Oil Company. Now he flew above the mighty Irrawaddy and all the jungles and temples of the road to Mandalay. He flew in a cloud of claustrophobia, oppressed by the thick, humid atmosphere and the dense vegetation which crowded in from all sides. He missed the emptiness of the desert, the feeling that each flight drew a line on a clean page instead of adding one more mark to a mass of scribble. He missed the sand and the rocks and the Mediterranean beaches and the Baghdad bazaars and the tennis tours and the bridge parties.

The money wasn't so good, either.

CHAPTER EIGHT

Battle for the Atlantic

SIR ANTHONY EDEN began his retreat from power in a
DC-7C airliner on personal charter from B.O.A.C. He left
London Airport at seven o'clock on the night of November
23, 1956, at the height of the Suez crisis. He flew to the West
Indies as Prime Minister when the British invasion forces
were observing an uneasy truce in Egypt and the British
Government was under fire all over the world. Eden was to
return from his health holiday three weeks later, still Prime
Minister, but less than a month from having to resign on the
grounds of a physical exhaustion which exactly symbolised
the state of his Suez adventure.

The first signs of that exhaustion were clearly apparent as
Captain Anthony Christopher Loraine watched Eden come
aboard his DC-7C, that November night. The Prime Minister
walked firmly across the fifty yards of tarmac from the Royal
Lounge to where the airliner was waiting in No. 1 Bay, but
looked tense and tired. He was seen off by a group of
Ministers, including the Earl of Home, Secretary for Com-
monwealth Relations, and Mr. John Profumo, Parliamentary
Secretary to the Ministry of Transport and Civil Aviation.
Travelling with Sir Anthony in the 69-seater aircraft were
Lady Eden, two M.I. 5 officers, and Dr. Kenneth Bergin,
B.O.A.C.'s medical superintendent of air services. Eden faced
a bill for £750 for his charter flight to Montego Bay, in
Jamaica. The charge would have been higher had not the

DC-7C been due to go as far as Bermuda in any case as part of " crew familiarisation " training.

Captain Loraine, at 46 one of B.O.A.C.'s senior pilots, was looking forward to this flight. The DC-7C's, known as the Seven Seas, were the Corporation's very latest airliner and were not due to go into service on the North Atlantic routes until the following January. The Prime Minister's charter had the added interest of being the first commercial flight by a land plane to make a non-stop crossing of the 3,440-mile leg from London to Bermuda.

Eden's journey was not without incident. Three hours out from Bermuda, Loraine was informed by his cabin staff that Dr. Bergin had been called into action. Loraine had visions of the international drama which would envelop him and his aircraft if the Prime Minister became desperately sick, perhaps even died, high above the Atlantic, a thousand miles from land. There was little he could do but warn Bermuda to provide an emergency reception for their landing. Dr. Bergin came forward to the cockpit. "Is the Prime Minister going to be all right?" asked Loraine. " Oh, he's fine," said Bergin. " It's one of the M.I. 5 men. He was taken violently ill without any warning. Some sort of fever. I've given him sedatives and he should be all right until we get to Bermuda."

The Seven Seas landed at Bermuda at 6.40 on the morning of November 24, took off again at eight o'clock, and reached Montego Bay at 12.45—7.45 local time. The DC-7C's flying time of 18 hours 25 minutes was a record for the 4,700 miles from London. The Prime Minister was met by Sir Hugh Foot, Governor of Jamaica, and then went to stay at a secluded bungalow called Goldeneye, the holiday home of Ian Fleming. Fleming was later to become world famous as the author of the James Bond thrillers but at this time he was described as an ex-naval commander. The suspense centred on Eden's political future and the twenty detectives posted among the palm trees and poinsettias stood guard over the sick premier with a stolid air which never suggested the image of 007 to emerge from a typewriter in the same bungalow.

Loraine, who began his flying career with a small charter company at Croydon before joining Imperial Airways in 1932, had come to regard himself as something of a specialist in charter flights to influence the course of modern history. On the morning of June 19, 1940, five days after the fall of Paris to the Germans, he flew a B.O.A.C. flying boat to a lake at Biscarrosse, forty miles south-west of Bordeaux, in a dramatic bid to avert the capitulation of France. On board were two French politicians, M. Plevin and M. Monnet, staunch supporters of General de Gaulle. Loraine landed at Biscarrosse knowing no more than the two Frenchmen wanted to meet the French Government, then based at Bordeaux. Only when they were going ashore from the lake did they instruct Loraine to prepare for a flight to Algiers instead of returning to England. He pointed out that his instructions from B.O.A.C. did not mention the possibility of going further than Biscarrosse. "We have chartered your plane," said Monnet, "and we give the instructions. It is our intention to return from Bordeaux with the entire French War Cabinet. You will fly them to Algiers and from there they will announce that France will continue the war from North Africa. Your flight will ensure that our two countries remain Allies in the fight against Germany."

"In that case," said Loraine, "I would like some charts of Algiers harbour. I've never landed there before. It won't be much use to anybody if we carry the French Cabinet off to Africa and I go and kill us all putting this flying boat down in a strange harbour. Give me some charts and I'll try not to do that." The Frenchmen promised to ask for the charts in Bordeaux. After they had gone, Loraine and his crew were left on the lake in an unarmed flying boat, knowing the German Army was advancing rapidly in that direction. They had seen Panzer columns heading for Biscarrosse when they flew in from England. A German reconnaissance plane flew over the lake that morning, circled at low altitude, and flew away again. Loraine waited all day and all night for the Frenchmen to return. They arrived shortly after dawn on

June 20 while German bombers were attacking Bordeaux. There was no sign of the French Cabinet and Plevin and Monnet were deeply depressed. "There will be no flight to Algiers after all, captain," said Monnet. "We failed in our mission so there is nothing to do but return to England." Loraine took off from the lake at 8.30, carrying as refugees Maurice Monteux, B.O.A.C.'s Paris manager, and his family. The Monteux family arrived at the lakeside to beg a lift on the flying boat only a few hours ahead of the leading German tanks. Loraine could see the tanks as he began his flight home and was grateful that the Luftwaffe's fighters had not yet mastered the art of keeping up with the Panzers.

Another B.O.A.C. flying boat went into Biscarrosse even later than Loraine. The pilot was Capt. D. C. T. Bennett, the Australian who was afterwards to establish the war-time Atlantic ferry and Bomber Command's "Pathfinder" force, and then become a controversial operator in post-war aviation. Loraine had flown as Bennett's navigator on the first experimental transatlantic crossings by Imperial Airways flying boats in August 1939. Less than a year later, Bennett was landing on a French lake in the middle of an area swarming with German tanks and motor cycle patrols. He was making contact with the remnants of the Polish Army, still attempting a fighting retreat across France. When Bennett flew out of Biscarrosse, he had taken on board General Sikorski, the Polish war leader, Sikorski's daughter, and members of the Polish general staff. The flying boat took off over the heads of a German column and the Poles stood defiantly at the windows with drawn revolvers, prepared to exchange fire with enemy machine guns. Fortunately, the appearance of a civilian flying boat took the Germans by surprise and Bennett made his escape under cover of smoke blowing over from French oil tanks burning on the coast.

The failure of Monnet's and Plevin's attempt to get the French cabinet to Algiers led to another charter flight by Loraine. Once again he began the operation not knowing his final destination or the real purpose of the mission. On the afternoon of August 4, 1940, he was told to prepare his Royal Mail flying boat, Clyde, for a flight to West Africa instead of its scheduled crossing to New York. He was to take eight passengers to Lagos but that part of the journey beyond Lisbon was also to be regarded as a proving flight for a new service to West Africa. Britain's air routes to the Middle and Far East had been cut by the fall of France and Italy's entry into the war. A service to Lagos would be the first stage of a wide detour around the Mediterranean area.

Loraine faced a formidable challenge. He had to cover 5,000 miles never previously flown by flying boats. There was no special information about harbours, no reception facilities, no servicing organisation, no re-fuelling arrangements. He was going to have to maintain war-time radio silence and manage without weather reports. He was also under strict orders not to land in any part of French Africa—making a single leg of the flight as long as a non-stop Atlantic crossing. Above all, there was a need for urgency. " Get to Lagos with all speed," Loraine was told. He did some shopping for whatever charts were available at the Admiralty charts agents in Poole, without time to arrange for the cost to be charged to B.O.A.C.'s account. So the leader of this vital, urgent enterprise had to pay for the charts out of his own pocket on the promise that he could claim the money back on expenses when he returned from his flight into the unknown.

Loraine's crew consisted of Captain W. S. May, as second pilot, and Radio Officer Cheeseman. The Clyde arrived at Lisbon, at 2.26 p.m. on August 6 and Station Officer Rogers was taken on board to deal with whatever engineering problems developed along the route. The passengers had proved to be Colonel de Larminat of the Free French Army and seven members of his staff. They travelled without the usual luxury of the C Class Short flying boat. The walls were stripped of upholstery and the floor was bare. But the Clyde was carrying every possible gallon of extra fuel and had an all-up weight of twenty-four tons—the largest load this type of aircraft had

A.T.D BLACKBUSHE | | E.T.A LIN
0744 CAMBRIAN SW 1128
0856 B.K.S BR 1257
0709 DERBY TD 1119
0719 DERBY GZ 1139
0912 EAGLE VH 1244
0828 EAGLE VL 1150
1000 DAN-AIR SU 1430
A.T.D CROYDON
0808 TRANSAIR TC 1135
A.T.D FERRYFIELD
09.. AIR KRUISE ZB 1325

Charter companies have special-
ized in airlift operations brought
about by international tensions.
ABOVE: In 1956, charter planes
rescued refugees from the Hungarian rising against the Russians.
RIGHT: In 1947, they saved
43,500 people from the massacres
which followed the partition of
India and Pakistan. BELOW: In
1948, they helped to launch the
"technical miracle" of the Berlin
airlift.

Harold Bamberg, preparing for a V.I.P. flight with his chief pilot, Ca
Harold Watkins (the man who learned to fly from a frozen lake in Finland
trace the beginning of the British Eagle fleet to the Halifax bomber, Red ▮
which he bought with £500 cash and a £3,500 over draft.

Bamberg's proudest moment came when he merged with the Cunard S
Ship Company and put Boeing 707's on transatlantic routes. Then, in Febr
1963, the Atlantic venture ended in defeat, he spoke to a mass meeti▮
employees from a maintenance platform in a London Airport hangar
announced he had bought back control of the company to re-build its fort▮

Monique Agazarian

Dr. Graham Humby

Capt. Homer Cochrane

Capt. Marian Kozubski

Capt. Bill Bright

ever lifted—when Loraine began a night take-off in Lisbon harbour. The flying boat's forward lights were on for the run along a flarepath laid out across the water. In all this blaze of light Loraine and May saw what they each thought to be a slim searchlight beam ahead of them. It was not until Loraine had actually lifted off that May realised the beam of light was merely a reflection of their own lights from the sail of a small fishing vessel directly in the path of the flying boat. It was too late to put down again and the Clyde did not have enough altitude to turn away from the fishing boat.

May shouted to his captain but Loraine was fully occupied with his take-off procedure and did not have a clear view of the fishing boat because it was more to May's side of the aircraft. Seeing the mast fast approaching, the second pilot wrenched at the controls and tilted the flying boat on to its port wing-tip. The port wing must have come within a foot or so of the water while the starboard wing rose sharply and apparently cleared the fishing boat. Only next morning was a complete section of the starboard aileron seen to be missing. A great gash in the wing on the far side of the outer engine showed how close the expedition had come to disaster before it could explore a single mile of the new route.

Daylight found the Clyde following the west coast of Africa after a night flight across a thousand miles of ocean, with Loraine navigating entirely by the stars. He arrived at Bathurst in the Gambia shortly before noon on August 7. A piece of sheet aluminium from an abandoned Lufthansa base at a nearby airfield offered a solution to the problem of replacing the damaged aileron. Royal Navy fitters patched up the wing with the aluminium, using heavy brass nuts and bolts to make a crude but effective joint. After a night's sleep, Loraine took the Clyde on a thirteen-minute test flight and found that the aileron worked perfectly. The Free French passengers, still something of a mystery to Loraine, returned on board after lunch. Leaving Bathurst at 2.57 p.m. the flying boat alighted at Freetown in Sierra Leone just three hours later. This short hop, no more than 450 miles, was to take on fuel. The re-fuelling tender turned out to be a clumsy steel barge, weighing several hundred tons. Loraine made urgent signals for it to turn away from his moorings. One nudge from a barge of that size could wreck his flying boat.

Re-fuelling was postponed until next morning. Loraine tried to find an alternative to the tender but soon despaired at the lack of facilities. There seemed to be no pumps and no pipelines. To complicate matters, the flying boat was rocking in a five-foot swell across the harbour. Hearing of a sheltered bay some way up-river, he hired a motor launch to go and see for himself. His patience was strained when the launch's engine seized and another launch had to tow him to a buoy at the place which had been recommended to him. The second launch left him at the buoy and went on to a village a few miles further up the river. While waiting for the launch to return, Loraine worked out how he could taxi the Clyde to this bay and tie up to the buoy. A lighter carrying drums of petrol could also tie up there and native canoes would ferry the drums between the lighter and the flying boat. That way, there was no risk of collision.

A few minutes after that comforting thought, Loraine was floundering in the river and shouting for help. The second launch, coming back to take his launch on tow, approached the buoy too fast, lost control, and crashed into him. Loraine's launch sank beneath him and he was well soaked by the time the other launch was able to get back to him. Loraine had a further soaking when re-fuelling at last began at dawn next morning. He stood on the wing throughout a tropical rainstorm directing operations. His raincoat was in use as an umbrella over the fuel intake while the natives hoisted the heavy drums out of their canoes and on to the wings, then emptied the contents through a funnel. The work went on until daylight was fading and still only a thousand gallons had been taken on board.

Loraine taxied back to his moorings in the harbour. He took off in rough water at 6.50 a.m. the following day and completed a 1,300-mile flight to Lagos by 3.51 p.m. He reported to the B.O.A.C. Regional Manager and assured him the proving flight had been a great success. The information he had gathered since leaving Lisbon would make it very possible to establish a regular flying boat service to West Africa. Since that had been the whole objective of the Clyde's mission, Loraine presumed he would drop his Free French passengers and return to England. The Regional Manager made two corrections. The Clyde's objective was now extended to Leopoldville in the Belgian Congo, another 1,200 miles to the south. And the Free French would be going with him.

There was a delay of eight days before the Clyde was cleared for the flight to Leopoldville. During that time Loraine interpreted sufficient rumour to be sure his passengers were engaged upon a political mission of the highest order. The Governor of Nigeria was personally involved in the preparations for the flight and one of de Larimant's junior officers, in a less secretive moment, assured Loraine he would be helping to decide between war and peace in a large part of Africa. Loraine was more concerned with aviation problems. His flying boat, designed specifically for the North Atlantic, was already experiencing over-heating troubles. Now he had to cross the Equator and go far south where the increased humidity would mean a loss of engine power.

The flying boat left Lagos, at 5.35 a.m. on August 19, and the ten-hour flight to Leopoldville was made with some apprehension. Loraine had to skirt French Equatorial Africa along almost his entire route and the French authorities were strongly in favour of the Vichy Government which had come to terms with the Germans. De Larimant and his men appeared distinctly nervous of being intercepted by French aircraft. They stressed to Loraine that it would be a disaster for the Allied cause if they were captured by pro-Vichy forces. He could only order his crew to keep extra watch and hope the 160-m.p.h. flying boat would not have to try and run away from any fighter patrols. In fact, there was no sign of other aircraft at all. Loraine flew across the tropic sea with all the lonely detachment of a Victorian balloonist. He could almost imagine the flying boat suspended in the sky while a continent passed by across the horizon.

The mouth of the Congo river drew level with them in mid-afternoon and Loraine headed 300 miles inland towards Leopoldville. On reaching his destination he had to circle overhead while work was completed on a mooring being prepared for his arrival. The mooring was ready at half-past three and the flying boat landed safely amongst the rocky shallows of Stanley Pool between Leopoldville on the Belgian side and Brazzaville, on the Vichy French bank of the river. The Clyde was moored in no-man's-water between two different causes. From this position de Larimant set about plotting a wholesale change of allegiance in his country's African colonies. Early next morning, a boatload of French officers slipped out of Brazzaville and kept a secret rendezvous on board the flying boat. They represented the French Cameroons and Lake Chad Territory. After a passionate speech by de Larimant, a document was signed in the Clyde's saloon pledging the two colonies' support for General de Gaulle. It was an epic desert march by a Free French column from Lake Chad, commanded by General Le Clerc, which helped to outflank Rommel's Afrika Corps in the decisive battle of the Tunisian campaign three years later. But for the meeting on the Clyde, the Allies might have been fighting instead for control of Central Africa.

De Larimant received no delegation from the French in Brazzaville itself, strongly committed to the Vichy government at this time. Ian Scott-Hill, a B.O.A.C. official in Leopoldville, knew that Colonel Carretier, commander of the French Air Force units across the river, was particularly interested in long-range aircraft and had himself made a flight between Africa and South America. Scott-Hill sent a message to the colonel, inviting him to take a launch out to mid-stream and inspect the B.O.A.C. flying boat while it was still there. Carretier had been impressed to hear of the Clyde's pioneering flight from London and was quick to accept the invitation. De Larimant received Carretier on board and after a tour of inspection the two men sat down to discuss local politics. Carretier revealed himself as a Free French sympathiser but explained that the colonial administration was staunchly Vichy. After a long discussion he was beginning to talk in terms of a coup d'etat and a change of local government. De Larimant offered the support of Free French elements already conspiring in Brazzaville. The result was a brief action some days later, establishing a new administration and bringing the whole of French Equatorial Africa into the war against Germany.

Loraine saw little of de Larimant's activities. The flying boat was in need of a complete overhaul before attempting the flight back to England. With no proper servicing facilities available, Loraine had to rely on Rogers, the engineer, doing the best he could. One of the oil coolers developed a fault on the way from Lagos and needed attention. Loraine was not very happy about the other coolers. The air-intakes were not big enough for these latitudes. He anticipated more problems through over-heating before he was clear of the tropics. Loraine was right. A second oil cooler gave trouble on the return flight to Lagos on August 22. He spent most of the 1,200 miles trying to hold the aircraft at a speed and height which gave the most effective flow of air across the coolers. A fuel leak was also discovered at Lagos and had to be repaired. There was a welcome drop in temperature as the flying boat continued north but more faults developed. The automatic pilot failed, adding to the physical strain of a mission which had lasted for more than three weeks when Loraine finally alighted in Poole harbour on August 28. He was a sick man. A severe attack of malaria developed after he made his report and he was put to bed for six weeks. It was January 1941, before he was fit to return to duty. The Clyde was no more. The flying boat had broken from its moorings in a violent gale during an overnight stop at Lisbon, and became a total wreck.

A year later, Loraine was co-pilot when Winston Churchill flew to Washington for the meeting with President Roosevelt which authorised the production of an atomic bomb. Loraine gave up his place in the cockpit while the Prime Minister took over the controls of the chartered flying boat for two hours of the 27-hour flight from Stranraer and so qualified as an honorary sky tramp.

The State airlines have indulged in charter flying alongside their regular services ever since the principle of Government subsidies, established by Churchill as Secretary of State for Air in 1921, helped to bring about the formation of Imperial Airways. One of Imperial Airways' first charters was for an airliner to fly over London while a party of Mayfair socialites danced the Charleston at 4,000 feet. Easily the company's most flamboyant customer was Captain Alfred Loewenstein, a Belgian financier, who set out to impress his fellow millionaires by chartering nine aircraft from Imperial Airways as his personal fleet, flying in formation under the command of Gordon Olley. Loewenstein's enthusiasm for air travel led to his death when he mysteriously fell out of an aeroplane over the English Channel.

Both B.E.A. and B.O.A.C. competed strongly with the independent companies for charter business after the war. They carried British athletes to the Olympic and Empire Games throughout the world, opera and ballet companies to Russia, symphony orchestras and military bands to America, football teams and their supporters to European Cup games, shipping directors to launchings in foreign shipyards.

B.E.A. have tended to concentrate on *ad hoc* charters . . . such as the South American millionaire who complained that the scheduled Comet service to Munich left London ten minutes too early for his personal convenience. He paid £1,500 for a 132-seater Vanguard to take him and two friends to Munich at the exact time he preferred. As part of the V.I.P. service, the airliner's galley was prepared to serve a banquet during the flight and the millionaire was offered an elaborate menu, specially printed to carry his name. He waved the menu away, saying : " Nothing to eat, thank you. We're only going to Munich for a business lunch and want to get back to London as soon as the meal is finished." B.O.A.C. preferred to find more regular charter work and came to dominate the group holiday traffic on the North Atlantic routes as well as carrying out extensive trooping movements. By 1962, the Boeing 707 was so widely established on the Corporation's scheduled services that Comets, Britannias and DC-7's were available for charter flights, making B.O.A.C. the biggest charter operator in Britain.

Loraine's trip to the West Indies with Sir Anthony Eden was not his first V.I.P. charter to that part of the world. Three years before, he had flown the Queen and the Duke of Edinburgh to Bermuda and Jamaica at the start of their first Commonwealth tour. Through Bermuda passed some of B.O.A.C.'s less distinguished but highly profitable charter traffic in the opposite direction . . . coloured immigrants heading for Britain's Labour Exchanges. And via Bermuda came the challenge to B.O.A.C.'s exclusive use of the Union Jack on the prestige route between London and New York. The challenger was Harold Bamberg, of Eagle Airways, making his most spectacular gamble of all.

In 1957, he began to re-equip the Eagle fleet with DC-6C's and the latest Viscount turbo-prop airliners. Eagle Airways (Bermuda) Ltd. was incorporated in May of that year and within twelve months was operating a successful Viscount service between New York and Bermuda. That was Bamberg's first toehold in America, his first bid to break B.O.A.C.'s transatlantic monopoly. The second bid came with the appearance of Eagle Airways (Bahamas) Ltd. in 1959 and the start of services between Nassau and Miami. Eagle also began regular flights linking the Bahamas and Bermuda, and established a " Sky Coach " service between London and Bermuda.

With these opening preliminaries completed, Bamberg made his big call. The stakes were high, no less than the sale of 100 per cent. control of the Eagle organisation to the

Cunard Steam Ship Company. Then, as chairman of the newly formed Cunard Eagle Airways, he applied to the Air Transport Licensing Board for permission to operate a daily service between London and New York, and in July 1961 he was awarded a fifteen-year licence to operate on civil aviation's "Blue Riband" route. B.O.A.C. objected strenuously but Bamberg had taken advantage of the previous year's Civil Aviation Act by which the Conservative Government had finally repealed the principle of a State monopoly of scheduled services.

Fifteen years after buying his first Halifax bomber for £500, Harold Bamberg placed a £7,000,000 order for Boeing 707's with the triumph of a trampship finally overhauling the *Queen Mary*. On November 21, 1961, he was outlining the great prospects ahead to a Cunard board meeting in Liverpool, presided over by Sir John Brocklebank, when he was called into an outer office to take a telephone call from his secretary in London. He walked back into the board meeting and said: "Gentlemen, we have lost our North Atlantic licence. You look like being the owners of three redundant Boeing 707's." Mr. Peter Thorneycroft, Minister of Aviation, had upheld B.O.A.C.'s appeal against the Cunard Eagle service.

Even then, Bamberg would not admit defeat. He called Cunard's North American branch managers to an emergency meeting in a Bermuda hotel, took delivery of two Boeings, and in May 1962 launched a London-Bermuda-Nassau-Miami service. The service promised to be so successful that he began to plan a second application for the London-New York licence. But within a month the Cunard Board had joined with B.O.A.C. to form B.O.A.C. Cunard Limited, a £30,000,000 company to take over all Cunard Eagle operations in the Western Hemisphere. Bamberg was a helpless spectator to the closing down of his original undertakings in Bermuda and Nassau, and the surrender of the Boeings and some of his best pilots to the Corporation which he had set out to challenge. The Cunard Steam Ship Company retained control of Eagle's European operations but showed little enthusiasm for Continental services or holiday flights to the Mediterranean. Bamberg watched his proud fleet of old allowed to dwindle to seven aircraft. His venture on the North Atlantic had met with disaster on a *Titanic* scale.

Captain Loraine was flying regularly on B.O.A.C.'s New York route when Cunard Eagle first won its operating licence and he sensed the Corporation's feeling of an enemy within the gates. After the attack was repulsed and the licence revoked, he helped with the mopping up operations by taking command of one of the Cunard Eagle Boeings absorbed into B.O.A.C. His first flight was from New York to Bermuda and was delayed by a hurricane. The second flight brought the Boeing smoothly back to London Airport where Loraine's landing was watched with glum envy by members of Eagle's unemployed aircrews.

"A most enjoyable trip," said Loraine. " The 707 is quite the nicest plane I have ever flown. The next best must be my old twenty-ton flying boat—and not even a Boeing could compete with that if you ever want to charter an aircraft for some secret mission up the River Congo."

CHAPTER NINE

Success is not Enough

MOST New York banks do not open on Saturday. Captain Bill Bright, a freelance ferry pilot, arrived in the city as a B.O.A.C. passenger late on Friday evening, November 25, 1960, and met a two-day delay in obtaining the money to pay for the DC-4 airliner he had come to collect. He was acting on behalf of Trans World Leasing, a British company which was buying the aeroplane from Capitol Airways. Bright had to wait until Monday to collect the cash from the Manhattan bank where he was expected. There were other formalities, including a War Department clearance, to be completed. Then he joined a flight to Washington, held a conference with Capitol engineers waiting for him at the airport, and finally went to be introduced to the DC-4, standing in its hangar with the jaded patience of an aeroplane which has been too long out of the sky.

Bright made his examination of the aircraft and pronounced himself ready to make an immediate departure. " But don't you think you should take her up and around on a test flight," said one of the ground engineers. " This plane has been out of service for some time." It was now late afternoon and Bright indicated the darkening November sky. " Not much point in doing a potted test by flying round in circles when it's already too dark to see very much," said Bright. " I've got to fly to Boston as an export airport before I can get out of the country. If I go now it can be my test flight as well, and I can make an early start across the Atlantic from Boston first thing in the morning." The mechanic raised a further detail. " But where's your crew, captain? You can't fly a four-engined plane like this across the Atlantic all on your own. The weather's going to be dirty at this time of year and you know there's no pressurisation to lift you over the top."

This was a problem which had concerned Bright for the past three days. An American pilot had been contracted to share the flight with him and by all the economics of ferrying that would have been an adequate crew. But the American did not contact Bright at his New York hotel on Friday, as arranged in advance. A whole series of telephone calls over the weekend failed to trace him. There was no message from him at Washington airport, no clue whether he was sick, no longer available or perhaps merely delayed.

" The crew will be joining me at Boston," said Bright, a man of cheerful confidence. " But if you get any stragglers through here tonight you might tell them to hurry after me because I'm off first thing tomorrow."

The DC-4 took off at 6.40 p.m., the floodlit Washington Monument glowing out of the darkness like a piece of illuminated grotto. Twenty minutes later Bright began to cough and rub his eyes. Soon he was choking, and blinking needle-sharp tears. He was aware of smoke swirling in the soft light of his instruments. Instinctively, he opened one of the cockpit windows. Then he shut it again because the effect was merely to draw more smoke and fumes into the front of the cockpit. Bright grabbed the oxygen mask to his face and reached down at the side of his seat to turn open the oxygen valve. It was a one-handed struggle to open the valve and the valve was stuck firmly closed, probably from disuse. Bright held a handkerchief over his face, prepared to believe the oxygen supply would have been empty had his left hand been strong enough to turn the valve.

The situation in the cockpit was now becoming desperate. Bright was breathing through his handkerchief with the greatest difficulty. The smoke smarting in his eyes made it almost impossible to see his instruments, never mind trying to maintain a proper look-out ahead of the aircraft. As far as Bright could tell the trouble was inside the fuselage and there was no sign of flames to show an actual outbreak of fire. A strong smell of rubber led him to suspect the fumes came from an electrical fault within the instruments. He made a brief radio call to Washington airport, saying he was returning for an emergency landing, and then turned off everything electrical. This left him to make an entirely visual approach, peering out at the night from a smoke-filled cockpit. The Washington Monument showed up again below his port wing but vaguely this time, like a lantern submerged in a muddy pool. The lights of the airport seemed dim and distant as he began his approach, then sparkled wildly through the tears in his smoke blackened eyes when at last he put down into the glare of the runway. It had seemed the longest, most tentative landing of his career. Bright was sure he would have been overcome by the fumes early on in the approach if the cockpit had not begun to clear slightly once the electrical equipment was switched off. He sat in the DC-4 at the end of its taxi-ing, threw open the windows, and coughed and choked over the fresh air which rushed into his lungs.

"Thought you weren't going to do a test flight," said the same Capitol Airways engineer when Bright walked into the hangar. "Get me your expert on electricals," said Bright, no longer cheerful. Within forty minutes the trouble had been traced to the VHF radio, the faulty instrument removed, and a fresh radio installed. The DC-4 took off again at 7.40 p.m. and reached Boston uneventfully, two hours later. There was still no news of Bright's American co-pilot and when he failed to appear next morning Bright considered flying the plane to England alone. There was no telling how long he would have to wait for the American, assuming the man would eventually turn up. Boston was not the easiest place from which to organise a replacement pilot at short notice.

Bright thought of the weekend he had wasted in New York, unpaid overtime since a ferry contract carries a flat fee. He also thought of collecting both pilots' fees as some sort of consolation. "That's for me," decided the man who was in the process of having to sue one of his previous employers for outstanding wages. "I'll take it up on my own. We would fly it one at a time if there were two of us."

Only when he was flying to Goose Bay on the first leg of the crossing did Bright admit to himself a glow of pleasure at the prospect of piloting a large aircraft across the Atlantic single-handed. He began his flying career with the R.A.F.'s 138 Squadron on special operations over war-time Europe, dropping Allied spies and saboteurs as far inside Germany as the suburbs of Berlin itself. That gave him a relish for occasionally flying beyond the rim of certainty, something he sensed with no more heroics than a mountain guide enjoying the challenge of a sheer face after too long in the foothills.

The late-November weather became steadily worse during the afternoon as Bright flew further north and he landed in a blizzard at Goose Bay in Labrador. Bright climbed down from his cockpit by a ladder he had borrowed at Washington and made his way through the snow to the Customs office. "You flew in from the States in this weather?" said the Customs officer, and he registered more surprise when Bright announced that he would be continuing his flight to London in a little more than an hour. "I'm going to London myself in a couple of days," the Customs officer explained. "I've got a ticket booked with T.W.A. and I can't wait to get over there and see what England is really like. I've never been there before "

" Pity you've got a ticket and that you've got to wait until Thursday," said Bright. "I might have offered you a lift." He arranged for a Royal Canadian Air Force jeep to give him a lift to a self-service restaurant at the far end of Goose Bay's military airfield. After a leisurely meal, and a wash to freshen up, he telephoned his flight plan to the control tower. There was no jeep available for his return journey to the aeroplane, meaning more than a mile's walk in the breath of the blizzard. As he came up to the DC-4 something stirred between the landing wheels and a snow-plastered figure stepped into sight, carrying two suitcases.

"Does that offer of a lift still stand?" asked a voice which Bright recognised as the Customs officer's. "I've got my leave brought forward and I've cancelled the ticket. I didn't want to miss you so I've been waiting here for the best part of an hour, hoping that you would have room to take me." Bright saw that the man was almost trembling with cold from his long wait on an exposed runway. "There's plenty of room for you," he said. "Come on board." The Customs officer was obviously puzzled to get into an airliner by following the pilot up a ladder into the cockpit but he chose to make no comment. "Which seat should I take?" he asked. Bright threw open the door to the passenger compartment and told the Customs man to sit wherever he chose. For the next few minutes Bright busied himself with his preparations for take-off. He glanced back down the plane two or three times and received a smile from the Customs officer sitting halfway along the sixty-seat fuselage.

Bright had actually taken off and was climbing to 8,000 feet when there was an apologetic tap on his shoulder and the Customs officer spoke in a tiny voice: "Where are the others? The rest of the passengers? I'm the only one back there."

"There aren't any other passengers," said Bright. "I thought I explained it was a ferry flight. That's why I told you to take your pick of the seats."

"So there are no passengers but me," said the Customs officer. "But where are the rest of you? You don't mean there isn't a proper crew for a big four-engined plane like this?"

"Well, there should have been a crew," said Bright, "and it's a long story why I'm flying this all by myself, But don't worry about a thing. I can look after everything this end o you just go back there, put your feet up and enjoy the trip. You'll never get to England any cheaper than this."

The Customs man was cheered by this last point and went back to his seat. For the next two-and-a-half hours Bright maintained a speed of just under 200 m.p.h. on his course to Sondre Stromfjord, which lay north of the Arctic Circle on the west coast of Greenland. The weather continued to deteriorate and he had no idea of what conditions lay ahead. Goose Bay control could provide him with no information of weather at Sondre Stromfjord when he set off and the VHF radio, replaced at Washington after his emergency landing, had failed within the first hour of his flight towards Greenland. It was 9.30 p.m., just beyond the point of no return to Goose Bay, when the Customs officer touched Bright on the shoulder again. This was no apologetic tap. This was the anxious rap of a man who had just looked out into the blackness of the Arctic night. " I was shining my torch along the wings to see if there would be any ice and I saw oil gushing from one of the engines. It's all over the wings like tar. Does it mean the engine is going to blow up? What are you going to do about it?"

This was a bad moment to pose such questions. The DC-4 had only enough fuel to go on to Sondre Stromfjord and there was no telling what the weather was going to be like there. Frobisher, in north-east Canada, was an alternative, but Bright had even less idea of what kind of weather to expect there and he was unfamiliar with the airfield. His radio was out of action so that he could not call up for information. Oil on the wing sounded ominous even though his instruments showed no loss of pressure from any engine. Perhaps the Customs man had spotted an oil leak just as it started. If Bright could make a quick diagnosis there might yet be time to save the engine from serious damage.

One more technical problem kept Bright in his seat when he wanted to hurry back to the passenger compartment and see that oil for himself. He had discovered that the DC-4 did not have the automatic pilot control which he had taken for granted in deciding on a solo flight across the Atlantic. That meant he could not leave his seat throughout every minute the plane was in the air. So how could he go and make an assessment of the situation when somebody had to remain at the controls?

The Customs man touched Bright's shoulder once more and unwittingly provided a solution. It became an unwilling solution when Bright installed his solitary passenger in the pilot's seat but the Customs officer was made to see there was no alternative.

" I won't be a minute," said Bright. " Just keep your hands and feet exactly where I put them and don't move anything. Look straight ahead and just imagine it's on a set of rails instead of in the air."

Bright went back into the passenger compartment and felt the hollow gloom of a deserted theatre. He never considered this was a part of his aeroplane when there were no passengers—just a line of empty seats trailing after him across the sky. He shone the Customs officer's torch out along the starboard wing and saw a thick black mass of oil, about nine inches wide, stretching behind No. 2 engine. It looked very serious. Then, he crossed to the opposite window, shone the torch along the port wing and saw a similar amount of oil stretching from No. 3 engine. He went back to have another look at the starboard wing and returned to flash the torch out of one of the port windows again. There was no doubt that the same amount of oil was spread over the wing behind each of two engines. How much oil he could not tell since oil is like blood in its capacity for spilling a pint and making a gallon of mess.

While the Customs man sat stiffly at the controls of the DC-4, 8,000 feet above the Atlantic, Bright looked out from the passenger compartment and tried to decide whether two engines could develop the same mysterious fault at the same time in exactly the same way. If they could and had, he was going to have to cut both engines and try to struggle to Greenland on only half-power in still worsening weather. It was a grim prospect. He went back to the cockpit and took over the pilot's seat to the abject relief of the Customs officer who later admitted he had begun to wonder if perhaps Bright had baled out and left him sitting there until the fuel ran out. The instruments still showed no change of pressure or temperature in the two suspect engines. " We've got nothing to worry about," said Bright. He was talking to the passenger but reasoning with himself. " They must have overfilled those engines with oil at Boston and the overflow would have frozen on the wings as soon as I took off. I wouldn't see it from here in the cockpit, and I suppose the glistening effect of the oil being frozen makes it look like a fresh leak even now. But it can't be, not making exactly the same pattern on each wing. It's too much of a coincidence. Anybody that unlucky would be so out of luck he shouldn't expect to live long, anyway. We'll ignore the oil and press on."

Bright realised that if he was making the wrong decision two of his four engines might suddenly seize solid, with the added risk of the propellers then refusing to feather. This extra drag would give little hope of making Sondre Strom-fjord. The Customs man sat down in the co-pilot's seat " It's lonely back there on my own," he said. " I'd rather stay up front with you."

There were 500 miles of the North Atlantic to cross before Bright could be sure his diagnosis was correct. Like all experienced pilots, he knew that flying was a business confined to the line of dilemma between ultra-caution and over-confidence. There was little commercial future for a pilot too hasty in cutting engines and making emergency landings when the engineers could find nothing wrong with his aircraft. But there was little future of any kind for the pilot who always pressed on regardless of his instruments or such omens as oil on the wing.

Sometimes the dilemma balanced on more than technical considerations. Taking off from Blackpool municipal airport for America in April, 1959, Bright heard such a banging from one of his DC-4's engines that his obvious course was to turn back and request an engineer's examination. But his passengers were heavyweight boxer Brian London and his supporters, who had just been given a civic farewell on their departure for Indianapolis and London's world title fight with Floyd Patterson. Television cameras were recording the scene at the airport and Bright could imagine the general embarrassment if the local hero was returned less than five minutes after take-off. Bright decided to fly the 130 miles to Prestwick, knowing the engine could be attended to there without turning a mechanical failure into a public exhibition. But the banging ceased as suddenly as it began and he carried on to Reykjavik, in Iceland, according to his flight plan, with the engine behaving perfectly. Then, during take-off from Iceland, the banging resumed. Nine hours of ocean lay ahead and this time there was no alternative but to go back to Reykjavik. The airport engineers were unable to trace the fault. London's party arrived in America a day late after waiting for a replacement engine to be fitted. The return flight to Blackpool was without incident. Brian London had been knocked out in the eleventh round so this time there was no civic party, no television cameras. "Surprised you ever left in the first place," one of the airport workers said to Bright. "One of your engines was making such a clanging when you took off the Mayor could hardly hear himself speak."

Bright was listening for the same kind of ominous noise as he flew his solitary passenger towards Greenland. He had made two misjudgements on the Brian London flight in not going back to Blackpool when the distinguished audience for his take-off had been well aware something was wrong, and then in thinking the faulty engine could cure itself. Was he making a bigger mistake now by ignoring the warning signs of a double engine failure? Shortly before midnight the lights of Sondre Stromfjord appeared below and Bright knew he had made the right decision. He landed safely, with all four engines working smoothly, and afterwards, climbed up on the wings to see for himself that a small amount of oil had overflowed from the two inner engines and frozen to a pattern formed by the air flow. There was no mechanical fault.

Stopping only to re-fuel, he set off over the Greenland ice-cap for Keflavik in Iceland and a late breakfast, and then pressed on to London Airport. He arrived in the mid-afternoon of November 30 after flying the DC-4 for all but three minutes of the twenty-five-hour flight. Those three minutes were when the Customs officer took charge. The Canadian set foot in England with some degree of aircrew nonchalance, having kept Bright well provided with hot coffee from Greenland onwards and worn out the battery of his torch slipping into the passenger compartment every fifteen minutes to make sure the engines did not produce any further drama. Bright has never seen him since but on subsequent flights through Goose Bay he was an innocent listener to steadily more colourful stories of the time a Customs man thumbed a lift on the end of a runway and ended up flying an airliner across the Atlantic.

Ferry flying was very much temporary work for Bright at a time when his career was making a bold change of direction. Nine years as a pilot on B.O.A.C.'s Far Eastern routes after leaving the R.A.F. had left him weary of Corporation routine. He joined Eagle in 1954 when the company was expanding to take on Middle Eastern trooping contracts, and then he moved on to Independent Air Travel, a fast-growing company controlled by Captain Marian Kozubski.

Kozubski, a bearded Polish war hero, and a veteran of the Indian, Pakistan and Berlin airlifts, was establishing himself as the most dashing, most controversial operator in the business. He created an international incident when his Skymaster was forced down in Albania by MiG fighters for violating Communist air space. His company was the first to be fined for exceeding the safety restrictions on pilots' flying time. He complained he was being victimised by an airport commandant and sent a tractor to tow the commandant's car into a lonely stretch of countryside. He drove his own Jaguar with the dash of a man who had driven in the Monte Carlo Rally, and survived a spectacular crash on his way to London Airport to take over one of his aeroplanes. In four years, he progressed from a single Dove, largely engaged on ferrying racing pigeons across the Channel to starting points in France, to owning a fleet of ten airliners.

Then on September 5, 1958, there were only nine. One of the company's Vikings crashed into houses at Southall, killing seven people. An official inquiry decided the plane was overloaded, maintenance had been neglected, the pilot who died in the crash was tired, and the airline's overall policy was to keep its aircraft in the air regardless of regulations.

Bright witnessed from within the disintegration of Independent Air Travel in a hostile blaze of publicity. He stayed on after Kozubski's departure to help organise a new company, Blue Air, and was dejected when that failed, too, and 120 employees were thrown out of work. Bright joined another short-lived charter company with the title of general manager and left by taking the directors to court for his salary. He began freelance flying as a ferry pilot while bringing to life an old ambition to start an airline of his own. His previous business enterprises, an antique shop and a florist's, had been modest sidelines to flying but he enjoyed the hint of manipulating his own destiny. Now he wanted to launch a charter business which would begin with the profit of all the mistakes he had seen in other people's operations.

Coming into charter flying nine years after most of his ex-R.A.F. contemporaries, Bright could see that the wild, free-for-all pioneering days were over, a Klondike corrupted by its own fool's gold. A converted Halifax bomber, bought as war surplus for £500, was able to make a profit of £220 in twenty-four hours on the first Berlin airlift, by managing six trips in a single day. The civilian version of the Lancaster bomber could average a net profit of £1,500 a month on the same operation. The second Berlin airlift, meat strikes, rail strikes—these provided highly profitable operations which convinced so many independent airlines that there really was a goldmine in the sky. The last thing all this did was prepare them for finding long-term markets of their own or teach them the elementary business of costing their charters realistically.

Bright had seen that when the airlifts and strikes were over—even between one airlift and the next—most of the smaller operators struggled to find work of any kind, grateful for charters which barely covered their overheads and making no provision for replacing their cheap, war surplus aircraft with commercially produced planes. As early as 1949, economists were warning owners of £4,000 war surplus Dakotas that each plane needed a paid mileage of 20,000 per month, earning £5,000 to allow for the fact that a suitable replacement would cost £60,000 in five years time. The warning came when an operator was reckoned to be doing very well if he could find 7,000 paid miles a month for his Dakotas.

During his spell with Eagle, Bright was impressed by the foresight of Harold Bamberg in buying Lunn's travel agency to guarantee tourist flights for his own airline. The need to make only one profit between them made both sides of the business even more competitive. His period with Independent Air Travel also convinced Bright that there was nothing basically wrong with Kozubski's policy of gaining maximum use of each aircraft. What was wrong was having a ground administration which could not achieve the same high pressure efficiency.

Bright registered his own charter company in the summer of 1960 at the very time when a large proportion of the existing operators were preferring to be amalgamated under the title of British United Airways. Managing director of the new group was Freddy Laker, whose financial surrender to Airwork two years earlier had merely gained him access to a more powerful boardroom and given greater scope to his business instincts.

The ex-flight engineer, who survived in aviation only by turning old bombers into saucepans, now took charge of a £20,000,000 enterprise and insisted the day of the little man was over.

Mustering his life's savings of £3,000, Bill Bright begged to disagree. He found a partner to add another £1,000 to the business. The name they chose, World Wide Aviation, was rather ambitious for a company with only £4,000 as capital, no staff, and no aircraft. Between his freelance ferry flights, Bright spent the summer and autumn organising charters and obtaining the necessary licences to operate. In December, he began operations with a three-week holiday flight to the Middle East, a Christmas tour of the Holy Land. The pilot was the company's chief and only pilot, one Capt. W. Bright. By sheer coincidence the aircraft was the DC-4 he had brought across the Atlantic single handed. He took it on hire for a year, with World Wide undertaking to carry out all servicing and repairs. Bright knew this was the most expensive way to operate but he needed to start flying to raise the money to buy aircraft of his own. Like so many charter companies before it, World Wide was going to have to operate on credit in anticipation of revenue yet to be earned.

A major need was some sort of scheduled flying, a regular income not dependent on the seasonal spurts of tourist traffic to the Mediterranean. Bright found the answer in Iceland where he won a contract to provide a London-Reykjavik link for the transatlantic service of Loftleidir, the Icelandic airline. On the strength of this, he hired another DC-4 on similar terms and began to construct his ground organisation. World Wide was based at Gatwick Airport with an operations manager and an assistant, a chief engineer, two engineers, and a secretary. An accountant and another secretary worked in the London office, in Regent Street. There was also a commercial office with a commercial manager. Wages for the ground staff totalled £150 a week and Bright engaged five complete air crews to guarantee full use of the aircraft. He needed a minimum of a thousand paid hours per aircraft per year bringing in a total of £250,000 to break even. He was sure he could safely exceed that figure.

In March, 1961, World Wide began to live up to its name. One of the DC-4's was placed on a year's contract to Sabena, for United Nations operations in the Begian Congo. Bright flew the plane to Leopoldville himself, curious to see how the civil war was going. The previous September he had flown one of the first British charter planes into the Congo when independence exploded in blood and flames. He and an old friend, Pete Palmer, both without regular jobs, had hired a Viking for a spell of sky-tramping around Africa. They arrived in Entebbe at a time when all communications with the Congo had ceased to exist. Bright and Palmer, appreciating the charter business to be found in a state of anarchy, pressed on to Elisabethville and put the Viking down between the anti-aircraft barrels scattered on the runway. At Elisabethville they were hired by officials of the Union Miniere to discover the fate of the company's European employees at Bakwanga, in South Kasia. This was the site of the world's largest open-cast diamond mines and the Europeans were feared lost after early reports of looting mobs ravishing the whole area.

Smoke was still rising from burnt-out empty villages as the Viking approached Bakwanga. The Union Miniere's European estate, a plot of exclusive suburbia dropped in the heart of Africa, was intact but utterly deserted. There was not the slightest sign of life on or about the local airstrip. The two fliers circled overhead and felt the chill of wondering if they were the only men alive in this whole exotic wilderness. Then, Bright landed the Viking and they caught the glint of Congolese Army jeeps and tommy-guns among the trees. Bright and Palmer were soon to agree that Congolese soldiers wore their uniforms and carried weapons in a manner which inspired confidence only in one's worst fears. The two pilots remained in the aircraft until a Union Miniere jeep arrived to take them to the European estate by way of several road blocks manned by trigger-excited Congolese troops. The deserted streets and gardens of the European district, as seen from the air, were explained by finding the entire community living in a state of siege in the centrally placed sports and social club. Wild-bearded Bel-

gians, armed with only a few revolvers between them, asked
for news of the massacres and pillaging which they felt must
be drawing near. Some hurried to gather up the personal
belongings they had with them to claim a place on the Viking's first flight out of Bakwanga. In all, fifteen flights were
needed to complete the evacuation because many of the
Belgians gathered courage from the aircraft's link with the
outside world and insisted on the furniture and ornaments
from their bungalows being taken out as well.

The Congolese Army remained a vaguely hostile audience
throughout the airlift but did nothing more than brandish
tommy-guns and accelerate their jeeps dramatically. Bright
came to the end of the evacuation firmly convinced the early
troubles of the Congo's independence would have been
stemmed had the individual Belgians owned parts of the
country instead of largely being employees of the Union
Miniere. Then, like the Kenyan farmers in the Mau Mau
days, they would have stayed to hold on to what was theirs
and complete anarchy would have been avoided.

Bright went back to the Congo in March 1961, as managing
director of World Wide Aviation and this time had something
he was determined to hang on to—his own business. Any
threat to the DC-4 was now a personal threat because it was,
in effect, his aircraft and represented the principal income of
the company he had waited so long to establish.

The civil war between the Congo Federal Government and
the breakaway state of Katanga became a very personal matter
for Bright when he landed at Luluabourg on July 4, 1961,
to re-fuel during a flight from Leopoldville to Elisabethville,
the two rival capitals. On board the DC-4 were a Katanga
general and his staff officers, and an escort of forty Katanga
troops. They were returning home after visiting Leopoldville under a flag of truce to discuss possible peace terms.
Government officials had given them a cordial send-off from
Leopoldville but a very different kind of reception was waiting at Luluabourg. The airfield was swarming with Congolese
troops, in a much more aggressive mood than Bright ever

encountered at Bakwanga. He advised the Katangans not to show themselves at the windows of the aircraft, and then stepped down on to the runway to meet a Congolese major who appeared to be in charge of the airfield. Bright pointedly adjusted the hand grenade which he carried, clipped to his shirt pocket, on all Congo missions. There was a spare grenade in his brief case in the cockpit. Bright discovered during the airlift from Bakwanga that wearing a grenade was a visiting card accepted without question by Congolese soldiers of all ranks and temperaments. He had never thrown a grenade in his life and had little idea of how to throw one. He wore it as a personal H-bomb—a deterrent which had failed the moment it no longer deterred.

The major was suitably impressed by the grenade. So were the soldiers, armed with tommy-guns, who clustered behind him. " I understand you have Katanga troops on board," said the major. " They must leave the plane immediately." Bright explained that the aircraft was on charter to the United Nations and the Katangans were returning home under a flag of truce.

" My instructions from Leopoldville were not to allow them to leave the aircraft in Congolese territory," he said. " We have stopped here only to re-fuel. If you will let me take on petrol we can leave within the hour." The major said that the re-fuelling could begin but that the aircraft must not leave until he could get in touch with his colonel for instructions.

Bright went back on board to find the Katangans nervously peeping through the windows at the gathering mass of their enemies. He went into the cockpit where his co-pilot, Tony Strickland-Hubbard, pointed out the Congolese soldier stand-ing on guard in front of the aircraft, his tommy-gun directed at the cockpit. " This has the smell of a trap," said Bright. " These Congolese were expecting us, they knew we had Katangans on board, and they wanted them off. You can guess what would happen if they set foot amongst that itchy-fingered lot. We'd have a massacre in which the aircraft would certainly get shot up and very likely you and I as well."

"I thought these Katanga chaps were guaranteed free passage," said Strickland-Hubbard, a pleasant young man whose occasional sky tramping was a form of escape from his life of leisure in the South of France as a Woolworth heir. "Why should they wave them off from Leopoldville and then want to kill them here?"

"Because that's how they do things in the Congo," said Bright. "It would outrage the U.N. to kill their guests in Leopoldville. It would be a lamentable misunderstanding, a tragic accident, if they happen to go and get themselves killed on the way home. What bothers me is that it needs only one bullet to be fired and they'll all start shooting. Thank Christ I made the general's escort stick their rifles and tommy-guns in the hold. They can't get at them no matter how jittery they get."

Bright went back to his passengers and found the general's staff officers had drawn their revolvers in face of the steady build-up of Congolese troops on the runway. He insisted to the general that his officers must surrender their revolvers if they wished to remain on the aircraft, pointing out that a few revolvers could not possibly hold off the Congolese if they chose to attack and might well provoke such an attack. The Katanga officers were reluctant to hand over their revolvers but the general insisted they should do as the pilot asked. Bright collected up the revolvers and took them into the cockpit. He returned to the passenger compartment in time to see the Congolese major climb on board, followed by a dozen heavily armed soldiers.

"My colonel will soon be here," said the major. "But first I must inspect your passengers." The Katangans, now completely defenceless, shrank back into their seats as the Congolese subjected them to a fierce scrutiny. Bright followed the Congolese along the length of the aircraft and could only guess what was being said in the long, heated argument between the major and the Katanga general. Bright would

have preferred the Katangans to say as little as possible because a single word could inflame the whole situation. But
the major came back down the aircraft in a more relaxed
mood, seeming particularly pleased because the passengers
were unarmed. It was impossible to tell if his pleasure carried
any sinister significance but Bright was sure the revolvers
were safer out of the way in the cockpit. There was a bar on
board the DC-4 and Bright invited the major to join him for
a drink. The major was happy to accept and the relaxed
atmosphere which quickly developed in the bar seemed to be
communicated to the troops outside. They stopped pointing
their weapons at the aeroplane. Numbers of them began to
drift away from the runway. The local petrol bowsers—
barrels of fuel and portable pumps trundled out on trolleys
—were moved into position and re-fuelling was started.

A few minutes afterwards the Congolese colonel arrived.
Bright and the major left the bar to meet him on the runway.
The colonel's attitude was as stiff as the major's had been
before half-a-dozen large whiskies. "You have Katanga
soldiers on your aeroplane," he said. "I must insist they
leave the aeroplane and are handed over to me." Bright
fingered the hand grenade on his shirt and suggested that
was impossible. Even if there was no massacre on the spot
and the aircraft was allowed to leave, the incident would
almost certainly wreck his Sabena charter and ruin World
Wide Aviation's business reputation. Who would want to
use an airline which abandoned an entire load of passengers
before they were even halfway to their destination? The fact
they were all murdered shortly afterwards would ensure full
and lurid publicity. As captain of the aircraft, Bright was
determined not to surrender his passengers. As managing
director of World Wide Aviation, he could not even contemplate such a thing. "No," he said firmly, "my passengers
have been guaranteed safe passage and I cannot allow them
to leave the aircraft."

The colonel was not obviously displeased by this attitude.
Bright sensed that the colonel and major were not very confi-

dent of controlling their own men once the Katangans appeared. The refusal to surrender the passengers provided an excuse for the colonel to pass the responsibility to his superiors. He left the airfield to make a telephone call to Leopoldville. " Do not attempt to take off until I return," he said before he went. Bright saw him talk to the airfield manager at the far end of the runway. A messenger ran across to the men in charge of the petrol bowsers and re-fuelling was stopped with only a third of the petrol Bright had requested taken on board. " Looks like we're here for the night," said Strickland-Hubbard. It was now 4.30 p.m. At 6.30 they were still waiting for the colonel to return. The DC-4 had been sitting at the end of the runway for five hours in all and now radiated a passive weariness, which was absorbed by the few remaining on-lookers. The guard originally posted in front of the aircraft had been succeeded by a more casual Congolese. He gradually drifted away to join some of his comrades grouped round a cooking pot some three hundred yards to the left. Bright was relieved to have the tommy-gun removed to that range. If the guard had ever thought to put a single burst into the plane's tyres the DC-4 would have needed guarding no longer. Take-off would be impossible.

There were signs of agitation from the passenger compart-ment. The Katangans feared the coming of night and the prospect of sitting out there in the darkness, unarmed and surrounded by their enemies. Bright tried to re-assure the Katangans. He thought it much more in character for the Congolese to postpone any further action until the morning in the hope that somebody in Leopoldville would then be prepared to take the necessary decision. " But we still don't know what that decision will be," said the Katanga general. " Cannot you take us out of here before then?"

Bright had been thinking along those lines ever since he landed. Attempting a surprise take-off would have been suicidal earlier but the chances were much better now that the Congolese were lulled into this relaxed state. They obviously thought the plane could not leave because it had only a third of its fuel. But Bright had calculated that with what he had on board when he landed there was just enough fuel to make Elisabethville. With the approach of darkness, the Congolese probably assumed the plane could not leave until morning, anyway, since Luluabourg airfield was not equipped for night operations. But there was still enough light for a take-off—if Bright waited no longer. He looked at the guard, engrossed in the happenings around the cooking pot, and said to Strickland-Hubbard: " Tell them to sit tight back there. We're going."

Everything depended on the engines firing first time. With four engines to fire the odds were high. Bright reckoned he would have half-a-minute's start over the Congolese at the most, assuming they were suitably surprised. The first engine fired first time and heads were turned towards the DC-4. The second engine came in after 15 seconds. Bright set the aircraft rolling as the Congolese troops began to run in his direction. Another 15 seconds and the third engine opened up. That was enough for Bright to go through with the take-off. He sensed, rather than heard, a hail of tommy gun bullets from the guard who had deserted his post. He saw jeeps with machine guns mounted pull on to the runway from the airfield's administration area and head to cut off the DC-4. The fourth engine came in just 45 seconds after the first. Bright lifted off with the jeeps well short of him. They fell away beneath the port wing. He could imagine a farewell volley from the machine guns but the aircraft climbed away, completely undamaged. Four hours later he landed in Elisabethville and restored the Katangans to their own. World Wide Aviation had honoured its obligations.

Shortly afterwards, a charter aircraft belonging to another British company was destroyed while on the ground at Luluabourg. A second was shot up by a Government fighter while parked at Elisabethville. A third disappeared in mid-flight. Bright's DC-4 escaped any further drama, its flights largely divided between ferrying U.N. troops and transporting large quantities of soap. Bright never understood the need for such a cargo. Large areas of the country were desperate for food and medical supplies and his aircraft was chartered at great expense to fly in soap. If it did not make sense it made very good business.

Business would have been even better had the DC-4 not been a British registered aircraft and so required by British regulations to return to its home base for maintenance and clearance after every 300 hours. This had to be done even though the aircraft was being serviced at the Leopoldville base of Sabena, an international airline. The flight to Gatwick and back took 40 hours so the aircraft could operate in the Congo for no more than 260 hours in every 300, a considerable loss of efficiency. World Wide's second DC-4 was sometimes needed to help out in the Congo. Otherwise it became increasingly occupied with inclusive holiday tours during the summer of 1961.

This was a period with a high mortality rate for small British charter companies. The Civil Aviation Act of 1960 was now in force, its strict safety requirements forcing up overheads, its intricate licensing procedure making charter work less and less flexible. Although the new regulations offered long-term advantages to reputable British operators, they suffered from the immediate disadvantage of not applying to foreign competitors. German charter companies, previously few and small, using British pilots mainly, suddenly moved into the British market in increasing strength. Like aircraft of American companies which began to operate from Luxembourg under aviation's equivalent of a flag of convenience, the Germans could sit on the tarmac at Gatwick and pick up business at short notice while British firms were still filing an application for the necessary licence. Foreign operators could also undercut on prices without the same rigid limitations on aircrew's flying time, without having to replace aircraft components on a calendar life basis, regardless of wear and tear. Some other countries have since adopted similar requirements but there were heavy casualties among British companies during the interim period.

Several travel agencies, including a high proportion in the Midlands, found themselves without the charter planes they had booked for the summer of 1961. World Wide's DC-4 was offered as a replacement although Bright knew he was taking on a schedule drawn up for Argonauts, a more sophisticated version of the DC-4 which was pressurised and about twenty-five knots faster with Rolls Royce Merlin engines.

The World Wide aircraft's lack of pressurisation meant extra fuel bills on flights to Northern Italy by having to go round instead of over the Alps. A slower speed over a long distance demanded non-stop operations to keep up to schedule during weekends at the height of the holiday season. Bright's care in setting up his ground staff was rewarded by the DC-4 maintaining its service smoothly throughout the summer.

World Wide Aviation came to the end of its first year of operations, showing a net profit of £14,000 on a turnover of nearly £300,000 and having increased business booked for 1962. Yet, by March, World Wide had suspended all operations and Bright was looking for a job. The annual report of the Air Transport Licensing Board which appeared in August 1962 stated that a total of ten operators had gone out of business in the past year and warned charter companies against being " grossly under-capitalised."

Bright was certainly not over-capitalised with only £4,000 behind him. But the direct cause of his failure was that too many charter transactions suggest a tottering human pyramid. The airline operator of inclusive holiday flights is directly involved with the public who book the holidays, the organiser offering the holiday, the agency arranging the holiday, and the hotelier providing the holiday. If any one member of that pyramid falls down he takes the rest with him.

Bright had £40,000 worth of bounced cheques to show how often the pyramid collapsed financially during his one season of operations. The owner of the aeroplane is always in a vulnerable position because he provides by far the most expensive part of the whole operation, and tends to get paid last of all.

One other reason for World Wide's failure was the delay in being paid by Sabena for the Congo charter. The delay was no more than is usual in dealing with any very large-scale commercial establishment having a complex system of accountancy and not favouring quick cash transactions. Bright was kept waiting for several weeks, even months, for sums of up to £25,000, never doubting that he would be paid but not getting it in time to keep up with his overheads. That meant borrowing money to meet his wage and fuel bills, and that meant yet another bill when the interest had to be paid. Without the bounced cheques, Bright would have been able to hold on for the Congo money. The two things together were too much for a company with £4,000 of capital and no assets.

Within a year of World Wide Aviation disappearing from the scene, the Congolese Republic had formed its own air force. The officer in charge of flying operations was Captain Joseph Viatkin, the Russian-Dutch-Scottish charter pilot who became one of the personalities of the Berlin airlift. Now, he directed movements between twenty-two airstrips scattered through the African tropics, attracted like many other sky tramps by the hint of adventure and the firm promise of £100 a week. The "Force Aerienne Congolais" began with a fleet of four aircraft, three DC-3's and a DC-4 leased from British companies. Viatkin had a personal reason for preferring to fly the DC-4. Bill Bright and he had been in the R.A.F. together and had crossed paths many times on charter work. The DC-4 in which Viatkin showed the Congolese flag to its troubled people was the same aircraft in which his old friend gave the Canadian Customs man a lift to London, via the Arctic Circle.

Capt. Joseph Viatkin (left of picture) veteran of the Berlin Airlift, was flying with the Congolese air force in 1962—in time to help in a very different form of airlift.

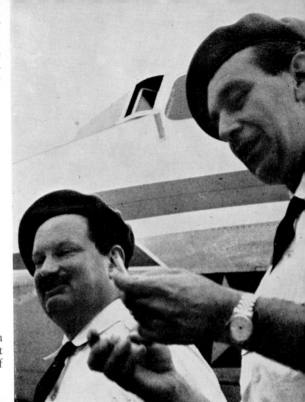

BELOW: Nuns rescued from the turmoil of civil war wait to be flown to the safety of Leopoldville.

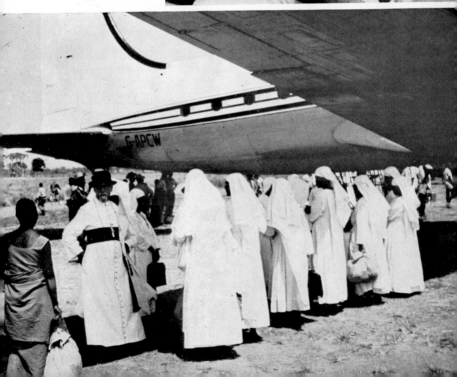

Charter work has an endless variety. RIGHT: Lloyd International fly horses of the Swiss equestrian team to the Olympic Games in Tokyo.

BELOW: Charter operator Cliff Luxton (left) hears TV personality Hughie Green re-construct their escape from Russian fighters in the Berlin air corridor. Journalist Jim Preston (right) was their passenger.

Helicoptor pilot Alan Green (TOP) switches to a horse between flights in the mountains of Iran.

ABOVE: One of the Bristow Helicoptors fleet engaged in off-shore oil operations in the Arabian Gulf.

Freddy Laker (right), once a scrap dealer and now managing director of British United Airways, Britain's largest independent airline. The movements of his world-wide fleet of aircraft are plotted at Gatwick Airport by Captain Cecil Bebb (below)—the charter pilot who helped to make history in July, 1936, when he flew General Franco from exile to start the Spanish Civil War.

CHAPTER TEN

Pilot to the Heavenly Host

CLIFF Luxton was out of bed at five a.m., two hours earlier than he needed to get up for his flight from London Airport on Saturday morning, March 30, 1963. He had taken his wife a cup of tea in bed, washed, shaved, put on his uniform, packed his travelling bag and taken his wife a second cup by 5.30. From then until six o'clock he paced the living room of his flat in Denham, opened his travelling bag at least six times to check the contents, and tried unsuccessfully to force some cereals down into a stomach with the hollow restlessness of a sea-shell held to the ear. That restlessness had become a definite twitch deep inside him by the time he was driving towards London Airport and the aeroplane waiting for him there.

Luxton, a small deliberate Welshman with a long expressive nose, recognised that twitch and all the other symptoms as familiar travelling companions. They had set out with him on every flight he had ever undertaken in over thirty years of flying, ranging from wartime bomber raids to crop-spraying, from Atlantic crossings to Mediterranean holiday tours. He presumed that expectant mothers had the same kind of apprehension on the way to the delivery ward no matter how many times they had been there before.

Turning into the airport, Luxton drove his car past the huge terminal buildings, the sprawling hangars and workshops, the offices of independent companies with world-wide contracts. He picked his way between the litter of giant air-liners, stretched out dead-eyed and stiff in the grey early morning like fish on a slab, and headed for the small executive aircraft which wasn't even his. It was an Aero Commander merely on hire for the day.

Owning an aeroplane has come to have the social status of running a string of racehorses. Which makes owning a *fleet* of aircraft outrank all but film producers and minor royalty (top royalty having an air fleet of their own called the Queen's Flight). The scrapbooks of aviation are thick with photographs of proud operators reviewing their massed aircraft, carefully arranged to a perspective suggesting half as many more aircraft than there really are. One pre-war company issued an aerial picture of its fleet of eight aircraft drawn up on the runway with a solemn explanation that only seven could be seen because the photograph was taken from the eighth.

This Napoleonic urge to stretch profitable one-plane companies into precarious empires in the sky has long been a major cause of disaster—physical and financial. Passengers and crews have died in too many heavily mortgaged aircraft serviced by too few ground staff with not enough spares. Investors have been ruined by the depreciation of surplus aircraft standing around on the runway waiting for the next group photograph. And very often those same aircraft next appeared swelling the ranks of a mass review by an even more ambitious rival.

All this was a temptation Luxton had resisted with the modest contentment of a man practising monogamy in a harem. Even in the immediate post-war years when a surplus R.A.F. bomber could be bought for £100, he decided that flying aeroplanes was a better proposition than owning them. He preferred to work as a freelance, finding his charter business first and then hiring somebody else's aircraft to do the job. The arrangement meant that the little Welshman was no social threat to his film producer neighbours in Denham, by never actually owning a single plane let alone a fleet, but it also meant that the worry of how to make the aircraft pay for themselves between charters belonged to somebody else.

One of the hangars he drove past on his way across the airport was where nine hundred employees of Cunard Eagle Airways had been called together by Harold Bamberg earlier that month and assured they were not going to be declared redundant or taken over by British United Airways.

"I know how unsettled you have all been since we lost our North Atlantic licence," he said, speaking from one of the maintenance platforms. "We also lost some of our best people when B.O.A.C. took over eighteen of our crews at the time of their arrangement with Cunard. And our European operations have been allowed to dwindle. As long as we were owned 100 per cent. by Cunard there was nothing I could do about it. That is why I have now bought back control of the company to try and put the Eagle back in the air in the biggest possible way."

The applause was for the squire returning from the wars to restore his estate. Harold Watkins, standing at the back of the hangar, felt like one of the oldest retainers. He had been with Eagle for more than half of the twenty-three years since he first flew from that frozen lake in Finland. The Eagle fleet, of which he was still chief pilot, now resembled the Finnish air force in one respect, having only seven aircraft and nine hundred people involved in flying them.

In little more than a year from Bamberg's speech in the hangar, Watkins would be recruiting fresh crews to operate fourteen Britannias, seven Viscounts and two DC-4's, with six BAC-111 jets on provisional order.

The company was to buy control of Starways, the private airline operating from Liverpool, win an important Far Eastern trooping contract from Freddy Laker's B.U.A. and compete with B.E.A. along thirty-two scheduled services in Europe. Harold Bamberg had come back to the centre of the gaming table, bidding for power with all the discreet flamboyance of the golden eagles which decorate the walls, the table lamps, the cigarette boxes and the ashtrays of his West End penthouse.

Cliff Luxton had flown with Eagle many times but only on a freelance basis. He was happier on the outside of large organisations. The only hint of a power complex was in the Ruritanian profusion of gold braid about the uniform he designed for himself and his title as managing director of CJL Aviation—which turned out to be a company with a nominal capital of £100, his wife Mabel as the only other director, and a telephone number where he could be reached day or night. The twitch in Luxton's stomach stirred with each ring of that telephone because every new job was a new idea, flying a different plane, with fresh places to go. His stomach relaxed only at the moment a flight actually began and he could become absorbed in the familiar procedure which embraces the strangest cockpit.

He climbed into the Aero Commander at London Airport that morning and admired the sheer beauty of £50,000-worth of small aeroplane. President Kennedy was using the same model as his personal aircraft and Luxton rated it the finest piston-engined executive plane in the world. He began to wish the day's flight was to somewhere more exotic than Douglas, Isle of Man. Then he remembered that the most colourful charters can begin with little glimpse of what really lies ahead.

There was the large, well-dressed Dutchman, who walked into Luxton's office one winter day in 1951 and asked him to provide thirty-six walkie-talkie outfits and two powerful short-wave transmitters. Luxton was based at Croydon Airport then and had taken to dealing in war surplus to maintain the fortunes of CJL Aviation during lean periods of flying. This was an exceptionally lean period. The company's bank balance stood at 4s. 8½d.

"What price would you ask for that much equipment?"

asked van Leeuwen. "Always supposing you know where to get it."

Luxton knew where to get it. There were short-wave transmitters and generators going cheaply at an American base in Lancashire and the Canadian forces were selling off ex-paratroop walkie-talkies. He reckoned £200 would buy the lot, plus £150 for transport and other overheads plus whatever he could get for his own time and trouble.

" Might get away with a thousand pounds," he said, preparing for some hard bargaining. Van Leeuwen opened his brief case, took out £1,000 in £5 notes and handed them over.

" I was a Dutch naval officer," he said. " I know you were an air force officer. We are both gentlemen. I trust you will have the equipment here by the end of the week."

Four days later, Luxton had the whole consignment safely installed in a workshop he rented at Croydon. In the early hours of the following morning, he had to get out of bed to take a personal telephone call from Amsterdam. Van Leeuwen came on the line, congratulated Luxton on his efficiency and added: " There's a KLM Convair leaving London at 9.15 a.m. A ticket has been bought in your name. Will you please come to Amsterdam. I want to talk to you."

Luxton thought of the easy money he had made in the past four days and happily accepted a free trip to Amsterdam. He was met off the plane at Schipol Airport, driven into the Hague in a Mercedes saloon, installed in a luxurious hotel room, and given £20 in Dutch currency as " spending money." That evening he was entertained to dinner by van Leeuwen and two of his friends, one a newspaper editor, the other the chairman of a famous brewery company.

" We have a very fine aeroplane, a DC-3," said the brewer. " We would like you to come to Geneva with us to see it and then sell it for us at a good price."

Luxton could not see any possible connection between this proposition and the radio equipment back at Croydon but he was enjoying his new standard of living. Next day, he joined them on a Swissair flight to Geneva and inspected a superb specimen of a DC-3 which was introduced as belonging to the brewer but having been on loan to the Swiss Red Cross.

"I can get you somewhere in the region of ten to twelve thousand pounds," said Luxton. The Dutchmen were easily delighted and left for Amsterdam having pressed upon him a first-class air ticket to London, two packets of nylons for his wife, and large boxes of chocolates for his two children.

"Can't say I understand this at all," Luxton told his wife when he arrived home with the presents. At the back of his mind was an idea that the Dutchmen were involved in a big construction project in Africa or the Far East. The radio equipment would be useful for linking a series of scattered labour gangs. They were probably selling the DC-3 to raise money for a more suitable aircraft for this kind of work.

Next morning Luxton began to make inquiries about possible customers for the plane. He heard that a Canadian by the name of Green was in the United Kingdom to buy a DC-3 for an American company. He traced Green to the offices of Scottish Aviation at Prestwick, told him about the plane by telephone, and Green expressed immediate interest. Luxton put in a call to Amsterdam and arranged with van Leeuwen to have the DC-3 flown over to Croydon the same day. Green was already at the airport when the plane arrived for his inspection. The Canadian was slim and fair-haired with eager, almost boyish eyes and a sharp line in business talk.

"It's a deal at £12,000," he said, "subject to examination by an engineer, satisfactory proof of the title of ownership, and a chance to study the log book to establish any accident history."

Luxton passed on these conditions to Amsterdam and went home to await developments. At 1 a.m. the next morning he was out of bed to take another Continental call from van Leeuwen—this time from Brussels. "There are tickets reserved for you and Mr. Green on the KLM flight to Schipol Airport this morning," he said. "The sale can be completed when you reach Holland."

Luxton and Green duly arrived in Amsterdam, were met by the same Mercedes and taken to the same hotel in the Hague. Van Leeuwen greeted them in the expansive foyer and ordered drinks at a table which commanded a view of the main entrance. It was then that the business took a furtive turn which would have amused Luxton had not van Leeuwen's manner been so earnest.

The Dutchman broke off a pleasantly formal conversation with Green to lean across the table towards Luxton. "Mr. Luxton," he said, "when you have proved we can trust you implicitly I can reveal exactly the enterprise on which my friends and I are engaged. But first, I want you to do something for me tonight. In a few moments a man will come through the door of this hotel. He won't look at us or talk to us but he belongs to our organisation. He is a courier of ours and tonight he is taking something very valuable to Brussels by train. We have reason to believe his mission is going to be interfered with on that train. We want you to follow him, watch what happens and act on your own discretion."

Green's first reaction had also been to treat this cloak-and-dagger talk as some kind of joke. But now the smile on his face had grown wary as if this was turning into a joke of doubtful taste. Luxton was aware of Green's feet shuffling under the table and he tried to reconcile van Leeuwen the conspirator with the brisk businessman who arrived at Croydon or the friendly character who sent him home with nylons and chocolates. Before he could think of a suitable question, van Leeuwen gave a quick nod in the direction of the hotel entrance. "This is the man," he said.

Luxton looked at the man who walked into the foyer, walked past their table without a blink of recognition, sat down at another table some twenty feet away and ordered a drink. He was about fifty, grey haired, wore horn-rimmed spectacles, was well-dressed. He placed a brief-case and his homburg on the seat beside him while waiting for the drink. Luxton would normally have imagined him to be a Civil Servant. If the man knew van Leeuwen, he ignored him in a convincingly natural way, sitting at a table which must have been carefully chosen to give Luxton the best possible view of the man he was to follow.

"Will you do this for us?" van Leeuwen asked. "It is important you do."

There was an uneasy pause before the pilot said: "If it is so important I must know more of what all this is about." Further shuffling from Green seemed to remind van Leeuwen of the third person at the table. His reaction was to call for the Mercedes to be brought to the front of the hotel to take the Canadian to meet the brewer. "He has all the documents," said van Leeuwen. "You can complete the deal with him. It is his aeroplane, after all."

Green went reluctantly. He did not like to leave his companion alone in a scene set for some sort of espionage. Furthermore, he did not relish the idea of going off alone to an unknown rendezvous with another member of the conspiracy. "I'm a man of quick decisions," said van Leeuwen, pleasantly as ever, but with an urgency to his mood. "You have seen the plane. If you want it I suggest you take the car outside." Green remembered his reason for being in the Hague and went out to the Mercedes.

Van Leeuwen then suggested that he and Luxton should go to a room in the hotel which had been reserved in his name. Once there he said: "You have met some of the people in our organisation. Do we seem honest and fair?"

"You've been very kind," said Luxton. "Very honourable, most straightforward."

" In that case, can you get me thirty-six parachutes and an aeroplane which can carry all the radio equipment you have bought for us, and twelve men over a distance of two thousand miles without touching down?"

Luxton instinctively recalled a well-informed rumour that Flight Refuelling Ltd. were anxious to sell off one or two of their Lancasters. These had their bomb bays converted into fuel tanks and could fly almost halfway round the world. " I know just the aeroplane and could get it for five or six thousand pounds," said Luxton.

That price promised a handsome profit since he had recently bought a brand new Halifax bomber for another client at £2,500. " But you still haven't told me what I am getting into."

" What I am to tell you is between one officer and a gentleman and another. As you know, the Dutch Government had to withdraw from Indonesia in 1949 and hand over to elements which many Dutchmen believe to be planning the establishment of a Communist regime in the East Indies. I belong to an organisation dedicated to preventing such a regime."

Luxton sat in the hotel room and wondered if what was happening to him now could possibly have any association with the original inquiry about some quite harmless war surplus. His theory about the big construction project had been shattered by the mention of parachutes. Even the best paid labour gangs would not go to work by parachute.

" We need what we have asked you to get for a small expedition which we plan to land in Indonesia and recover certain property worth many millions of pounds. This property belongs by right to Holland and not Indonesia so there is no question of theft involved. I must tell you it might be tough, it might be rough. But all you have to do is obtain the equipment and fly us near enough our objective to use the parachutes. Surely a pilot is not committing a crime if his passengers choose to jump out of his plane in the middle of an apparently peaceful flight. What they do when they reach the ground is their business not his."

Luxton decided not to question this kind of reasoning. He doubted if an Indonesian court would accept it, but his conscience could when he recalled the 4s. 8½d. which was his bank balance until this Dutchman came on the scene. Before then, his only work in weeks had been an air-taxi trip for Morton Aviation. He made just over £2 flying a woman racehorse owner to see her horse run at Nottingham —and won £25 with a desperate gamble on what she told him about the horse on the flight north. The Indonesian venture was going to be a much bigger gamble but it was one he felt he could not refuse.

"All right," said Luxton, "Tell me about this courier you want following."

The little Welshman got into the same carriage as the distinguished Civil Servant type on the night train to Brussels. The carriage was in the form of one long compartment and Luxton chose a seat where he could watch the courier through the reflection of a mirror. He could see the brief-case containing papers which van Leeuwen considered to be vital to the whole scheme. The brief-case lay on the seat at the man's side, not too near to look obviously valuable, not too far away for him to grab should he be attacked. Luxton studied his fellow passengers and tried to decide what an Indonesian secret agent would look like.

Nothing happened on the journey. At Brussels, he saw the courier get into a car which had been described to him by van Leeuwen. He went to a telephone kiosk and called van Leeuwen at his flat in the Hague. "Your courier arrived safely," said Luxton and realised it was the most melodramatic message he had ever sent in his life—including his early career as a radio operator on war-time missions and on epic flights across the Atlantic.

"Very good," said van Leeuwen, and his quiet complacency made Luxton wonder if the whole trip had been some sort of test of his reliability. "Perhaps you will now return to England and get the aeroplane and parachutes."

Luxton was back in the reassuringly drab surroundings of his Croydon office next morning. He telephoned Flight Refuelling to make a bid for one of their Lancasters but learned they had been withdrawn from the market because they were needed for a new charter contract. He next tried B.O.A.C. and inquired about a fleet of Yorks left over from the merger of British South American Airways. B.O.A.C.'s chief sales manager was delighted to offer the pick of the fleet at £5,250. This was slashing Luxton's profit margin on the deal but the Dutchmen had proved good customers and the York would be even better for what they wanted than the Lancaster. The York had a bigger fuselage and would carry the twelve parachutists in much more comfort. Luxton put £250 of his own money as a deposit and began to recruit a crew from among mutual friends who were also finding it a hard winter.

"I can't tell you much more than it's a very special job which is going to be very well paid," said Luxton. "You're on the payroll from the moment you say 'yes'." Two pilots a flight engineer and a navigator were happy to settle for those terms. One of them went to collect the thirty-six brand new parachutes which Luxton had bought at £5 each from a war surplus dealer in the East End of London.

Then came a call from B.O.A.C. to say that the Lancashire Aircraft Corporation wanted to buy the whole fleet of Yorks. If Luxton couldn't pay the balance outstanding on the York he wanted within seven days, it would have to go to Lancashire Aircraft with the others. He telephoned van Leeuwen in Holland and asked for the money to be rushed across. "Afraid we can't raise that much cash so quickly," said van Leeuwen. "Try and hang on to the plane for at least a fortnight. We have the money but we just cannot reach it at the moment."

Luxton took a chance and called on Freddy Laker at the

headquarters of his Aviation Traders in Buckingham Palace Road. He and Laker had become drinking acquaintances through meeting at sales of war surplus equipment.

" I hear you are in the market for Yorks," said Luxton. " Well, I've just about the best York there is in the country and you can have it as soon as I've made one flight with her, at the same price I'm paying for it—£5,250. The trouble is I'm short of the odd £5,000 for a couple of weeks until some money comes through."

Laker called in his secretary and wrote out a cheque for £5,000. " Watch what your doing," he said as Luxton went to leave. " Don't go knocking *my* York about, will you?" The plane was formally bought from B.O.A.C. and within a week van Leeuwen had arrived with the money to clear Laker's loan. " But the York is yours when this one trip is over," Luxton promised.

He sensed that the trip was very near when yet another telephone call from van Leeuwen in the small hours of the morning instructed him to take the next Sabena flight to Brussels. A similar Mercedes was waiting at Brussels and this time there was a drive of about an hour along country roads to the south of the city. The journey ended when the car turned into the rear entrance of a hotel in a small village. Luxton glimpsed three more Mercedes parked in a barn before he was led inside the hotel and introduced to a man sitting behind a table in a private room.

Luxton described the man to his wife when he returned home: " My first impression was of immense strength. He had a neck like a bull and short bristly hair and drummed on the table with fingers like great bananas. His shoulders were so broad I thought he was even bigger than van Leeuwen—who was a big man himself. Then this character stood up and I could see he was only about 5 ft. 8 ins., with long muscular arms hanging down almost to his knees like a wrestler. He said, ' I expect you've heard of me. I'm the one they call Turk Westerling!' "

The British Army knew this man as Captain Raymond Westerling, who fought with Australian troops in North Africa and with the British commandoes in the Far East. In Indonesia he was wanted by the authorities as the ruthless leader of his own "Army of the Heavenly Host," a resistance movement based in West Java and pledged to destroy the Republican Government. His exploits had created the colourful image of some kind of jungle Robin Hood.

Westerling's nickname of "Turk" could be traced back to his birth in Istanbul in 1919. His father was a Dutch antique dealer and his mother was French. He married an English nurse from Wolverhampton after a two-week wartime romance which ended in divorce. His hatred for the Indonesians was said to stem from the murder of his second wife, a Eurasian girl, during the war of independence in which he led a Dutch commando against the rebels. Luxton was correct in one observation. Westerling was a professional wrestler for a time before a world war gave him a wider choice of opponents.

Now he sat in the Belgian hotel and outlined to Luxton his plans for continuing his private war with Indonesia. " I know where the so-called Indonesian Government has precious stones worth about five million pounds hidden away up-country in Indonesia," he said, speaking English with a transatlantic accent. "All this equipment you have been gathering for us so efficiently is to enable twelve of us to parachute in and grab these precious stones which rightly belong to Holland. One plan is that you drop us from the plane and then fly straight back to Europe. But we might decide to clear a strip in the jungle and have you come back to pick us up. We'll settle that detail later. I'm sure the whole operation will be very easy and straightforward. But it's only fair that you and your crew should know that somebody might start shooting at you. If you aren't keen, just forget and we'll get another crew."

Luxton flew back from Brussels feeling increasingly apprehensive. Had he allowed himself to drift too deeply into all this? Would the crew want to go through with it once they knew what was in store for them? Twelve hours later, Luxton and one of the pilots he had hired for the expedition were flying back to Brussels in a Consul aircraft hurriedly chartered at Croydon Airport. An even more dramatic telephone call than usual from van Leeuwen had explained that the Belgian authorities were ordering him and Westerling out of the country on the suspicion of activities contrary to international law. " Mr. Westerling cannot fly on a scheduled flight because most of the countries in Europe will not allow him in for fear of complicating diplomatic relations with Indonesia," said van Leeuwen. " Get any available plane and come and fetch us out of here."

Plain clothes policemen and security agents escorted van Leeuwen and Westerling on board the Consul when it landed at Brussels. From there Luxton was instructed by Westerling to make a flight plan for Tangier. At Tangier, the leader of the Army of the Heavenly Host climbed down to earth from the steps of the Consul and waved cheerful goodbyes as the plane took off on the return flight to London, with van Leeuwen still on board. Luxton anticipated immigration difficulties at London Airport after the trouble at Brussels but the Dutchman had a brief interview with a detective in a private room and suggested a telephone to a certain number in the Hague. The call was made. Van Leeuwen was cleared for immigration with smiles all round. Not for the first time, Luxton suspected that the Westerling enterprise had secret backing in high places in Holland.

Luxton asked van Leeuwen if he should pay off the crew now that the plan would have to be called off. " Not at all," said the big Dutchman. " We go ahead and pick up Mr. Westerling somewhere along the way." The relief which had been mounting within Luxton all the way back from Tangier suddenly gave way to deepest gloom. This whole business had got steadily out of hand and yet at this stage there did not seem any way of not getting even more deeply involved. Three days afterwards, he and the crew were at Hurn Airport loading the radio equipment and parachutes into the York. Van Leeuwen had already arranged for the plane to be switched to Dutch registration. Luxton thought the nature of their cargo might cause trouble with Customs when they flew the York across to Amsterdam. But there were no objections from the Customs. Van Leeuwen had seen to that, too.

For the first time, Luxton began to experience genuine alarm. These arrangements were too smooth, too inevitable. It was all beginning to run away with him at a frightening pace—as if he'd handed over control to an automatic pilot and now couldn't get back into the seat himself. The end came when van Leeuwen produced a Dutch crew for the York and asked Luxton to join them on a flight to Czechoslovakia to pick up the firearms for the expedition.

" No," said Luxton, " This is too much. It's getting a bit too tricky with arms coming into it. Quite frankly, I'd rather you left us out of it from now on. Take the York— it's your plane. You've got all the other equipment, too."

Van Leeuwen's charming manner indicated he was not surprised. He gave Luxton £1,000 in £5 notes to pay off the English crew and told him to keep the balance as his own commission. " When we've finished with the York," he said, as they made their farewells, " we'll bring it back to Amsterdam and you can sell it for us to your Mr. Laker."

Luxton was never to see or hear of that York again. He watched the newspapers for many months for stories of Westerling's parachute raid but nothing ever appeared. Then, in 1958, he read that Westerling had disbanded his Army of the Heavenly Host and was living peacefully back in Holland, opening a night club and planning an unlikely career as an opera singer. Van Leeuwen has yet to reappear on the scene.

Luxton had good cause to remember the Westerling affair when he sat in the cockpit of the Aero Commander at London Airport eleven years later and prepared for the flight to the Isle of Man. His client for the day was the Canadian who bought the conspirators' DC-3—the same Mr. Green. Except Luxton and millions of television fans now knew him as Hughie Green, TV's top quizmaster.

Green, once a child star of the music halls, was already something of a show business veteran when Luxton first met him at Croydon Airport. He had starred in Hollywood films and Broadway plays. But he was little known in Britain where the BBC's decision to end his radio talent show, *Opportunity Knocks,* in 1949, led to a five-year difference with the Corporation, culminating in a long and expensive law suit. By 1951, Green, a war-time ferry pilot, had had to take a job as European representative for Atlantic Aviation and it was in that capacity he bought the DC-3 from van Leeuwen's friend.

Luxton and Green kept in touch afterwards. They worked together ferrying ten ex-military Neptunes across the South Atlantic to the Argentine in 1955. Then came commercial television and Green's fame grew with the success of *Double your Money.* Luxton was kept busy providing executive aircraft to take him on business and publicity trips all over Britain and Europe.

The flight to the Isle of Man on the morning of March 30, 1963, was to take Green to a meeting in Douglas. Travelling with him was holiday camp tycoon, Billy Butlin, himself a flying enthusiast and a contestant in the *Daily Mail's* London-Paris air race of 1959, competing in his personal Spitfire.

Green and Butlin joined Luxton on board the Aero Commander in time for take-off at 8.30. The flight took ninety minutes. By two o'clock the meeting was over, and the plane was heading south for Bognor Regis where Butlin was to preside that night over an important charity dinner at one of his holiday camps. Green was at the controls and put the plane down on a private grass-surfaced airstrip adjoining a refrigerator factory about half a mile from the holiday camp. Butlin shook hands and walked towards a car which had been awaiting his arrival outside the factory. He left not realising the plane had landed in a confined space without needing to use its brakes. The wheels dugs into two large patches of boggy ground on touch down and brought the plane to a halt with a skid and slight swerve which Luxton and Green found ominous. They walked across to examine the skid marks and then paced out the 800 yards of the strip while considering how best to make their departure. Luxton noted that a gas-holder more than 100 feet high stood in the middle of a gas-works beyond the far end of the strip, directly on the only available line of take-off.

" The only thing to do," said Green, " is to stick the tail right into the fence at the bottom of the field to give us every possible inch, I'll stand on the brakes and gun the engines like mad, then let her go with a bang. When we reach 70 m.p.h. you give me quarter-flap and she'll come up like a rocket. It's a bloody nuisance about that mud we hit touching down. I'll keep her well over to the other side and we should miss it."

Taxi-ing down to the bottom end of the field the plane twice sank into other patches of mud which they had not noticed. Luxton climbed down each time, stuffed long tufts of grass under the wheels, and pushed and heaved to get the plane clear. Then they reached the end of the field, turned round, revved the engines while the plane strained against its brakes, then suddenly went racing away towards the far fence. At 70 m.p.h. Luxton applied quarter-flap. The extra lift increased the speed to nearly 100 m.p.h. and Green lifted the nose wheel for take-off. At that moment the main wheels dug into another unsuspected patch of bog and the plane's speed fell away. Luxton had visions of the plane trying to tear itself off the ground at low speed and flopping right into the gas-works.

" Cut! Cut! " he said. " She's not going to make it."

As he spoke, Green cut both engines and clapped the brakes full on. The plane slithered off the grass airstrip, crashed through the boundary fence with a tremendous bang, and ploughed into a ditch which seemed to be littered with large blocks of concrete. Luxton felt the plane hit one block and cannon away to hit a second block. The wings fell away and the top of the cabin disappeared. He was already undoing his seat belt when petrol began to spurt in all directions. The plane was still moving forward, tearing itself apart over more concrete blocks. A wheel flew overhead as the undercarriage was torn away. Then what was left of the fuselage came to a halt and Luxton knocked off all the switches before he and Green scrambled clear of a pile of wreckage which had been a £50,000 aircraft. Except for cuts and bruises, they were unhurt.

First on the scene was Billy Butlin. He took them back to the holiday camp and insisted they became his guests for the charity dinner and stayed overnight. Luxton and Green were relieved to have this opportunity of relaxing after a frightening experience. Green spent the evening in deepest depression. A passionate advocate of greater use of light aircraft, he feared that the accident might attract sensational publicity and prove a blow to the whole cause of executive flying. He found little consolation in Luxton's reminders that it was his first accident in many years of flying, that it happened on a recognised operational airstrip, and that their landing at Bognor had been included in the flight plan approved by the air traffic authorities before take-off from London.

Green was more cheerful next morning when they were up early to drive to Kidlington Airport, near Oxford, in a car borrowed from Butlin. He had some business calls to make on the Continent followed by a television show in West Berlin on the following Thursday. Green had intended to travel with Luxton in the Aero Commander which now lay in the rubbish dump. The drive to Kidlington was to find a replacement and they succeeded in hiring a twin-engined Cessna 310. Luxton thought it tactful not to mention exactly why they needed a replacement. They flew the Cessna down to London Airport that afternoon and met there again the following morning. A magazine journalist, Jim Preston, joined them for the trip to cover Hughie Green's television show in Berlin.

Geneva was their first stop for Green to join a business conference. Next day they flew to Stuttgart where Green, still active as an aviation salesman for all his television commitments, spent the evening with a prospective customer for a new jet-engined light aircraft. Shortly after lunch on Tuesday, April 2, the Cessna stood at the end of the runway at Stuttgart Airport and waited for the control tower to pass on the formal approval of the plane's flight plan to Berlin. This had been submitted by Luxton on arrival at the airport and the procedure called for the flight plan to be sent by teleprinter to the Berlin Control Centre. Berlin would then flash back the necessary clearance. Green was to pilot the plane while Luxton acted as radio operator and Preston sat behind.

"We have your clearance, Oscar Kilo," said a voice from Stuttgart Control. "Fly Airway Green I—Frankfurt. Climb and maintain altitude 9,500 ft. After passing Frankfurt contact Berlin Control on frequency 118·1 megacycles. Join the Berlin Corridor at Mansbach. Good day and thank you."

The first stage of the flight went smoothly. Luxton spoke to Frankfurt Control and had his altitude confirmed at 9,500 feet before being handed on to Berlin Control. From Berlin he was assured that he entered the corridor on course at Mansbach and was proceeding down the centre line of the corridor. "We have you nice and clear on our radar, Oscar Kilo. You are clear to Gatow R.A.F. airfield."

At 2.20 p.m. the Cessna was flying above thick cloud and below a deep blue stretch of sky. "This is the first aeroplane I've ever flown in," said Preston. "I never thought flying was so beautiful." Luxton made a routine check of his position with Berlin. "On course and dead centre," came the reply. "You are cleared to Gatow." There was a pause and then the voice added; "Incidentally, you have a stranger approaching fast from behind at five o'clock."

That was Luxton's side of the plane and he turned to look over his shoulder at the white cloud and blue sky beyond. Suddenly a MiG fighter, displaying large red stars on its wings and fuselage, came out of the cloud and flew in front of the Cessna. The MiG rocked its wings and lowered its undercarriage—the international signal for "Follow me and land."

Luxton called up Berlin and asked for instructions. He was advised to stand by and after about twenty seconds he was told: "Oscar Kilo, you are still cleared to R.A.F. field Gatow at 9,500 feet." The MiG repeated its signals when Green held to his course, then the Russian fighter banked steeply to the right and approached the Cessna from behind. As Luxton turned his head, the whole front of the MiG's wings lit up and he could see zig-zags of tracer flash past the cockpit, interspersed with ball ammunition which exploded into puffs of black smoke and sent pieces of shrapnel flying in front of the windscreen.

"Christ, the madman's firing at us," said Green. "Call up Berlin and see what's supposed to be going on." Luxton's call was referred to Berlin military control, there was another long pause and then a fresh voice said: "Oscar Kilo, you are still clear at 9,500 feet to Berlin . . . By the way, our radar screens show another stranger approaching fast at eight o'clock." Luxton looked to the other side and saw a Yak 25, a large twin-jet fighter, flash up out of the clouds to reach an altitude about five or six thousand feet above the Cessna. The Yak pilot then put his plane into a vertical dive to pass immediately in front of the Cessna. The Yak created its sonic boom almost on the nose of the Cessna which was twisted over on its starboard wing tip by the force of turbulence. Gravity forces pulled the fuel away from the port engine which stopped.

The Cessna was falling on its side for 2,000 feet before Green could re-start the port engine and level out. Luxton was frantically calling up Berlin for some practical advice or promise of help and he had to raise his voice as the MiG approached from behind again and opened fire once more. The only response from Berlin was the same baffling, infuriating routine statement: "You are still clear to R.A.F. field Gatow." An emergency was first acknowledged with a firm "Negative! Negative!" when the pilot of a Pan-American airliner further up the corridor called Luxton to say: "Brother, my heart bleeds for you. Try and get in the cloud."

"Negative!" said Berlin. "The Russians will have radar gunsights so the cloud will offer no escape. Try not to take avoiding action too obviously."

Green was visibly exasperated by Berlin's idea of aerial diplomacy. While the MiG kept up its firing from behind, the Yak was now flying from left to right immediately overhead at about 600 m.p.h. Each time the blast from its twin jets left the Cessna rocking like a dinghy in the wake of a torpedo boat. Green hung on to the controls and said: "My bloody mouth's dry Cliff. I don't know how much longer this little crate is going to hang together." Like Luxton, he had lost all sense of time and the distance they had covered along the corridor. Every time the MiG hurtled to the attack, he was cutting back the Cessna's speed to seventy m.p.h. so that the fighter and its tracer went flashing past. He threw the throttle wide open when the MiG turned back to get ready for a fresh attack.

"Oscar Kilo," came a message from Berlin, "You are five miles from R.A.F. field, Gatow. Suggest steep approach through cloud." The Yak was too late to intercept this move and the MiG managed only one burst, splitting the cloud with its red flashes of tracer, before the Cessna burst into clear sky immediately above Gatow airfield. Green went straight in and made a good landing. His humour was restored by the time he had taxied over to where a group of Army and R.A.F. officers were waiting. He appeared from the plane with all the certain sparkle of a television personality and refused to blame the Russians for what happened. "Those planes were hired to do that by a rival quiz show," he said. "I definitely recognised the MiG pilot as Michael Miles . . ."

Behind the scenes, Green was to press for a full explanation of what went wrong with the clearance for the Cessna's flight plan. The Berlin authorities suggested the Russians were challenging the right of private aircraft to use an air corridor which they claimed was allocated to the Allies only for the provision of essential public services to and from West Berlin. Certainly, the Russians refused any promise of safe conduct for the plane out of Berlin once Hughie Green's television programme was completed on Thursday night.

"To be quite frank," an R.A.F. officer told Luxton, "the Russians have indicated pretty firmly that this time they will really shoot that plane out of the sky if it tries to get back along the corridor." The same officer came up with a suggestion when Green and Luxton announced they were not prepared to abandon somebody else's aircraft in the middle of Europe. "Why not take the northern corridor to Hanover?" he said. "It's only sixty miles long—half the distance to Mansbach. Make a dash for it around dawn and you might get clear before the Russians wake up to what's happening . . ."

At 6 a.m. on Saturday, April 6, the Cessna was wheeled out of its hangar at Gatow on the far side of the building from the wood where Russian observation posts record all movement in and out of the airfield. The familiar twitch in Luxton's stomach was of a stronger tension this morning as he climbed on board and sat beside Green. Then the engines started, the plane taxied on to the runway and moved straight into its take-off, leaving the Russians in the wood to strain through their night glasses in the half light and try to decide what kind of aircraft was leaving so suddenly.

The needle of the airspeed indicator was pressing the red danger line at 225 m.p.h. as Green headed the Cessna at tree-top height into the Hanover corridor. He knew that Berlin Control had held off all other traffic but not for the Cessna's convenience. The idea was to keep other aircraft clear of a possible attack by the Russians. Green held the Cessna at an altitude of fifty feet all the way, uncomfortably low for jet fighters and the most awkward height for anti-aircraft systems on the ground. The West German frontier was reached in less than twenty minutes without the slightest interference. Luxton's radio received a message from Hanover Control: "Good morning, Oscar Kilo. Trust you had a very pleasant flight to-day."

Luxton announced Oscar Kilo's successful escape from Berlin with a one-word reply to Hanover Control. "Nuts," said the managing director of CJL Aviation, free for the first time in four days to forget about MiG fighters and Yak jets and tracer bullets and shrapnel. It was just seven months and three weeks since he read an article in *The Times* which solemnly recorded "the passing of the heroic age of aviation."

CHAPTER ELEVEN

Enter the Helicopter

FIVE of the passengers in the speedboat watched impassively as the helicopter clattered towards them across Weymouth Bay. Alan Green, the sixth passenger, assessed its line of approach with the eye of an experienced helicopter pilot and waited for the Westland S51 to take up its position, 500 feet above the speedboat's wake. He was well aware that his whole future in flying would depend on what happened in the next few minutes, four miles out to sea.

Alan Bristow sat at the controls of the helicopter and reflected that the future of a whole industry could depend on the sure aim of the man sprawled full length on the floor of the cockpit. Lt.-Col. L. V. Stewart Blacker, once of the 3rd Turkestan Rifles, squinted through his monocle along the sights of the modified anti-tank gun, protruding from the open doorway of the cockpit, and took aim at the forty-gallon oil drum being towed behind the speedboat on a twenty-foot float.

Blacker had helped to make the gun himself, one of many inventions during a colourful military career in which he worked on the development of the 3.5 inch infantry mortar, introduced firing through the propeller arc to the Royal Flying Corps, and produced the P.I.A.T. anti-tank gun in the most desperate days of World War II.

At 67, he now travelled in a helicopter across Weymouth Bay with the total confidence of the man who took part in the first flight over Mount Everest, back in 1933. The gun in his arms was a variation of the famous P.I.A.T. which he had created in the garden shed of the stately home in Hampshire where he was living in retirement.

Green heard a muffled explosion from the helicopter when Blacker opened fire, then came a clanging impact from behind the speedboat as a missile tore a hole in the oil drum. There was an immediate tightening of interest from Green's five companions in the boat. They watched closely while the helicopter hovered in position for Blacker to fire nine more missiles. Three narrowly missed the drum as it rolled wildly on its float in the wake of the speedboat. The other six were resounding direct hits, the last knocking the drum from its mounting and into the sea. Green sat discreetly apart from the other passengers while they discussed the demonstration with thinly disguised enthusiasm on the way back to shore, and during the drive to a disused naval air station at Henstridge in Somerset. There they were greeted by an obviously excited Bristow. " Gentlemen," he announced, " if that oil drum had been a whale you would have been £2,000 richer after Colonel Blacker's first shot—with six more whales killed in the next ten minutes. All that from two men and one helicopter. Think of the results you would get from sending a whole fleet of helicopters into the Antarctic all using guns like this. They would kill more whales than all the whaling ships of the world put together."

The five men who accompanied Green in the motor boat were the representatives of a Dutch whaling company. But Bristow knew the Scottish, Norwegian and Dutch whaling interests were so closely linked that he was talking to a cross section of the entire industry. He explained how a missile fired from an airborne whaler's gun would electrocute the whale on impact, the harpoon being linked by cable to a powerful generator on board the helicopter. Death would be instantaneous and virtually painless compared with the traditional method of " playing " a harpooned whale like a ninety-ton salmon on the end of half-a-mile of cable from the catcher-boat's foredeck, a hazardous procedure taking anything from a few minutes to two hours. Whales killed from the air would be automatically inflated by a cartridge of compressed gas contained within the body of the missile, and left floating on the surface to be collected by tow-boats and brought to the factory ship at its convenience.

"Obviously there are many snags that still need sorting out," said Bristow. "That's why I asked you to come down and see the show. We need your financial backing to go ahead and perfect this idea. But I do believe we have shown you enough to-day to prove beyond all doubt that it could be something like ten times more productive to kill whales from a helicopter. If we can hit an oil drum seven times out of ten at a range of 100 yards we can fire our missile into the stomach of an eighty-foot whale every time."

The Dutchmen came to Weymouth with the stoic reserve of sailors whose every voyage lasts six months. They went home, carrying Bristow's burning eagerness between them. And long after they had gone, he stood by the helicopter, assuring Green and Blacker that the incident out in the bay would revolutionise an industry which had not come up with anything as dramatic since the Norwegian Svend Foyn invented the heavy calibre harpoon gun in 1865.

Listening to Bristow's salesmanship, Green was reminded of the first time he met the man who was now his employer. Sub.-Lieut. A. G. Green of the Fleet Air Arm, a reluctant transfer to helicopters from the fighter-bombers which he considered the "real hot stuff," was posted to a detachment of 771 Squadron at Portland in 1945 and told to report to Sub.-Lieut. Bristow. In front of an old seaplane hangar, housing the Sikorsky R4 helicopters mounted on floats, he was received by an aggressive, prematurely bald young man with the words: "Take this brush and sweep the seaweed from this slipway." Bristow had little regard for the niceties of naval discipline where his helicopters were concerned. He gave his fellow officer the task of driving a fifteen-cwt.

Bedford truck which towed the helicopters out of the water, up the slipway and into the hangar. Green, an inexperienced driver, was once so absorbed with the ponderous behaviour of the truck that he began to tow the helicopter into the hangar before Bristow, the pilot, had time to switch off the engine and stop the rotor blades. According to Green, the Wrens at Chatham afterwards complained about the language which rang out from the cockpit.

Bristow's concern for his precious machine gave no hint that he, too, was an unwilling convert from fixed wing aircraft. In 1944 he was switched from fighters to become one of the Fleet Air Arm's first helicopter pilots. He served with the Merchant Navy earlier in the war and had been torpedoed four times. That seemed to his superiors an excellent qualification for this rather eccentric form of flying machine which they then envisaged as a secret weapon for combating the U-boat menace in the Atlantic. Bristow flew a helicopter for the first time and embraced its possibilities with a passion which Igor Sikorsky himself could scarcely have matched on September 14, 1939, when he finally established the helicopter as a legitimate form of air transport instead of a flying freak of no real purpose.

Seven years after Sikorsky's historic flight, Lieut. Bristow stood on the slipway at Portland, waved the glossy brochure he had received from the manufacturers for America's very latest helicopter, the Sikorsky S51, and assured Green : " These things are going places. Another six years and they will have created a whole new world of aviation." The prophecy proved as optimistic as Bristow's efforts to force sports-car performance from the fifteen-cwt. Bedford truck he used to drive between the naval station and his home at Osmington Mills. But with the same enthusiasm he did his personal best to make the prophecy come true.

On leaving the Fleet Air Arm, he joined Westland Aircraft as a helicopter test pilot. Four engine failures in one day could not even faintly crumple his evangelical faith in helicopters. Between testing flights, he organised training courses for foreign pilots, and demonstrated to British Army units the use of helicopters in building Bailey bridges from the air.

On September 30, 1948, he landed a Sikorsky S51 in the Place des Invalides, Paris, to complete a journey of forty-six minutes twenty-nine seconds from St. Paul's Cathedral, in London. A Bristol 171 helicopter had carried special mail to Biggin Hill where a Meteor jet went on to Orly airport and the waiting Bristow. This London-Paris record stood until the *Daily Mail* air race of 1959 when it took all the massively elaborate efforts of the Royal Air Force, using more advanced aircraft, to bring the time down to forty minutes forty-four seconds.

Seven months before his triumphal landing in Paris, Bristow went to the rescue of three keepers isolated for twenty-six days in Wolf Rock lighthouse, eight miles off Land's End. He flew from Culdrose aerodrome in the face of a forty m.p.h. gale and in spite of Trinity House reluctance to risk his machine in such conditions. Finally exasperated after forty-eight hours of standing in readiness, he set off on his own initiative at 6 a.m., on the morning of February 7, 1948. At his request, the local lifeboat put to sea to stand by in support of the operation. Bristow thought it simpler not to explain his flight was unauthorised. Arriving at Wolf Rock and meeting the full blast of the gale, he hovered over the top of the lighthouse and began to lower sacks of food on a steel cable. One of the keepers instinctively fastened the end of the cable to the rail of the tower. The helicopter immediately lost all freedom of movement and Bristow sat helplessly at the controls while his machine swung on the end of the line, banging its wheels against the lantern house when caught by sixty m.p.h. gusts. The situation was saved by Bristow's mechanic, Les Swain, who had insisted on joining the flight. He produced a pair of wire cutters, opened the cockpit door, and hung far over the edge of the doorway to reach and cut the cable. Released from its anchorage, the helicopter shot clear of the lighthouse like a cork from a champagne bottle and, with 200 lbs. of food already delivered to the keepers, Bristow returned to Culdrose in the mood to celebrate such a merciful ending to his errand of mercy.

The official reaction at the airfield was distinctly chilly but Bristow was to receive the Royal Aero Club Medal for the mission made in defiance of all normal procedure. Later that year, one of Westlands' senior executives received a punch on the nose when he tried to challenge Bristow's uncompromising attitude to flying. The blow cost Bristow his job and with it all prospect of helicopter work in Britain. Proud to suffer for his cause, he crossed the Channel to become chief pilot and manager of a French helicopter company. Now there were fresh audiences to impress, new customers to win. As chief pilot, he flew a helicopter under the Eiffel Tower, towed water-skiers down the Seine, went crop-spraying, trailed advertising banners, took aerial photographs, did film stunt work, and danced an aerial quadrille in Serge Lifar's " Ballet for Helicopters," performed before 500,000 people at Orly Airport.

As manager, he travelled to Indo-China and sold thirteen helicopters to the French Army, helping to set up its very first helicopter unit. Then, a pilot again, he accepted a temporary commission as a Special Service Officer in the French Foreign Legion and led those same helicopters on desperate missions at the height of France's colonial war in Indo-China. Flying with a bandolier of grenades strapped around his waist and with a tommy-gun under his seat he operated in direct support of the most forward troops and even landed behind the enemy lines to rendezvous with secret agents. Demonstrating that helicopters could be used by night in the most difficult terrain, he put down in a jungle clearing to rescue four wounded survivors of an ambushed patrol. Two of them travelled back to safety outside the cockpit, lashed in stretchers secured to the helicopter skids. The other two were strapped into their seats with Bristow sitting in the middle and praying that his overloaded machine would manage to claw sufficient lift from the unhelpful tropical atmosphere to rise clear of the treetops. The passenger on his left had a bullet lodged in his brain and was spared all the flickering tensions of the flight to a front line hospital where a Frenchwoman surgeon performed the operation which saved his life. Awarded the Croix de Guerre for such exploits, Bristow faced each fresh challenge of the helicopter's versatility with the glee of a preacher about to confound a doubting congregation.

Green proved a zealous if less aggressive disciple of the cause. The one-time invoice clerk at the L.M.S. railway station in Manchester, flew helicopters throughout Europe and Africa as a crop-sprayer for the first five years after leaving the Fleet Air Arm in 1947. Then, in the autumn of 1952 he headed for the Antarctic on board a Norwegian whaling ship. His job was to use a helicopter as a spotter aircraft for the factory ship's attendant fleet of whale catchers. Walrus flying boats had been tried for this role but their use was restricted by bad weather for they could only alight on the water. Green was one of the first pilots to fly a helicopter in the Antarctic. But not the first—as he realised when he received a letter from Bristow, explaining that he had been down there the previous year. The hero of Indo-China had returned to France in 1950 and met a demand that he should take out naturalisation papers if he wished to remain as manager of a French company. Bristow preferred to walk out instead, and went looking for work as a freelance pilot. That was how he came to join the crew of a whaling ship owned by Onassis, the Greek shipping millionaire, and took part in the first successful trials of the helicopter as a whale-spotter. His letter to Green at the start of the following season contained useful advice on flying helicopters in Antarctic conditions and also carried the warning that Bristow would be returning to the scene this year with a rival Norwegian whaling ship. The two ex-Fleet Air Arm colleagues were not to meet in the Antarctic but Green was called from bed at six o'clock one morning in the first half of the long voyage to the whaling grounds and taken to the radio cabin to hear Bristow's voice boom across several thousand miles of ocean: "Where are you, Green? I've put in three hours flying already this morning. You can't move around here for dead whales."

When Green's ship moved further south into the latitude of days without night he was soon making the same kind of early start as a matter of routine. A 3 a.m. briefing by the whaling manager would summarise the whereabouts of the catcher-boats and choose the fresh area to be surveyed from the air before Green climbed into his helicopter as it sat on its landing platform, firmly lashed down against the heavy Antarctic swell. The machine remained secured while the rotor built up to maximum revs. Then, at the moment when the ship reached the highest point of its see-saw motion, the helicopter engineer released the picketing device and Green rose sharply above the cluttered, industrial outline of the 23,000-ton factory ship. She bristled with derricks, cranes, winches, masts and aerials like a slab of dockyard accidentally put to sea. The slipway to receive the dead whales was slashed through the stern with the blunt precision of a railway cutting. In front of the twin funnels was the so-called Hell's Gate, dominating the main deck where a 100-ton whale could be completely dismembered in the space of half-an-hour. Green knew that the same deck would be swilling with blood by the time he returned from his flight.

The helicopter turned away to the south-east, flying at 500 feet above a Mediterranean-blue sea. Whaling takes place during the Antarctic summer and the temperature is normally little lower than freezing point. On this December morning the sun was so bright three or four hours before it would be dawn in Britain that Green had to pull down the dark visor of his flying helmet. He flew over the green and blue cathedrals of icebergs, some up to 200 feet high and half-a-mile long. Penguins shuffled to the edge of the icebergs as he went past and their flippers flickered with excitement.

It was easy to imagine the penguins as the dapper little people that their appearance suggested. They were the only hint of native humanity in all this bleak, barren continent. Green had touched down in the middle of the Arabian desert and found a crowd of inquisitive Arabs around his helicopter within ten minutes. He had force landed in the African jungle and had been greeted by the local missionary out for a walk. But now he flew into the terrible loneliness of Antarctica, feeling as apart from the rest of the world as a spaceman in orbit round some frozen planet. " The time to worry," Green thought, " is when you find yourself waving back to the penguins."

He came across the first of the whales near the edge of the ice-pack, where it stretched with a dazzling glitter into the white blur of a far horizon. The whale was blowing its vapour twenty-five to thirty feet into the air so that steam seemed to be leaking from beneath the sea. Then Green drew overhead and looked down upon the most graceful monster known to creation. This was also the largest monster in creation—the blue whale, as big as twenty-five elephants, its 100 to 120 tons making it twice the size of the more northerly sperm whale which inspired the fanciful legends of Herman Melville's *Moby Dick*. Green admired, as always, the perfect streamlining of the blue whale's body, the dark, blue-grey colouring shown to the sky. Then the huge creature leapt clear out of the water with the exuberance of a young salmon and displayed the delicate pink and white of its stomach before returning to the sea with the clean plunge of an Olympic high diver. A few seconds later the point of its entry smoothed into a circle of oily calm water which lingered as the whale swam on. This was the " slick," what the hunters knew as whales' footprints. A flick of the whale's tail caused this same effect each time it submerged after surfacing to blow and betrayed its course as obviously as if it grew legs and tried to scuttle to safety across the Antarctic snows.

Blue whales do not usually swim in large groups and the helicopter continued to the east in search of more numerous targets. A horseshoe-shaped bay in the ice provided what Green was looking for—ten fin whales, each about seventy-five feet in length, swimming within their Antarctic lagoon in a blissful school. He called up the factory ship and began to recite a sequence of numbers from his code for the day. Radio communication was on an open frequency and great care was observed to prevent rival whalers from intercepting messages from the helicopter. Even negative reports were helpful to the opposition in sparing them the trouble of investigating an empty area. News of sighting a whole school of fin whales, the second largest variety, would be accepted as an open invitation to join the chase.

"Nine, three, five . . ." Green began in the day's sequence for "I am among whales." Then he caught sight of another larger school and something of his excitement must have shown in his voice. "Forget the code," called the factory manager. "If there are that many whales just give us a bearing to steer and the catchers will get there as soon as they can."

Green began to circle above the whales and let down his trailing aerial to transmit his homing signal. Within an hour the first of a dozen catchers came steaming into sight at about fifteen knots. These were trim little vessels of 700 tons with a railed-in catwalk between the bridge and the harpoon gun in the bow. The catcher's captain is also its gunner, almost always a Norwegian and an acknowledged celebrity of the industry.

The whales were unaware of the helicopter's presence overhead. Green had once accidentally dropped a smoke float and hit a whale on the nose but it swam on undisturbed. Now, as the catchers closed in, the whales sensed the propeller vibrations in the water and began to swim faster and faster in all directions. The faster they swam, the more often they had to surface to breathe, the more streams of vapour attracted the catchers, the more slicks trod across the water to give away their escape routes. Green looked down on the slaughter which followed with the hopeful revulsion of a man instinctively on the side of the whales, always hoping they would learn not to run away but submerge and stay still until the catchers went away. Instead, the 1½-cwt. harpoons plunged deep in the whales' bodies at a range of 50 yards and tore great wounds when a grenade exploded three great barbs into the flesh. Killer harpoons finished off each dying whale before it was winched to the side of the catcher. The body was then inflated with compressed air and left to be collected later, a little red flag planted on each whale to identify its owners by right of killing. A dozen whales had been killed by the time Green began his return flight to the factory ship and the little red flags were flying from so many grey and bleeding mounds that he felt he was passing over a flooded golf course. He tried to remember where he had read something about " if whales could only scream we'd never shoot another whale."

Before his first Antarctic expedition was over Green had grown to admire the high skill and business efficiency of whaling even if his sympathies remained with the creatures who ended up in the vast cooking pots beneath Hell's Gate with the stench of a million fish and chip shops frying on bad oil. He never complained about the stench. Like other helicopter pilots he experienced the sensation of utter blindness in one of the Antarctic's sudden thick fogs and had his calculations of the factory ship's position confirmed by the distinct smell of bubbling whale oil which reached him at a range of twelve miles.

The blank vastness of the Antarctic tested a pilot's confidence in his instruments. Flying one of the small Hiller helicopters with an endurance of no more than 4½ hours even carrying extra fuel tanks, Green was always conscious that a navigational error could mean a forced landing in the sea with the nearest catcher perhaps several hours away. He wore a rubberised immersion suit, sealed at the wrists, ankles and neck, but knew he would not survive for long in Antarctic water. The alternative was landing on an iceberg, but the danger here was the overwhelming sheer whiteness of an iceberg as the pilot made his approach. He could lose all sense of position and direction in a sudden white-out. Bristow once had to put down on an iceberg and reported the sensation of being lowered into a bowl of milk. While he sat in his machine and waited for help to come he heard the creaking of the iceberg as it prepared to split in two. All he could do was wait to see if his half would roll over when the break occurred, plunging the helicopter to the bottom of the sea. When the iceberg finally cracked apart, his portion stayed firmly upright and he watched the other half turn a majestic somersault.

Green remembered Bristow's experience the day he came to the end of a patrol along the edge of the icepack and his Automatic Direction Finder indicated that he should head into the ice to reach the factory ship. His own sense of direction suggested this must be wrong even though the glaring loneliness of the ice could have led him on to completely the opposite course, even though the ADF needle pointed firmly the way he should go. Green had to decide between his instincts and the basic rule of flying that a pilot should always have trust in his instruments. It was not a narrow choice. The needle and his mind were pointing in totally opposite directions. If he chose wrongly he would be flying 150 miles over the edge of the world of survival. Green had an idea that he might have lost his ADF aerial which would mean the direction of the instrument's needle bore no relation to the homing signal transmitted from the factory ship. The only way to check the aerial would be to put down on the ice and see if it was still there. Green was reluctant to do this. He always thought of the icepack as the backyard of Hell, tempting in its beauty but cruel and destructive. Bristow's tale of the white-out effect indicated a strong risk of misjudging any landing on the ice and wrecking the helicopter, radio and all. The catcher boats would never find him then. On the other hand, he could fly on without checking the aerial and if he went the wrong way he would be forced down when he finally ran out of fuel.

Making a glum study of the icebergs below to see if one conveniently resembled the flight deck of an aircraft carrier, Green noticed an iceberg near the far horizon which carried two tall glistening spires of ice. " Why that's the one like Cologne Cathedral," he thought. " I flew over that on the way out so home must be that way, at least." Once over and beyond Cologne Cathedral, Green looked ahead and picked out a long, thin, lop-sided iceberg he also remembered from the outward flight. From there he caught a distant glimpse of an iceberg whose wedding cake silhouette was also familiar. In this way he made his way safely back to the factory ship in complete contradiction of his ADF instrument, which was afterwards found to have lost its aerial as he suspected. Green could fly home from memory because the helicopter pilots were expected to look for icebergs of distinctive shape to use as landmarks for catchers being called to a sighting of whales. An iceberg was rarely of the same shape or in the same place for more than a day but this was enough to help whalers closing in on a pack of whales. In Green's case, the Antarctic's spectacular ice formations saved him from the most hazardous dilemma he faced in two seasons of whaling.

Between seasons, Green met Bristow back in England and first heard his revolutionary idea for shooting whales from helicopters. A company, called Air Whaling Ltd., was formed in 1954. Bristow was the managing director, Alan Green the chief and only pilot. George Russell Fry came as financial manager, and Jack Woolley, Bristow's engineer in the Antarctic, joined as technical director. Andre de Geiter, a young Frenchman, who had been Green's mechanic, parted company to become a helicopter pilot himself—and a spectacular flying career was to be cut short most ironically when he died in his bed during the Agadir earthquake.

Fry and Woolley specialised in the unspectacular earthbound aspects of the helicopter business although their

contributions were to prove every bit as dramatic as those
of the fliers. Fry, quiet and precise, went back to his City
desk after the war as a partner in an old-established firm
of accountants with a very special gold watch to keep him
punctual for appointments, including the one which brought
him Alan Bristow as a client. The watch was one of six sent
to Bomber Command by an anonymous South American
admirer to be presented to the pilots who made the most
raids on Berlin. Squadron Leader Fry of 103 Squadron
qualified easily for the watch. As an accountant, he faced
only difficulties in helping Bristow found his company.
Bristow had no money, no assets, no contracts. Bankers
regarded helicopters with the gravest suspicion and insurance
companies were openly horrified. " His plans excited all my
old flying enthusiasms," said Fry. " But the economics of
the thing scared me stiff." By City standards, Fry's early
missions to raise credit for Bristow were as hazardous as his
wartime visits to Berlin. But he recorded the same stubborn
sequence of success and, once actively in business, the company was never to know another financial crisis. For Fry,
however, there was one casualty in the course of his self-
styled " bank-raids." He lost his Berlin gold watch somewhere
along the way.

Jack Woolley started his working life as an aircraft
draughtsman and became a helicopter engineer to see the
world. He worked for Pest Control on crop spraying operations in France, Switzerland, the Sudan and South Africa
before joining Bristow in 1952 to go to the Antarctic. Air
Whaling's first contract sent him back to the Antarctic the
next season. He went with Green, supervising newly-trained
two-man crews of four Westland S55 helicopters bought by a
Scottish whaling company. It proved a disappointing winter
and there were no sensational results even with four long-
range machines out looking for whales. Woolley returned to
find Bristow more convinced than ever that the aircraft should
have harpoon guns of their own instead of merely spotting.
Using his drawing office experience, and improvising experi-

ments in ballistics, Woolley prepared a variety of plans for an aerial weapon. One idea was for a gun firing a harpoon loaded with curare, the deadly poison used by the blow-pipe natives of South America. Calculations based on the amount of curare needed to kill a twelve-stone man sought to establish the quantity required to dispatch a ninety-ton whale. Then a close analysis of the whale's blood system showed the vast creature's circulation to be so leisurely that it would have time to submerge and swim a distance of several miles before succumbing to the poison.

Research switched to a harpoon which killed instantly by electrocution. Here the snag was developing a generator light enough for the helicopter and powerful enough to kill the whale. Even Fry could not raise money for this scale of development without proof that the whaling industry would accept the new method. Bristow, impatient to obtain some reaction, decided to go ahead with a rudimentary form of gun and at least demonstrate the principle of harpooning from the air.

He interested Col. Blacker in the project and the man who invented his first mortar as a device for firing croquet balls eagerly modified his P.I.A.T. gun to kill dummy whales instead of tanks. The first trials were carried out with a fixed target on Bristow's airfield at Henstridge. Then came the highly successful demonstration in Weymouth Bay, in July 1955, leaving Bristow, Green, Fry and Woolley to wait for the official verdict of the Dutch observers with the nervous impatience of men on the brink of great things. Charter operators of fixed-wing aircraft were finding it increasingly difficult to stay in business in their traditional markets, and here were helicopters—so often dismissed by their critics as expensive toys—all set to move into a £20,000,000-a-year industry. If a whaling gunner could earn nearly £5,000 in three months using the relatively primitive method of a harpoon gun mounted on a boat capable of fifteen knots and needing a crew of twelve, how much more would a two-man helicopter crew earn using a gun which went looking for whales at 80 m.p.h.?

The whalers' verdict, when it came, was bitter and crushing. The industry, they explained, had been unable to expand in recent years and was facing signs of a recession. They just could not afford the large capital needed to develop the principle of a helicopter harpoon into a commercial proposition. In any case, they would be producing something which could mean that the world's whaling fleets would be rendered obsolete; there would be mass unemployment of whaling crews, and the national economy of Norway in particular might well suffer a severe blow. Bristow tried hard to show how the old whaling methods would be replaced by a more efficient, more prosperous new industry. When that argument failed he went from one whaling company to another, hoping to find someone prepared to lead the way. Fry furnished him with detailed figures indicating an increased profit margin of at least forty per cent. But the whalers of Europe are a tightly bound, conservative fraternity with a strong sense of loyalty. They all agreed the helicopter harpoon seemed a splendid idea but nobody was prepared to fire upon the established pattern of whaling.

Finally, the International Whaling Commission announced that helicopters being used for killing whales would be classified as catchers and companies employing these helicopters would have to reduce their fleet of catcher-boats accordingly. None of the whaling companies, it was clear, would ever agree to committing themselves to this untried method from the skies at the risk of surrendering numerical superiority to their traditional rivals on the sea.

Even Bristow, a salesman with the professional high-pressure optimism of a boxing promoter, finally had to admit defeat. He could not go ahead without the support of the whalers.

Green began to think Wilbur Wright was not far wrong when he wrote to a friend in 1906: " Like all novices we began with the helicopter but soon saw it had no future use and dropped it. The helicopter does with great labour only what the balloon does without labour and is no more fitted than the balloon for rapid horizontal flight."

In the summer of 1955 Green was left wondering just what sort of thing the helicopter *was* fitted for. Ten years after the war the charter aeroplane was having to settle down to the respectability of long-term contract work and building up its own scheduled services. The helicopter desperately needed to find some real significance and purpose of its own.

At one conference, Bristow sat across an empty desk from Fry and said: " We have a company, we have an organisation, we have ideas. All we need is some business." An uncertain future was resolved when an oil company offered a contract for maintaining and operating two helicopters which they had based in the Arabian Gulf. The machines were to ferry drilling crews and equipment between the Sheikhdom of Qatar and an off-shore drilling rig forty-five miles out to sea. Bristow accepted the contract and Green went out to the Middle East as chief pilot of the operation. Helicopters were not new to this kind of work in America, but they were being tried for the first time in the Middle East.

Green and his team quickly built up to a daily timetable of flights and demonstrated the reliability of helicopters as a permanent link between the shore and rig. They carried in men, tools, spares, and food. They brought out sick and injured workmen—a tremendous boost to morale in a hazardous operation with hospital now only a half-hour flight away instead of a five-hour trip by launch, weather permitting. The helicopters were turned back by weather only once in the first six months. During one period of four weeks, boats reached the rig on only two occasions. A helicopter was on board the night the rig began to break up in a sudden storm, in December, 1955. The helicopter took off for the shore with eight of the technicians packed in the cabin. Before it could return for more survivors the superstructure of the rig was swept into the sea, with the loss of twenty-two lives.

That meant the suspension of the Qatar contract but the oil company was well impressed by the work of the helicopters and transferred them to a seismic survey being under taken in the mountains of Iran. Helicopters had always been considered suspect in high altitude operations at high temperatures. Green cheerfully disproved another fallacy.

In 1957 Bristow Helicopters, as the company was now known, won a contract to carry out a helicopter service for off-shore drilling at Dass Island in the Arabian Gulf. This time Bristow had to provide the machines and he bought the first two helicopters to be owned by his company, Westland Widgeons. These were a development of the old Sikorsky S51, once again the very model which had inspired his ambitions as a young naval officer on the slipway at Portland. Within a few months he had bought more helicopters, two small Italian-built Bells with a third to follow. Two South American oil companies were prospecting for oil in Bolivia in the eastern foothills of the Andes, and had chosen helicopters as the best way of getting in and out of territory which was largely left blank on the map and labelled " Unexplored."

During the first week in August, Green was flying over the empty deserts of the Middle East. Before the middle of September he was in action in the dense jungles of South America. He left to take charge of the new operation with confident words from Bristow: "This is it. Now we really are going places. Two years ago nobody wanted to know us. Another two years at this rate and we'll be operating all over the world. There's a whole new field of charter flying opening up and the helicopter is making it all possible."

Green went out with Bill Petrie, the company's chief overseas engineer, and John Robinson, another engineer. They set up base in the village of San Borja, in the Beni province of Bolivia and assembled the Bell helicopters as they arrived in crates, delivered by DC-3 to an air strip which served the local abattoir. As the *helicopteros* worked on their machines, Bolivian *gauchos* rode past with herds of cattle which were slaughtered at the far end of the airstrip. The carcasses waited for the next flight out to the capital, La Paz. For Green the scene was uncomfortably familiar. It was as if his old whaling ship had followed him into the jungle.

The first stage of the oil prospecting involved a far flung sequence of geological exploration. A group of geologists would be taken by helicopter to a suitable site for an area camp. Each morning the geologists were lifted out of the camp and dropped one by one in the jungle with their little hammers and bags. Very often they were landed in river beds where a selection of rocks was conveniently exposed for collection. Each evening the helicopters returned to pick up the geologists with their rock samples and take them back to camp. Every ten days the whole area camp would be moved on to another site by a sequence of shuttle flights. The expedition's most fragile freight, ten hens to provide fresh eggs, was carried in a net slung beneath the helicopter. Green's log for such a mission in March, 1958, records: " Gained two eggs in flight—lost one bird."

Sometimes Green faced the problem of geologists needing to be put down in jungle so solid that he had to turn away in search of the nearest village and drop them there to organise local transport to their objective. On one occasion the nearest village for many miles was half a dozen huts cramped into a clearing too small for the helicopter to land. Green came down to within a few feet of the surface of a river running alongside the village and hovered above the water while Eddie Frankl, the Swiss geologist in charge of the survey, climbed down from the cockpit and splashed his way ashore to meet the villagers.

The noise of the helicopter had frightened the women of the village but native etiquette seemed to force their menfolk into a show of boldness. Wearing little more than sackcloth, they stepped forward to receive the young man who was dressed more for a suburban weekend than the role of a great white explorer, complete with trilby hat instead of the pith helmet the setting suggested.

Frankl could speak eleven languages, five fluently, although none of them was of any use with natives who spoke an obscure tongue in an even more obscure dialect. But his sign language carried all the confidence of a multi-linguist. In return for ten sheath knives, the jungle's most acceptable currency, he arranged to hire a dug-out canoe to reach his objective along a network of streams which tunnelled through the dense jungle. Frankl was already choosing his dug-out as Green rose from the village and the jungle closed in over his friend. The helicopter returned before dark and the geologist was waiting at the side of the river, holding a lively conversation with the natives by way of phrases he had learned from two villagers who paddled the canoe for him during the day.

Frankl climbed up into the cockpit with nothing more than the usual bag of rock samples to show for his day in the jungle. Green flew to pick up a survey party from a jungle clearing some weeks later and was asked to take on board two man-sized gorillas shot by a pair of natives employed to cut paths through the undergrowth or *pica*. He had once carried a live monkey when a geologist was being moved between two camps and insisted on taking his jungle pet with him. But dead gorillas were something different. " You can't get things of that size in a helicopter," he said. " They'll have to be left behind." The natives, standing proudly over their hunting trophies, were bitterly upset at this suggestion and the geologist was equally concerned. He pointed out the danger of labour troubles in the area if the *pica*-cutters' friends felt they had been denied a feast of gorilla meat and all the ceremony that went with it.

Green agreed to change his mind for the sake of public relations. He left the *pica*-cutters to mount guard over the gorillas and took the geologist back to camp where he

collected the freight sling. Then the helicopter returned
to the jungle clearing and carried the *pica*-cutters off to a
heroes' reception at their own camp with the gorillas riding
underneath in the position usually reserved for the expedition's precious hens.

Another form of wild life was jaguar, known locally as
el tigre. A survey party landing on the banks of a river
which was not marked on existing maps named it the Rio
Tigre after finding jaguar footprints in the sand. This was
beyond the Frankl Gap, a break in the mountains found by
Eddie Frankl, and south of the Rio Verdi, a river located
by Green. A young Dutch geologist was the first white man to
set foot on the banks of yet another uncharted river in the
same area. He called Green out of his cockpit to look at large
paw marks between the skids of the helicopter. "What are
these?" he asked. "Oh, those," said Green. "I would say
jaguar at a guess." "But I've got to stay out here on my own
for the next ten days," said the Dutchman with the genuine
alarm of a geologist on his very first foreign assignment.
Green helped to unload the tent, food, rifle, machete, and survey equipment on to the sand alongside the paw marks.
"Don't worry about those," he said. "You'll probably never
see the thing that left them. One of us will be back to pick
you up a week on Thursday. Be seeing you, sport." For all
his cheeriness, Green sympathised with the young Dutchman facing ten days alone in that wilderness. Another
pilot returned to collect him and found a thoughtful figure
sitting on the river bank, contemplating fresh traces of paw
marks. "I heard those jaguars every night," he said, "but
the funny thing is I never caught sight of anything."

The ten-day stay in the jungle was necessary to carry out
a topographical survey, the second stage of the quest for oil.
Otherwise the geologists returned to camp the same day and
were not equipped for a night in the jungle. That was the
prospect which faced John Robinson, one of the helicopter
engineers, when he offered to join a geologist, Tom Winkelmolen, in a search for rock samples along a fast flowing river.

Robinson, once a member of an R.A.F. mountain rescue team, saw the expedition as an interesting tropical ramble. Four exhausing hours after being put down by Green they had covered only two of the six miles to the clearing where he had arranged to collect them. At this rate they could not hope to reach there before darkness and the helicopter would have no clue to where they were. One solution was to return to the place where they landed but it had taken well over an hour to climb down the face of a fierce waterfall and there seemed little hope of climbing it from the opposite direction against the full force of the river. Winkelmolen announced that they must continue downstream until they found a gap in the vegetation which bridged the river for as far as they could see. Robinson found the going even more difficult for the next mile. The third member of the party, an Indian carrying the rucksack full of collected rocks, was physically distressed by the time they came to a spot where the treetops finally parted above the river. Robinson estimated that the gap was less than fifty feet wide. The rotor blades on a Bell helicopter described a circle thirty-five feet in diameter. " It will be a close squeeze but we can be picked up from that rock in the middle of the river," he said.

Getting to the rock was another problem. They were standing on a ledge thirty feet above the surface of the river. The overhang meant they could not climb down from the ledge without ropes and there was no indication that the bank became any lower downstream.

" There's only one thing," said Winkelmolen, and dived fully clothed into the river below. The Indian shrank from the edge and indicated he could not swim. " Come on brother," said Robinson. " In you go." The Indian went down into the water still wearing his rucksack and floundered to the rock in wild desperation. Robinson followed with more style but little less urgency. South America's dreaded flesh-eating piranha fish were normally found much farther down the Amazon basin, in more placid waters, but few Europeans cared to linger in any stretch of jungle river.

The three men huddled on the rock in midstream and hoped to hear the approach of Green's helicopter before the abrupt arrival of tropical night. Green found them with less than half-an-hour to spare, setting off up-river when they failed to reach the agreed rendezvous. From his cockpit there seemed only inches between the rotor blades and the trees as he eased the helicopter down to a position where one skid was resting on the rock. Robinson was the last to squelch into the cockpit, using the skid as the rung of a ladder. He watched the rock fall away beneath them until it sank from sight in this inland sea of inscrutable greenery. It had been a tropical ramble he would not choose to repeat.

The *helicopteros* worked in Bolivia for nearly five years, through mountain landslides and floods—when they lifted survivors out of devastated villages; through banditry and revolution—when as many as twenty bodies were seen hanging from public scaffolds in Santa Cruz.

In 1962, the oil companies finally ended the survey. Except for tantalising glimpses from the occasional wildcat well they had not found the oil they came looking for and the operation was wound up. Green and the rest of his team shared the oil men's personal disappointment but had the huge consolation of the helicopters' technical success in terrain where no other form of aircraft could have operated. For Bristow, a regular visitor to the jungle camps to put in a spell as a working pilot, the Bolivian adventure meant the end of his impatient years as a helicopter prophet and the coming of the great things he was hailing as a lieutenant in the Fleet Air Arm. The two helicopters he bought to begin work in Bolivia increased to a fleet of six within a year. Operations also expanded in the Middle East and the fleet grew even bigger.

The mergers establishing the British United Airways group, in 1960, brought Bristow Helicopters together with Airwork Helicopters, pioneers of crop-spraying operations, and produced a combined fleet of fifty-four helicopters compared with a total of fifty fixed wing aircraft in the rest of

B.U.A. There are now more than seventy helicopters, the largest fleet in the world, and still increasing in size.

While B.U.A.'s fixed wing aircraft work to an increasingly sophisticated routine of scheduled services and long-term contracts for trooping and holiday tours, helicopters still pursue unusual, hazardous charters in some of the most primitive areas of the world. " We are about the only bush pilots left in the business," Bristow will declare through the cigar haze of his chauffeur-driven Bentley on its way from a board meeting to his Mayfair manicurist. But he recites the company's far flung activities with a familiarity which comes from visiting each operation and flying every job. His helicopters can certainly claim to be the real sky tramps of to-day.

There are helicopters spraying bananas in the Dominican Republic, cotton in Rhodesia, rubber and jute in India. One helicopter ferries engineers and equipment between radio stations in remote parts of South Africa. More helicopters are helping to search for oil in the West African jungles and servicing off-shore rigs along the coast of Nigeria and throughout the Arabian Gulf region. Many of the company's most experienced staff are assembled in the North Sea area to take part in the great international hunt for off-shore oil and natural gas deposits. These men have shared and matched Green's flying exploits in five continents. Now, with Alistair Gordon as North Sea area manager, Johnny Johnson conducts operations from Germany, Spencer Allen is in charge of flying from Holland, and Clive Wright operates from England. Another long-serving expert, Bryan Shaw, leads a group of pilots based at Middle Wallop in Hampshire where Bristow Helicopters conducts the basic training course for the British Army's helicopter aircrews. And still Alan Bristow travels the capitals of the world in search of more and greater challenges for his flying machines.

" I love the challenge and the intrigue of the charter business," he once confessed in the middle of a three cornered telephone conversation with customers in Teheran,

Rome and New York. He was sitting at an empty desk in his otherwise empty office in a London skyscraper and between calls the telephones were returned to the floor to keep the desk-top clear as the flight deck of an aircraft carrier. " To stay on top in this business you need to know oil presidents and kings, cabinet ministers and rebels who might become cabinet ministers, civil servants who weave all the red tape and lawyers who think they know how to cut it. You've got to know the helicopter backwards and show your crews you can fly it backwards, if necessary. You must be prepared to go anywhere on this earth at any time of the day and night to take on anything that's worth doing. Then when you get the job in the middle of nowhere the secret is not to employ men who go native. I'd fire a pilot on the spot if I discovered he touched a glass of beer during a working day—even though his helicopter was sitting in the middle of the jungle, a hundred miles from anywhere. We may be bush pilots but we are *professional* pilots first, last and always. If there's any bush around it's just part of the scenery."

For Green—now too often confined to the company base at Redhill as operations director, with George Russell Fry and Jack Woolley completing the old Air Whaling team in adjoining offices—the scenery he found in the Antarctic, the desert and jungle served to dramatise his escape by helicopter from the life he might have led at his Manchester railway station. Towards the end of his spell in South America, he landed in an uninhabited stretch of jungle and joined one of the geologists on his search for rock samples, knowing it was safe to leave the helicopter unguarded. When they returned two hours later the machine had changed its colour to a deep violet and appeared to be quivering gently although the engine had been switched off and the rotor was not turning. The two men stood and stared for several moments of sheer fantasy. Then they went forward to investigate.

Fragments of the new colour began to break away and rise into the sky at their approach. The shimmering movement became stronger in some parts of the machine than others. " Do you see what it is?" said the geologist and he could not keep a childish excitement from his voice. " Butterflies! There must be a million of them. They've covered every inch of metal. The whole helicopter is buried in butterflies."

Butterflies flurried from beneath Green's feet as he climbed into the cockpit through the open doorway. Butterflies had to be dusted from his seat before he could sit down. Clouds of butterflies sprayed from the rotor blades when he started the engine. Trickles of butterflies fell from the cockpit canopy in protest against the sudden noise and vibrations.

The rest fluttered away when the helicopter rose sharply into the sky with Green and the geologist looking back at what seemed a wake of violet sequins. Alan Green never found an explanation for this jungle phenomenon. But if he had to explain what converted an invoice clerk to the restless life of a sky tramp he would suggest it was all part of the same chemistry which can turn a helicopter into a million butterflies.

8

CHAPTER TWELVE

Destination Unknown

WHAT next for the sky tramps? Is there a place for them in the glossy world of jet travel where the man who owns a single airliner must be a millionaire, where the filing cabinet is the procurer of all business so that even the unexpected has to arrive through the usual channels? How can the merchant venturers of the air compete with modern marketing techniques which offer a flight to any place on earth as one more packaged deal from an aviation supermarket?

Alan Green and the helicopter have established an extra dimension of charter flying. Cliff Luxton and his one-man, do-anything, go-anywhere CJL Aviation continue to exist with the colourful uncertainty dating back to his 4s. 8½d. bank balance in the days of Croydon Airport. Nearing retirement age, Anthony Christopher Loraine still captains a B.O.A.C. Boeing on the North Atlantic service and, in the absence of Royal tours and political missions, has the prospect of some horticultural society's charter excursion to a New York exhibition as an occasional escape from routine. Bill Bright, the operator who succeeded only to fail, now works for Keegan Aviation, buying, selling and demonstrating light aircraft for customers ranging from Texan businessmen to the Shah of Persia.

Harold Watkins and Don Ludbey contrive to get away from their desk duties with British Eagle and Lloyd International often enough to regard themselves as still faithfully married to flying, with domesticity merely a mistress. Maintaining the same concern for physical fitness which made him pace ten miles a day in his Russian cell, Watkins travels the world with his tennis kit in the cockpit and seeks a challenge at every destination. When Bob Batt flies these days, it is most often with a brief case and as a passenger, on his way to some sales or technical conference for Aviation Traders, a company progressed far enough from its saucepan and toothpaste-tube period to be manufacturing its own car-ferry aircraft, the Carvair.

But some of the sky tramps are already grounded. Joe Viatkin sells office equipment in London's West End and tries to trace an old comrade from the Berlin Airlift who is practising as a dentist in Lambeth. Having settled in Australia for his health's sake, Dr. Graham Humby has successfully revived his medical career to become one of Sydney's leading plastic surgeons, and charter flying's great empire-builder now plans to construct a private airstrip for his son and daughter who have both learned to fly. For Homer Cochrane, the desert flier, there is a return to his native Canada to take up an office job. And Monique Agazarian, the pleasure flying specialist, lives quietly in Beirut as Mrs. Monique Rendall, stay-at-home wife of a captain with Middle East Airlines.

The executive suite has long claimed Harold Bamberg and Freddy Laker. Bamberg does not miss flying, preferring to regard his boardroom as the cockpit of his largest airliner. "Running a large operation calls for the same sense of balance as the physical business of flying," he says. "In each case, the basic problem is to maintain a level course in face of an endless variety of opposing forces." He took violent avoiding action in February, 1965 when Britain's new Labour government confronted him with restrictions on private airlines' competition with B.E.A. on scheduled services. In a gesture reminiscent of his mass sales of aircraft thirteen years before as a personal protest against the monopoly granted to the State corporations by the post-war Labour government, Bamberg immediately scrapped British Eagle's domestic services in Britain and cancelled his plan to buy six BAC-111 jets for these routes. Then, having jettisoned this part of his load, he announced from his boardroom cockpit yet another change of course for British Eagle. Once more he was setting out to conquer the Atlantic, this time challenging B.O.A.C. for the rapidly increasing business in " group " charter flights to and from America.

For Laker, the boardroom is merely a hangar where ideas are checked over before he wheels them out into the open air and launches them to the skies. He bustles endlessly from one airport to another, the international tycoon who had the BAC-111 bus-stop jet built to his specification, who championed his own VC-10's when B.O.A.C. lost faith in theirs, and who finally captured the Corporation's South American routes. But Laker, the dealer, still finds time to buy or sell racehorses. And Laker, the flying man, never goes to bed without telephoning the night staff at British United's operations centre at Gatwick to ask if his pilots have reported any problems.

Within the operations centre, Cecil Bebb, founder member of the motley order of sky tramps, continues to stand at his blackboard and watch the planes go by. Flight BR 316, now making its passage across the board, is the same Whisky Zulu which delivered its ninety holiday makers to Palma a few hours ago. There are 120 passengers crammed into the Britannia for the return flight, and the reluctant emigrants from Majorca's beaches complain about the lack of knee-room with a Latin passion as fierce as their suntan.

One young woman passenger comes to the end of her fortnight in a luxurious hotel overlooking the Mediterranean by having to travel all the way to Gatwick with the broken back of the seat in front of hers tilted into her lap. It is an intolerable discomfort for a 28-year-old typist from Beckenham who has acquired a taste for iced champagne served on her private terrace. A few years ago, the typist might have accepted as an excuse for the broken seat a reminder that she was flying in a four-engined airliner at little more than twopence a mile—compared with fourpence a mile charged by British Railways to take her to and from her London office every day. But it is not an excuse to be contemplated at the close of her fourth Mediterranean holiday. "You never got this on B.E.A. or Iberia," she assures the hostess.

In fact, the typist's travels by B.E.A. or Iberia were also charter flights, costed with the same concern for each fraction of a penny per mile, equally liable to have a seat damaged on an aircraft so full that there is no alternative place for the inconvenienced passenger. It is one achievement of the independent operators that their customers now expect corporation standards of sophistication from charter companies less than fifteen years after the ex-bomber was their basic airliner. It is also another achievement that the State airlines have followed them so eagerly into the charter market. While B.O.A.C. and B.E.A. have flourishing charter departments, many leading European airlines—notably Alitalia, Swissair, S.A.S. and Iberia—have formed their own charter companies as specialised subsidiaries.

Most of the European and African scheduled services introduced by State airlines since the war were pioneered and proved by independent operators. One reason why the accident rate on charter flights durings the 1950's became more than ten times higher than for normal services was the inherent danger of aircraft flying along strange routes into unfamiliar and ill-equipped airports. Familiarity breeds contentment for passengers, crews and ground control as proved by the dramatically improved safety statistics in recent years. Cross-Channel air ferries, the charter companies' new idea for one of the oldest transport routes in the world, began and continued with an incredibly accident-free record although the car-carrying aeroplane poses considerable technical problems. The Continental holiday would certainly have remained a more exclusive status symbol without these air ferries and all the inclusive tours by air to such places as Majorca, Spain, Portugal, Italy, Sicily, Jugoslavia, Bulgaria and Greece. Charter companies are already flying to America, North Africa, the Middle East and India to establish the pattern for even more distant holidays. At the same time, they are building up their own regular, scheduled services throughout the world.

But only sixteen independent airlines survive from the sixty-nine in 1946 and the scores which have come and gone since then. Air Vice-Marshal Bennett, one of the casualties of the charter business, complains that flying has been overloaded with so many rules and restrictions that free enterprise of the air is denied all freedom. It is his verdict that aviation found its Elizabethan age after the war and surrendered it for a welfare state in the sky. Laker, the little man who set out to challenge a monopoly and is now establishing one of his own, believes the post-war boom was a freak of history which can never be repeated. He is convinced the number of independents must dwindle still further.

Two ex-managing directors have different views. Between family chores in the Lebanon, Monique Rendall day-dreams of a come-back to charter flying to develop a rich new market by concentrating on high-speed, high altitude executive aircraft which offered personal service in maximum luxury to expense-account passengers—an air-limousine to succeed the very basic air-taxi she used to fly from Croydon. Bill Bright has never formally wound up World Wide Aviation because he remains confident there is still a place for the small company seeking traditional charters. " I regard the year we were in business as a theoretical success," he says. " If only I could meet a fellow fanatic with £25,000 of uncommitted cash, we would be in business again tomorrow."

Harold Bamberg, who began with £500 cash and a £3,500 overdraft, experiences new stimulation in the increasingly complex nature of flying and the bigger stakes involved.

" When we started with the old bombers," he says, " the best man was the one who could improvise. Now he's the one who can get the best use out of the real thing—and that might include a 125-channel radio. I find that even more exciting than struggling across Europe with a Halifax full of apricots. But there's no reason why a small operator couldn't start up from scratch right now by finding the modern equivalent of a Halifax and those apricots.

" The real significance of all that has happened since is not how it happened or why it happened but the fact that it happened at all. I can't see why it should not go on happening. There will always be pilots who want to fly over the edge of a radar screen."